"*NLP for Teachers* is just the book I have been waiting for. It takes the complex terminology and techniques of Neuro Linguistic Programming and translates them into practical strategies for teachers in the classroom. It is packed full of excellent advice and useful activities that work on a profound level to alter behaviour and attitudes. If you follow the advice in this book and work through each section practising the techniques and using the tools, you will improve your teaching and leadership skills. If you also embrace the principles of NLP that relate to developing a high level of self awareness, rapport and flexibility you will also change your life and relationships – for the better. A must for your educational bookshelf."

al Consultant, Trainer,

AST, Sc

r Practitioner of NLP

"For those of us dedicated to the art of teaching, NLP brings new and deeper insights and understandings. This book gives practical, accessible approaches to help teachers and school leaders refine and develop excellent practice."

Liz Robinson, Head Teacher, Surrey Square Junior School, London

"Richard Churches and Roger Terry have written an impressively thorough and packed guide to NLP for teachers. It is based on the authors' extensive experience in the field, and the choice of contents is directly influenced by what teachers themselves have found most useful. It is well-illustrated, offers an engaging mix of explanation, examples and activities, and deserves to be a great success."

"The research zones are an especially useful and innovative feature. On topics such as mirror neurons, hypnosis, eye movements and more, Richard and Roger acquaint the reader with work in other fields that is relevant to NLP. The zones include full details of sources, and provide what is often a missing link in NLP publications. They offer a distinctive resource for anyone seeking a well-informed understanding of NLP."

Paul Tosey, Senior Lecturer in the School of Management , University of Surrey

"*NLP for Teachers: How to be a Highly Effective Teacher* is a rare book--unique and original ideas presented in so many different stimulating ways. You have idea sets, toolboxes, research zones, top tips, cartoons--a cornucopia of stimuli. Churches and Terry have produced something that not only will make you a better teacher, it will make any of us a better person if we soak in and act on the many clear suggestions. NLP for Teachers is at once a deeply practical and deeply theoretical book."

Michael Fullan, Professor Emeritus, OISE/University of Toronto

"This is a powerful resource for all those who wish to extend their portfolio of strategies to support effective learning and teaching. NLP offers a systematic, coherent and well tried range of techniques to enhance all aspects of communication. The book combines lucid expositions of theory, practical and relevant examples and a range of activities which support understanding and application."

"Education is a social process – this book demonstrates that it is no longer necessary to aspire to, or exhort, social skills – they can be developed and learnt. NLP offers a rigorous approach to personal effectiveness and enhanced professional expertise."

"The authors provide an accessible, relevant and directly applicable resource which has the potential to help classrooms and schools become emotionally literate communities."

John West-Burnham, Visiting Professor of Education, Queen's University, Belfast

"For those teachers who are clinical in their search for improvement, *NLP for Teachers* opens up a new way of examining classroom practice. The authors summarise the NLP approach in this comprehensive and insightful publication."

Alistair Smith a

"*NLP For Teachers*, by Richard Churches and Roger Terry, is a fascinating and extremely accessible book: it is full of information in a highly palatable format.

We highly recommend this book to every education professional who wants access to a set of tools that really work! - NLP - and who desires to grow his or her teaching, and - perhaps even more importantly - who really wants to rediscover what learning is truly about."

Dee Shipman, New Oceans

"… a great resource for all in the field of education. It contains a wealth of information on NLP, including the essential background to the most important tools and techniques.

One of the main strengths of the book is that it is directly aimed at classroom practice. As such, it is jam-packed with excellent advice and useful strategies as well as motivating and practical ideas. There is a bank of tips, Just Do It activities and a wide variety of NLP Toolboxes, all of which have immediate application to day to day classroom situations."

Use Your Edge **December 2007**

"I work in schools and teachers often ask 'What's this NLP all about then?'. I can now refer them to to a book that provides a clear and comprehensive guide to how NLP can help a teacher in the classroom. It's packed with the sorts of practical tips teachers like and I particularly like the section on running an NLP-based Inset day."

David Hodgson, author *The Buzz*

"This is an excellent resource for teachers and lecturers. This book will enable teachers to learn from practical application by the authors of their desire to improve teaching and learning skills and in particular personal effectiveness. I would recommend this as an essential resource for all teachers and lecturers and those who are studying for their Cert Eds."

John T Morris, Director, JTM Educational Consultants

"This is a book that you will want to come back to again and again whether you are an experienced or a newly qualified teacher. The authors unlock the complexities of NLP, giving practical and easy approaches in the classroom. Try out a couple of strategies, see their impact on learning and you'll soon be back for more. I speak from experience!"

Lyn Bull, Independent Education Consultant

"An NLP book that makes you sit up and take notice! Richard Churches and Roger Terry have provided an essential service to teachers by giving them the means to become excellent role models for the children they teach. The exercises are pitched at the right level for working with kids and for having fun, and the authors provide a comprehensive survey of the neurological research to support the principles of NLP."

Peter Young, author *Understanding NLP: Principles and Practice*

"*NLP for Teachers* combines a bright A4 format and accessible layout with detailed guidance and techniques on how to improve personal effectiveness as a classroom teacher.

Ideas from NLP have been gradually incorporated into education over a number of years, so it is good to see a book which brings the methods of NLP directly to bear upon the performance of the teacher and his or her interaction with pupils.

This is not just a compilation of practical techniques, however. It also has a substantial underpinning of theory. For those who want to probe deeper there are 'research zones' which include guidance on further reading, opening up the world of NLP more fully and going beyond NLP itself to the key figures who informed its development."

Julian Gill, Hypnotherapist www.aspiretherapyonline.com

"A Perfect Textbook to be used as you prepare and plan your most challenging lessons!

"A treasure chest of a text, I only have praise for this manual. Teachers who love teaching or who want to regain the love for teaching can use this book, which offers itself as a wonderful way to reinvigorate teaching practise using NLP.

"NLP is simply a set of wonderful techniques used to change around your own thinking so you are in a position of master your own communications in your Teaching practice. Anyone involved in the *communication of* teaching will immediately find the value of the book. Treat yourself well, but having this sort of support workbook around as acts to remind you to keep the communication relationship are the most in your teaching. It keeps you uplifted, balancing your dreams with practical steps in this set book.

"Anyone involved in pedagogy, will see how much communication most needs your attention in your teaching career. It teaches you how to prioritise your time, the most valuable commodity you own and to place within it the most fundamental communication skills. For any teacher in training or seeking to improve their classroom practise with NLP, this book emphasises, sound practises. Chapter by chapter invites you to try out different NLP exercises, which stretch and strengthen your existing talents, skills and natural gifts into the space between you, the students, parents, and colleagues you interact with.

"What's admirable about this manual is that it makes very clear those characteristics of effective teachers. E.g. your expectations that you have for yourself and others and how you might improve or reframe them if that is necessary. A book written with lots of respect for the teacher and the teaching experience. It redirects any teacher to put their attention on what they want to create in the class and to move on from feeling guilt or any other negative feelings generated from failed teaching sessions.

"For those who are especially sceptical, it provides lots of exercises which allow the sceptic to work things out for themselves. To test the material out for themselves. To put each section to the challenge and to notice for themselves the positive changes which occur in the classroom as a result of applying the various NLP exercises. To identify in precise and achievable outcomes, what you may want to accomplish. Chapters ask you to focus on your attitude. They each support you to put yourself into a decisive position. To decide how you want to communicate with learners. How to enjoy teaching and be generous about that too. Before further inspiring the reader to take more positive action, it shows how to plan out lessons from taking an internal approach. Lesson planning triggering and activating emotions, feelings, memories, and internal future representations teaching the teacher ho to assist them to create well formed outcomes bringing all their training together using all the inrwebL senses they have.

"Rapport, pacing and leading. Effective and aspiring effective teachers will get even more opportunities to praictse how to build rapport using specific language patterns. Known to influence learners, parents and colleagues.

"How to use praise in all its ways, is a major chapter of the book. Know how to use praise to get feedback from learners. Becoming skilled at how to use language to pay tribute to learners, parents and colleagues, increases your own flexibility to change their behaviour, language, or internal feelings about themselves. And this is all a seriously important part of learners taking action for themselves.

"Utilise everything
Each chapter teaches you to harness, and utilise where you are currently at in your teaching practise. Each has something to attach importance to as you put into use your treasures. It's a practical book, so it requires you to set up a programme of activity for yourself to learn and practice the material. It's a real great reminder text and rather than simply give you inspiration, it then gives you the most easy to apply NLP exercises.

"Memory and Anchoring

The two chapters, which show the teacher how to use the memory, and anchoring to create and recreate internal strengths, which learners can draw from, are exquisitely easy to follow and apply.

"More useful chapters!

a chapter on how to use questions in teaching, a chapter on defining what you value about teaching and updating those values if necessary so you remain flexible in the classroom whilst being true to self. And a chapter on motivation, which is key to learner retention.

"Personal 'favourite things I cherish', about the text are its size. It's big enough to carry around. It has jargon buster sections and its very clear illustrations that help to increase a person's rapport with the learners, parent or colleague. More than an introduction to NLP, it is a text you can use each day as you plan your communication messages for each of your lessons. Superb.

"Highly recommended: Should be on teachers mandatory reading list.

Deborah Rose, Therapeutic Hynotherapist for Stress Free Caring In the City, a WellBeing and Training Membership organisation for Social workers and Social care workers

"Richard & Roger's book is special in that it views teachers as thinking individuals who want the best results for their classroom while offering the "how" and not the "what" of teaching. The view of NLP offered in this book is up-to-date both in terms of NLP itself and academic research in areas that are relevant to NLP. What I really liked about *NLP for Teachers* is that it achieves a healthy overall balance. Theory meets practice and it is important because it is the basic concepts of NLP that can truly liberate you and give you control over your own behaviour, yet they are difficult to learn without immediately-practicable techniques. Both newcomers and experienced NLPers are given plenty to think about. The classroom is treated both as a group, with collective needs, and as a set of individuals, with specific needs. NLP is about being proficient in communication and those who will read this book and apply the concepts and techniques presented will be challenged and given the opportunity to be even better communicators than they already are."

Georgios Diamantopoulos, Doctorate researcher in NLP

"As a practising teacher who is mid way through NLP practitioner training, I am writing to thank you for *NLP for Teachers*. I read this book with huge enthusiasm because it not only clarified the essential ideas of NLP, but also rendered them in eminently practical terms and contexts for teachers. I have implemented many of the practices from the toolbox sections with great success and have networked much of the thinking with colleagues. As well as this, *NLP for Teachers* has led me in a number of other fascinating directions, one of which is mentoring. Inspired by *NLP for Teachers* (and of course my practitioner training) I have now written a school-wide NLP based mentoring programme which seems to have engaged the thinking of teachers and learners alike. The programme has undoubtedly contributed to a change in the school culture where learners are now becoming increasingly solutions focussed.

"So, a huge thank you to you both. I will certainly look forward to reading more of your work."

Ron Piper, Assistant Headteacher, Ridgeway School, Swindon

"This book is written for teachers as a practical text which provides opportunities to explore key areas of personal development and personal effectiveness. It focuses on the skills of:

Effective communication
- Influencing skills
- Managing emotions
- Setting positive outcomes
- Expanding repertoire of behaviours and increasing flexibility

"Having trained in NLP (Neuro-Linguistic Programming) myself, I am impressed with the breadth and depth of this book and I would imagine appealing both to a newly qualified teacher and to those who wish to develop and hone their skills and performance.

"It provides an 'Instant Training Day', a glossary of related terminology and a very comprehensive research section. The authors are to be congratulated on a well-structured book which is visually appealing and full of tips and activities."

Mary Mountstephen MA (SEN), Associate Editor, SEN Magazine

"This book aims to take the complex terminology and techniques of Neuro-Linguistic Programming (NLP) and turn them into practical strategies for teachers working at the chalkface.

"The book offers advice and activities to alter behaviour and attitudes, with a number of original ideas.

"The authors themselves say in their introduction that they are aiming to help teachers "bit the challenging mark of interpersonal and intrapersonal effectiveness".

"The pair are speaking from experience as well, having taught NLP approaches to more than 1,000 teachers and school leaders in the past four years.

"The book covers a lot of ground, looking at how to build rapport, thinking effectively, positive rewards, words to use with care, motivation, and paying attention to body language to name but a few topics.

"The advice is backed up with fully-referenced research, top tip boxes and advice on where to begin when it comes to applying the techniques you are reading about. There is also a useful glossary common NLP terms.

"The layout and design makes what could be a tough subject matter easy to read and digest."

Pete Henshaw, SecEd Magazine

"This book is the first of its kind to specifically tailor the powerful resources of NLP into the school context. It makes the connection with both pedagogy and classroom management, and allows easy application of the strategies. By respecting the professional craft of the teacher, this book raises the stakes, by offering teachers and school leaders another, more sophisticated look at how they are approaching learning in school. Thank goodness that we now have a resource to support the development of the interpersonal and communication skills that we all hold to be so crucial in effective practice in schools.

"The impact on learning and the work of the teacher in the classroom, to what extent and in which areas:

"In order for pupils to learn, they need to be in a "space" where that is possible. Rapport is a crucial aspect of this, and it was what the best teachers do instinctively. *NLP for Teachers* allows them to unpick this, expand and improve their skills, so that they can more quickly, effectively and consistently get children to be "ready to learn".

"An proper understanding of different preferences in learning and processing allows teachers to genuinely both understand where pupils are coming from, and also to ensure that they are fully meeting their needs. This is about a profound understanding of how the brain processes and stores information, and a sophisticated approach to subtly ensuring that all pupils have the best possible opportunities to learn.

"How the resource supports or enhances the everyday life or work of teachers, pupils or schools:

"The impact of *NLP for Teachers* goes well beyond the actual teaching and learning. For most teachers, managing challenging behaviour in and around class is a key concern. The NLP skills of rapport, reframing and state-management are highly effective in supporting teachers to effectively manage both themselves and their students. This can have a positive effect throughout the school - how teachers and pupils relate to one another, as well as teachers and teachers, and of course teachers and parents. By avoiding conflict, teachers are empowered to build strong relationships, which ultimately benefit the students, as well as supporting a less stressful work place. "

"Cost effectiveness in terms of educational aims and results - not just price:"

"*NLP for Teachers* presents a set of learnable skills which can be modelled, shared, coached on, and developed throughout the school community. My experience is that the "cascade" effect of these skills is both rapid and highly effective. Staff readily see the potential benefits to themselves, and are keen to develop the skills for themselves."

Liz Robinson Headteacher, Surrey Square Junior School, Southwark

"I fully endorse this book.

"It is highly accessible and of immense practical use. It is one of the few books that can inspire teachers to improve their skills and an educator and classroom practitioner to become a better teacher. It is innovative in that it does not require a teacher to replace any practice but allows them to improve their effectiveness through a number of techniques.

"All the techniques are easy to grasp and have high impact on classroom practice and learning. The techniques have an immediate effect and build into creating a highly effective learning environment. The book does not require any specialist resources or any expensive associated programme materials and can be applied to any subject or phase of education. As such it provides excellent value for money.

"It is rooted in the everyday life of any educational establishment with clear explanation of jargon and areas of further research that can be explored. It takes the very complex interactive process of teaching and simplifies what can be done to improve the practice for all.

"I highly recommend this as one of the best educational books this year."

Tony Crisp, Headteacher PRU

NLP for TEACHERS

How to be a Highly Effective Teacher

Richard Churches & Roger Terry

Crown House Publishing Limited
www.crownhouse.co.uk
www.crownhousepublishing.com

First published by

Crown House Publishing Ltd
Crown Buildings, Bancyfelin, Carmarthen, Wales, SA33 5ND, UK
www.crownhouse.co.uk

and

Crown House Publishing Company LLC
6 Trowbridge Drive, Suite 5, Bethel, CT 06801, USA
www.crownhousepublishing.com

First published 2007. Reprinted 2007, 2008, 2010.
Transferred to digital printing 2013.

British Library of Cataloguing-in-Publication Data
A catalogue entry for this book is available from the British Library.

Print ISBN 978-184590063-2
Mobi ISBN 978-184590184-4
ePub ISBN 978-184590350-3

LCCN 2006934875

Contents

Acknowledgements

Over the last four years, in conjunction with a number of fellow trainers, such as Henrie Liddiard and Lynn Murphy, we have been fortunate to have taught NLP approaches to well over 1,000 teachers and school leaders. Alongside specific training in Neuro-linguistic Programming, NLP tools have been incorporated into training delivered by trainers from Alistair Smith's training company (Alite): Will Thomas, Sarah Mook, Penny Clayton and Nick Austin (Alite and CfBT). Some material in the book first appeared in print in Teaching Expertise magazine (Churches and Terry, 2005; 2006a; 2006b; 2006c). We are grateful to Clare Smale the then editor of the magazine for her support in developing and first publishing this material. I (Richard) would particularly like to thank John West-Burnham for always listening to some very different ideas.

Alongside training teachers to use NLP we have continually kept one eye on exploring and researching which NLP tools are of most use to teachers and school leaders. This book is the result of using applied NLP with teachers together with the feedback we have received and the follow-up research that we have done. As such it is not a complete manual of NLP but rather a collection of those NLP tools, techniques and strategies that teachers have told us have made a difference to them in the classroom. Although there is evidence to support many NLP techniques and approaches from neuroscience, psychology and education, there are some approaches that just seem to work without (as yet) any real rationale to support them. Despite this we have included all of the things that we have had positive feedback on and, where appropriate, have included research evidence which supports (or at least sits in parallel to) the NLP techniques being described in the chapter.

We are also grateful for the support and encouragement of Surrey University's research programme in NLP and particularly to Dr Paul Tosey and Dr Jane Mathison for the access they have given us to their own research work and ideas. Also we should thank all the people at Roger's training company Evolution Training: the employees, trainers and various teacher participants who have directly and indirectly made a contribution—particularly Ali Mobbs for her outstanding illustrations. Thanks also to all those people who have given us support, encouragement and feedback in the production of the articles that preceded this book and the production of this book: Jenni Churches, Emily Terry, Dr Geraldine Hutchinson, Nick Austin, Liz Robinson, Claire McLean, Clare Smale and Heather Hamer. We would like to dedicate this book to our children: Sam, Lucy and particularly George, Richard and Jenni's son who died of cancer, aged 7, during the writing of this book.

Richard Churches

Roger Terry

August 2007

Introduction
Should you buy this book?

Teaching is about relationships as well as pedagogy. It is about feelings as well as facts and it is as much about what goes on inside your head as it is about what goes on in the heads of your students. It is about using your senses as well as your subject knowledge.

At the end of the day we all know that it is our mood when we enter the classroom that has the greatest effect on the children, our sense of motivation that drives the pace of the lesson and our abilities to relieve the tension in a difficult moment that creates the right classroom climate. Effective teaching begins and ends with our capacity to manage our internal responses and external behaviours.

There can be few jobs that require such mastery over interpersonal and intrapersonal skills, and the central importance of this area for teachers and school leader development is becoming increasingly clear (see West-Burnham, 2004; West-Burnham and Ireson, 2005). Because Neuro-linguistic Programming (NLP) is about personal effectiveness it offers teachers a range of tools and techniques to develop interpersonal and intrapersonal capacity, manage emotions and communicate much more effectively. At the same time there are specific approaches for getting in touch with who you are, so that you can truly connect to your moral purpose and values as a teacher, think deeply about what you do and have the skills to take effective action. In our work with teachers we have found that knowing what is important to you, what you want and having the personal effectiveness to act gives you the ability to link your values to your behaviours and to influence those around you to easily achieve what really matters. The link between values, behaviour and purpose is now recognised as being of key importance to effective school improvement (Fullan, 2001; 2007). We have included a specific chapter (The teacher within) on working with your values and exploring you identity. Is NLP the technology of emotional intelligence? Well, if such a thing exists, yes it probably is. It is certainly technology for developing interpersonal and intrapersonal competence.

> Is NLP the technology of emotional intelligence?
> Well, if such a thing exists, then yes it probably is. It is certainly technology for developing interpersonal and intrapersonal competence.

In writing this book we have not sought to present a work on pedagogy or teaching strategies. There are many excellent texts already available that cover these areas. Rather our intention has been to present a practical text that gives teachers the opportunity to explore the key areas of personal development and personal effectiveness. We believe that this area is not only under-represented in teacher education and training at the moment, but is also the key (in combination with effective teaching and learning approaches) to high teacher effectiveness. In our experience, it is this area that is often lacking or under-developed in less effective teachers, and the reason why two teachers can deliver virtually the same lesson (in the same way) to similar classes and yet have very different results.

In this book you will learn how to:

- communicate more effectively
- develop your influencing skills and approaches
- manage your emotions and feelings more effectively to help you to build resilience
- set yourself, and achieve, positive outcomes
- expand your range of potential behaviours and develop more flexibility

We have also included up-to-date **Research Zones** throughout the book that we hope will be of interest to the wider academic community as well as to teachers and others who work with children in a learning capacity. Chapter 1, *What's in a name?* contains some background information about NLP and its core concepts; the practical tool-based chapters begin with Chapter 2, *Blockbuster movies*. Chapter 14, *The magic number 7*, puts NLP into a wider research context in relation to what we know about consciousness and cognition and how early work in the field of NLP relates to current thinking. A final chapter, *Instant training day*, gives you a detailed set of training scripts to support you in delivering some NLP training yourself.

What have you got in mind?

At its heart this is a book about language and internal mental imagery, and how understanding this can transform your life and work as a teacher. Specifically it is a book about how to use the language and approaches of a group of extraordinary therapists (modelled by Richard Bandler and John Grinder in the mid-1970s) in the classroom. This early NLP research explored how therapists such as Milton Erickson, Virginia Satir, Frank Farrelly and Fritz Perls did what they did—the end result of which was the documentation of a wide range of tools, techniques and approaches. In doing this they discovered and unpacked tools, approaches and methodologies. These led to the development of specific techniques that are just as effective when used in everyday situations with everyday problems as they are when used with people in therapy. Indeed, over time, it became increasingly clear that there were specific strategies and approaches that many excellent communicators and achievers shared in common. Together these personal effectiveness and communication strategies have become part of what is known as NLP. Many of you will read this book and notice things that you have already learnt on courses and in books in recent years. The fact is NLP has been gradually being integrated into education over the last few years through the cascading and sharing of tools and techniques. This book will help you to understand where many of these ideas come from and how to use them effectively.

What you will not find in this book!

- **This is not a book about brain-friendly learning nor is it a book about how the brain learns.** If you are looking for a work on neuroscience and how the brain learns we highly recommend *The Learning Brain* by Sarah-Jayne Blakemore and Uta Frith (Blakemore and Frith, 2007) and the recent publication *Neuroscience and Education: Issues and Opportunities* by the Teaching and Learning Research Programme and the Economic Social Research Council (TLRP, 2007). There are also many helpful texts by Alistair Smith (2000; 2002; 2003; Smith and Call, 1999), Bill Lucas (2001), Guy Claxton (2002), Tony Buzan (2001) and others which provide a practical approach for those aspiring to plan their teaching and learning in a way that supports a more 'brain-focused' way of working. For a scholarly review of the potential impact of these approaches we suggest you look at the recently published research report *Learning to Learn in Schools* (Higgins et al., 2007). As NLP is primarily about communication, with yourself and others, you will find that the techniques and tools in the book complement any and all pedagogic approaches.

■ **You will not find pedagogic approaches in this book or anything that might replace your existing practice or training as a teacher.** Rather this book contains personal effectiveness tools and techniques with which you can easily enhance any existing good classroom skills and approaches, so that you can become highly effective in the classroom. In doing so you will find yourself becoming more influential in your delivery skills and more effective at managing yourself. This will enable you to have more energy and stamina, clarity and focus and the feeling of being completely in control of your emotions and purpose.

So what is this book about?

This book is about personal effectiveness. In a sense it is about the space between you and the students that you teach and the space within you when you are doing that. The type of knowledge that NLP represents is therefore a 'how to' rather than a 'what'. In a way it is technology for your mind.

> This book is about personal effectiveness. In a sense it is about the space between you and the students that you teach and the space within you when you are doing that. The type of knowledge that NLP represents is therefore a 'how to' rather than a 'what'. In a way it is technology for your mind.

Why we wrote this book

What our experience of using NLP with teachers tells us is that these tools and techniques can help teachers to hit the challenging mark of interpersonal and intrapersonal effectiveness more and more often. Our work over the last four years has taught us many things. In particular, we have learnt that that not every tool or technique works for everyone. This is almost certainly because we all have highly effective ways of dealing with the challenge of teaching. What is undeniable, from our experience, is that nearly every teacher we have worked with finds something that makes a real difference to them and their relationships in both the classroom and the staff room. At the end of the day the answer in teaching has to be in the territory of practitioner-led enquiry and in this spirit we invite you to work with the ideas and tools in this book and let us know what happens.

PENS

Learning NLP

Any good book about NLP should aspire to be a complement to hands-on practice and training. With this in mind we have included practical exercises throughout the book and a final chapter, *Instant training day*, which gives you seven interactive NLP training exercises that you can use separately or to deliver your own whole day training event in school. If you have not yet had the opportunity to attend NLP training by a recognised trainer or practitioner we would highly recommend that you do so. NLP is a set of practical skills and there is much to learn that can only ever be touched on in the context of a written text. Look out for training delivered by registered trainers of either INLPTA (International NLP Trainers Association) or ANLP (Association of NLP).

For those of you who are studying for a teacher training qualification, or who are doing a higher degree in education, we have provided **Research Zones** that give you useful references to research from outside of NLP that parallels and supports the model.

So should you buy this book? Yes, if you're interested in beginning to develop excellence in classroom communication skills. Yes, if you want to learn how to use powerful tools to support your personal and professional goals. Yes, if you just want to know how to feel good whenever you want to. In fact, anyone working in a school—teachers, subject leaders, phase leaders, senior managers, learning support assistants, local authority advisors and many others-—will want to buy it.

Getting the most out of this book

As well as containing lots of information about NLP and background to the tools and techniques, there are many practical activities for you to work on.

- *Just do its* are activities that will build your internal skills and capacity, and act as a prelude to the more advanced tools in the **NLP Toolboxes**.

- You will notice that there is some repetition of concepts in the book. We have done this so that you can really focus on working on a chapter at a time without having to cross-reference too much.

- We suggest that you take it a little bit at a time and play with the concepts and tools in your daily work, noticing how effective they can be in everyday situations. Once you have read a chapter and worked through the activities yourself, you may want to work through the activities again with a friend or a colleague. With some of the tools and techniques it is helpful to have someone read it out loud whilst you work through it. Discussing the activities afterwards can be really helpful.

- Set yourself the goal of taking two or three ideas, concepts and techniques at a time and have a day when you practise that one thing. Applying some of these strategies will be much more effective than simply reading the book.

- In general it is best to work through a single chapter in order as the approaches and learning become more advanced as the chapter progresses.

- *Research Zones* add academic depth to what is in the chapters but it is not necessary to spend time on these before working through the chapters and the tools.

- At the end of all the practical chapters there a box entitled More ways to start improving your classroom practice with NLP. These include a series of additional suggestions for getting started with the tools that are described in the chapter.

- Remember you don't need to absorb it all at once. Allow yourself time to work on one or two tools or approaches at a time.

Chapter 1
What's in a name?

Studying excellence

NLP is sometimes described as the study of human excellence. NLP studies not only what effective people do but also **how** they go about doing it. This includes the visible external behaviours/language of highly effective people, the internal mental processes that they use and the way in which they think. By applying these approaches and thinking you can achieve the same things in your own work and life. We are only just beginning to fully understand the power of our minds and the relationship between mind and body. Freedivers who dive to staggering depths without bottled oxygen are able to reach what is called a state of static apnea. They achieve this by banishing energy-sapping stress and fear. This represents an extraordinary mind game and is the opposite of adrenalin sports. Where adrenalin speeds up the metabolism freedivers slow it down. World champions can conquer the body's natural impulse to breathe for over nine minutes.

In NLP the process of studying the details of what people do, the ways they think, feel and behave is called **modelling**. Fifty years ago what differentiated an excellent golfer or tennis player from an average one was barely understood. What makes a top player has been analysed and videoed time and time again. Today you can have your golf swing or tennis grip analysed in great detail. This attention to the detail of excellence and effectiveness is what makes NLP research stand out from other studies of human behaviour and effectiveness. Out of such detailed studies came the body of knowledge that is NLP. Because NLP tools exist at the level of processes and communication skills they can literally be applied to any context to help you become highly effective, including the classroom. Today NLP is used to study the excellence and effectiveness of people in all walks of life and across all disciplines and fields. What has emerged is a wide range of approaches that are like 'software' for your mind.

The co-founders of NLP noticed that there were three fundamental characteristics of really effective communicators that were shared by all of the therapists, excellent communicators and influencers that they studied—these characteristics are also shared by effective leaders, salespeople and teachers. Firstly, be clear about what you are looking to achieve—know your outcome and have a grasp of what you want. Secondly, have the flexibility to adapt your behaviour and have a wide range of possible behaviours and responses. Thirdly, use your senses to notice if you are getting what you want so that you can adapt quickly and respond effectively.

The characteristics of teachers who achieve excellence in their lives and professional work

1. **Know what you want**—Identify precise and achievable outcomes. Know what the purpose and direction of your communication and action is. Specifically have clear internal pictures, sounds or feelings which come together to create your own internal representation of you doing the future action effectively.

2. **Know if you are getting what you want**—Sharpen the detail that your senses pick up so that you develop sensory acuity. Notice the responses of others in order to provide sensory feedback for you to ensure that you progress towards your outcome.

3. **Have the flexibility to change**—Be flexible in your behaviour, language and internal feeling. Continually adapt in order to influence and involve others in your outcome.

4. **Take action**—There is a real world out there. What goes on in your mind, and in the cinema that plays in your mind, is just a map.

Although much of NLP has parallels with recent studies from neuroscience and psychology, NLP as a form of knowledge is fundamentally a phenomenological one. As such it represents a body of knowledge about the nature of subjective human experience. NLP is best understood and learned by experience and through practice. Revisiting previous sections of the book and doing the **Just do it**s and other exercises again will support you in this.

Many of the highly effective NLP techniques included in this book are processes and skills drawn from the world of hypnosis. Following their detailed studies of therapists and excellent communicators Bandler and Grinder concluded that 'all communication is hypnosis' (Bandler and Grinder, 1979) in that any time a person communicates something to someone that requires them to experience that for themselves, a 'hypnotic-like' state is being induced. For example, if we were to begin to tell you about our recent holiday abroad, the feeling of the sand under our feet, the sound of the waves and the colours of plants and trees, you might well begin to create an internal image yourself. In this sense whenever anyone tries to communicate anything they are attempting to induce such a state. The primary way in which this is done is with words. Of course, you are not going to be able to put your classes into a deep trance and get them all up at the front pretending to be chickens after reading this book. Hypnosis is a much wider field than we are seeking to cover here; however, the core skills of excellent communication and influence are the same.

Following their detailed studies of therapists and excellent communicators Bandler and Grinder concluded that 'all communication is hypnosis' (Bandler and Grinder, 1979) in that any time a person communicates something to someone that requires them to experience that for themselves, a 'hypnotic-like' state is being induced.

Think for a moment and ask yourself, what is it that good therapists do?

We often ask this question in our training sessions and the list that appears on flips charts is invariably something like this:

■ Create positive change for people
■ Help people to change their behaviour
■ Communicate effectively

- Facilitate learning
- Change people's life
- Help people overcome difficult past experiences
- Support people to fulfill their potential
- Help people manage their behaviours etc.

These are all things which you expect to see in a really effective teacher. The bottom line is that the key skills of a therapist, like a teacher, are an ability to influence with words and to use language to create change. Understanding these sorts of tools is useful for any profession in which your use of language is your primary skill—as it is in teaching.

"Neuro"-linguistic Programming—what a terrible name!

And it is a terrible name …

Any good researcher in the social sciences, or in the physical sciences, will tell you that research can only tell you about what has actually been researched. A lot of claims are made about NLP and indeed many things have been promoted under the title Neuro-linguistic Programming since Bandler and Grinder did their original research at the University of Santa Cruz in California. What Bandler and Grinder actually researched were language patterns and the internal mental representations that were often created as a result of related techniques and approaches.

Those of you who are already familiar with NLP or who may be qualified to diploma, practitioner or master practitioner, will notice that some of the ways in which we talk about NLP are somewhat different from what you might be used to. The fact is that there is a revolution happening in NLP, largely as a result of university-based research programmes and the creation of formal master's level qualification in NLP at several UK universities. As is usually the case with new knowledge, NLP is constantly evolving and has done over the last 30 years. To be frank, NLP has taken on board some pretty wacky ideas at times. In writing this book we have been mindful to remove some things, whilst at the same time preserving those tools, techniques and ideas that in our own experience, and from feedback, we know can make a real difference to teachers on a daily basis.

Research Zone

Key influences on NLP

The term Neuro-linguistic Programming was used first by Richard Bandler and John Grinder at the University of California at Santa Cruz during the 1970s, and techniques first appeared in publication in 1975 (Bandler and Grinder 1975a; 1975b). They used the term to describe a body of phenomena and concepts which broadly support the view that humans can be seen as a single mind–body system, in which patterns of connection can be defined which link internal experience and language (the neuro and linguistic respectively) to behaviour (programming). Bandler was a student of mathematics and computer science, and Grinder a professor of linguistics. They were encouraged in their work by Gregory Bateson and the NLP model owes much to Bateson's work. In particular NLP has, from its inception, drawn significantly from key concepts that are to be found in Bateson's collections of writings *Steps to an Ecology of Mind* (1972).

NLP draws its influences from a wide range of fields most specifically: the hypnotherapy of Milton Erickson (Bandler and Grinder 1975b; 1975c), Gestalt therapy (Perls, 1969) and the family therapy approaches of Virginia Satir (Bandler and Grinder, 1975). Classical conditioning (Pavlov, 1927) is also applied in NLP and is known as anchoring.

For a number of years the field of NLP has been contentious. However, recent advances in neuroscience, as a result of fMRI research, have helped to put NLP into a wider research context. In particular, cognitive theories of hypnosis (e.g. Brown and Oakley, 2004) support the effectiveness and process of hypnosis and the effectiveness of hypnotic language and hypnotic approaches. Likewise, wider NLP tools and approaches are supported by research into mirror neurons (Rizzolatti et al., 1996), memory reconsolidation (Miller and Matzel, 2000), the effect of positive mental imagery (Neck and Manz, 1992) and work on micro facial expressions (Ekman, 2003).

A more detailed Research Zone that covers academic definitions of NLP can be found at the end of Chapter 14, *The magic number 7.*

Bandler, R. and Grinder, J. (1975a) *The Structure of Magic I: A Book about Language and Therapy*, Palo Alto, CA: Science and Behaviour Books

Bandler, R. and Grinder, J. (1975b) *Patterns of the Hypnotic Techniques of Milton H. Erickson, M.D.* vol i, Cupertino, CA: Meta Publications

Bateson, G. (1972) *Steps to an Ecology of Mind*, London: Paladin, Granada

Brown, R. J. and Oakley, D. A. (2004) An integrated cognitive theory of hypnosis and high hypnotizability, in M. Heap, R. J. Brown and D. A. Oakley (eds), *The Highly Hypnotisable Person: Theoretical, Experimental and Clinical Issues*, London: Routledge

Ekman, P. (2003) *Emotions Revealed*, London: Phoenix

Miller, R. R. and Matzel, L. D. (2000) Memory involves far more than 'consolidation', *Nature Reviews Neuroscience*: 1: 214–216

Neck, C. P. and Manz. C. C. (1992) Thought self-leadership: the influence of self-talk and mental imagery on performance, *Journal of Organizational Behavior*, 13: 7: 681–699

Pavlov, I. (1927) *Conditioned Reflexes*, London: Oxford University Press

Perls, F. (1951) *Gestalt Therapy: Excitement and Growth in the Human Personality* Verbatim, Moab, London: Souvenir

Rizzolatti, G., Fadiga, L., Gallese, L. and Fogassi, L. (1996) Premotor cortex and the recognition of motor actions, *Cognitive Brain Research*, 3: 131–141

The presuppositions (or mindsets) of NLP

Have you ever noticed another teacher talking about a class or a student and noticed that they have a completely different view of the student to you? Have you ever noticed this happen and realised that it was that teacher's expectations, beliefs and ways of thinking about that child or class that were probably at the heart of the problem?

Often in schools the way in which we think about things affects our behaviours and therefore affects and influences others around us. Over the last 30 years NLP has defined the critical mindsets that successful people adopt to help them achieve their potential. These are often referred to as the **presuppositions** of NLP. These have evolved within the field and from original modelling of therapists

and successful people in general. You will find these presuppositions expressed in different ways in various books, depending on the context that is being explored. The ten presuppositions that we have found to be most helpful for highly effective teaching are listed below. At the heart of these ideas is a fundamental principle: **we can't change anyone else's behaviour, we can only change our own**. This applies to children just as much as it does to adults, teachers, parents, friends and anyone else that we interact with. We can't always be sure how our changes in behaviour will affect others. However, being sensitive to the sensory feedback we get, and subtle signs and signals that we receive from others, we can become more adaptable and respond effectively to the behaviour of others.

We can't change anyone else's behaviour; we can only change our own.

Spending a few moments to reflect on these presuppositions will be helpful before you begin your journey through the practical chapters that follow.

Communicating effectively

■ **We are always communicating**

Everything we do in front of the children we teach in the classroom communicates in some way:

● the words we use

● small changes in our facial expression

● the way we stand

● how the way we arrange our classroom

● where we stand, etc.

Recognising this enables us to explore the details of our communication and the effect

it has others. In fact it is impossible not to communicate, and even saying nothing will communicate something.

▪ The meaning of your communication is the response you get

In many ways this is one of the most challenging ideas for teachers. It means that we cannot simply blame the lack of understanding about what we want on others. On first inspection this may seem a bleak idea, but in truth it is a liberating and powerful way of seeing the world in a different way. Knowing that it is ourselves that we need to change allows us to take full control of the only aspect of life that we truly have any control over—our own behaviour. Think about it, how do you get anyone else to do anything? The reality is that you have to act first.

▪ Resistance is the result of a lack of rapport

When you encounter resistance or challenge ask yourself—what sort of relationship do I have with this child, parent or colleague? Almost always, if there is not the mutual feeling of trust and relationship, that is rapport, resistance follows. Learning to build rapport is one of the key skills in NLP. In this book you will learn key skills that will enable you to build rapport effectively and quickly, whatever the situation or circumstance. Often teachers are approaching the classroom from the perspective of tasks, strategies and skills; children are operating at a much more fundamental level—the level of identity. They are usually more interested in who you are and what is important to you and they look for protection and nurturing. Being able to develop rapport effortlessly can help you to communicate on this level and transform the way you think, feel and behave.

How to think effectively

▪ The map that we create in our mind's eye is not reality

We are all acting and responding to our own internal maps of the world. These are the result of our experiences and the emotions associated with those experiences. Our maps are full of values, beliefs and memories. Some of these are helpful and some of them are not. The first step in the process of learning to have the flexibility and skills to communicate effectively and achieve your goals is to become aware of what is in your map and to recognise that it is just that, a map.

▪ The person who sets the frame controls the communication and the actions that happen

When children don't have a really clear understanding of what they have to do, what happens? We have all had the experience of setting up a classroom activity and then finding that it hasn't worked out. Often this is because we missed out an important part of the explanation or weren't clear about 'how' it was to be done. The same thing applies to all communication. The language we use powerfully affects the meaning that we communicate, whether we are aware of it or not. Taking time to be more aware of the hidden meaning in the language we use makes us much more effective. Fundamentally, whoever establishes the boundaries first will have set the markers for what follows.

▪ Everyone has all the internal resources that they need

NLP is essentially a positive set of ideas, beliefs, techniques and philosophies. At the heart of these ideas is the notion that if one person can do something so can anyone else. In other words, it's just a question of working out what that person does and applying it to ourselves. Often the things that make a difference are quite subtle or hidden and can be the result of internal imagery or just the language that we use with ourselves or others. At the end of the day we all have control over what we think and how we act.

Taking positive action

▥ We can all learn fast and from one-trial experiences

Think back for a moment to when you were training to be a teacher. How much easier is it to teach something, or deal with a classroom problem, for the second time or subsequent times? Our minds respond quickly to the memories that we have of things that we have done in the past, particularly when there are powerful memories associated with them, either positive successes or failures. Equally our minds respond just as quickly to the images that we create of future events. Creating positive mental representations of what we want enables us to effortlessly marshal our internal resources. So how quickly can you learn? Fold your arms for a moment. Now fold them the other way. How easy was that? It seems hard the first time doesn't it? Now practise folding your arms the unusual way seven or eight times. What happens when you repeat the experiment you first did swapping one way for another? With many things our mind doesn't need a lot of repetition to learn. NLP techniques definitely exist in this category of life and once experienced stay with you.

▥ Feedback is information; there is no such thing as failure

Knowing what we want and aligning our internal representations and imagery to the desired outcome is the beginning of the journey. Remembering that our map is not the reality, we also need to be alert to whether we are getting what we want. Feedback is not just about receiving verbal observations from others. By attuning our senses to the subtle details of what is happening around us we can know when we are getting what we want and when things are not going well. Noticing subtle signs and signals in the classroom can allow us to act quickly to realign what we are doing and to recognise when we need to do this.

▥ The person with the most flexibility has the most influence

How many teaching philosophies and ideas have teachers had to take on board in the last 20 years? And how many of them actually work all the time? Practitioners of NLP recognise that there is not a one-size-fits-all and that not everything will work all the time. At the end of the day, classrooms and schools are complex environments, and flexibility of behaviour and thinking gives us more choices and many more options. What NLP offers teachers is a wide range of possible behaviours and ways of thinking that they can use in their professional judgment, applying them when and where they make sense. The more tools in your tool kit the more jobs you can do. This has been illustrated time and again from the teachers that we have worked with.

Chapter 2
Blockbuster movies

How to plan successful lessons from the inside out and reach your outcomes

The movies you play in your mind are crucial to your success and effectiveness in the world, particularly the movies you create of future events. Research shows that excellent and highly effective people engage in positive mental rehearsal of what they want and what it will be like when they have got what they want. More recent research also bears out the importance of visualisation and mental rehearsal and these techniques are widely used by professional sportswomen and men. People who achieve realise that they are film crew, director, writer and producer of their lives and they take action in line with their positive mental maps of what they want as an outcome.

The way you hold your mental pictures, sounds and feelings has a profound effect on how you act in the world. When you learn how to create the best possible movies in your mind, what you are capable of doing, being and having increases hugely. In particular, ensuring that you have a rich and detailed picture of your outcome which is aligned with your values, can make the decisions you have to make, and the behaviours that you need to embed, seem effortless.

What you will learn in this chapter

In this chapter we will begin by developing an understanding of how our internal imagery affects our day-to-day behaviour. On one level this includes our memories, which often act as the triggers for behaviours and actions. Working with memories is explored in detail in Chapter 8, *Memories are made of this*. In this chapter we focus on how creating positive future representations, and movies, of what we want can increase our levels of motivation, our desire to achieve and the likelihood that we will succeed. With this as a starting point, we will experiment with creating future representations that will enable you to be resourceful and confident in the classroom.

Emotions, feelings and our 'internal state'

Have you ever noticed how the mood you were in before you went into a classroom to teach can leak into the lesson itself and affect the whole way that it went? Or how, if you felt bad at the start of the day, the rest of the day just seemed to carry on like that? In NLP we learn to pay attention to the changes that take place within us as we change emotional state, for example from anxious to relaxed or angry to happy. A key skill is to be able to take an inventory, or snapshot, of your current state of being. This is a quick and easy process, and becoming proficient at this skill will allow you to make many useful distinctions in your internal processing.

NLP Toolbox No. 1

Take an inventory of your internal state

First read the instructions, as you will be closing your eyes for some of the exercise.

Close your eyes and focus your attention inside. Become aware of the level of **self-talk** that you have at this moment, that voice inside that comments on your thoughts, actions and emotions. Is it loud or soft? What tone are you using to speak to yourself? For example, do you sound gentle or harsh, authoritative or friendly, urgent or relaxed? Do the words support and encourage, or is the voice critical? Just notice.

Then pay attention and notice your emotional state. What emotion is present? Are you excited, nervous, angry, happy, etc? Finally check your body—how does it feel, energised, tired, achy, do you have a pain anywhere, etc?

Open your eyes

Taking an inventory is a useful habit to generate because it will enable you to monitor the changes that you are making as you work to learn and explore the inner world technology that is NLP. You may have already noticed a change. In fact, just being aware of your inner state can change your outward behaviours and inner feelings—what Daniel Goleman refers to as the 'Self-Awareness dimension of Emotional Intelligence'. In NLP this is referred to as being able to **calibrate**.

Now we know how to take an **inventory** we are ready to notice what happens in more detail as we access a memory or a future representation.

Take a moment to think about biting into a really juicy lemon sometime in the future. Get a really strong image in your mind. What do you see? Notice all the details, the colour of the lemon, the light shining off the surface, the pores on the skin and the trickle of juice as you bite. Now notice the taste and feel of the juice on your tongue and in your mouth. Pay attention the sound that your mouth makes as you bite and move your tongue and lips. What words are in your head?

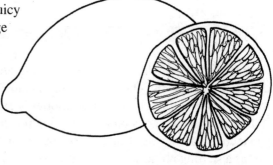

Did you notice that as you thought about doing this you began to shift your state? At a level below our conscious, analytical self our mind does not know the difference between an imagined reality and one on the outside. Merely thinking of biting deep into a juicy lemon, imagining the yellow fruit, smelling the citrus odour and experiencing the tartness of the flesh will begin to make your mouth water even though you have no lemon in your hands. Similarly, we can go bright red when thinking of something embarrassing when it isn't actually happening. Your mind affects your body and also your behaviours and this all happens before you're even aware of it.

Representations and the classroom

Our internal imagery and representations can produce real effects in our bodies and affect our capabilities in the world. These are also affected, of course, by our memories of past experiences—those of you who like the taste of raw lemon will have had a very different experience from those of you who do not. Think back to your time on teaching practice, or the first time you taught a lesson. If you create a fearful internal representation before teaching a class, what is likely to happen? How will you come over to the group? How will they be likely to behave?

If the last time you taught a class you had a successful lesson and felt great about yourself then remembering that before you teach them again will recreate all those feelings and many of the thoughts, leading to a further successful experience. Repeating this generates further success on success until you are unconsciously programmed to have great lessons with a particular group. On the other hand, this process will also happen at those times when you teach the 'difficult' groups. If a disaster occurs, and you repeatedly remember this before teaching the group, the chances are you will program yourself to have repeated difficult times with certain classes.

In his book *Social Intelligence*, Daniel Goleman notes how we are all connected to each other and how easy it is for humans to pick up on the inner emotions of another human being. This is particularly true in 'power relationships', such as those between teacher and student. This is because we are more likely to pay attention to our 'boss' or someone in authority. Students can easily tune in to your emotional inner state. We are all 'hardwired' to engage in this process through the activation of our mirror neurons. There is more about this in Chapter 3 on **rapport** (*We like like*). NLP takes this to a deeper level by exploring the *how*, in other words, what you can do about it. If you go into the classroom feeling fearful, or with internal representations that are triggering fear inside you, you might as well be walking in with a sign on your head that says, 'teacher who is scared of you lot!'

You can easily break this vicious cycle by making the decision to create positive future representations of events and to be clear about your outcome in relation to what you will see, hear and feel when you have achieved what you want. In sport this is often what makes the difference when top players come together for the highly emotional final of a competition.

Memories and internal future representations

Our memories and internal representations of the future are created, stored and coded in our mind with our five senses. You have already experienced that as we recall a memory or create a future image—our senses are activated and our mind reproduces the thoughts, sensations and feelings associated with that representation. Remember the lemon.

Research Zone

How our senses team up in the brain

Recent research demonstrates that our senses do not function as independently as was previously thought. Furthermore, in order to perceive what is going on in the world as a whole, all of our senses (visual, auditory, kinaesthetic, gustatory and olfactory) have to team up and work together. In some instances they actually appear to fuse together. For example, even the soundless image of someone talking is enough to stimulate the auditory cortex in the brain. This sensory integration happens very early in the process and therefore is likely to influence subsequent processing (Kayser, 2007; Macaluso and Driver, 2005; Kayser et al., 2005).

Kayser, C. (2007) Listening with your eyes, *Scientific American Mind*, 18: 2: 24–29

Kayser, C., Petkov, M., Augart, N. and Logothetis, N. (2005) Integration of touch and sound in auditory cortex, *Neuron*, 48: 2: 373–384

Macaluso, E. and Driver, J. (2005) Multisensory spatial interactions: a window into functional integration in the human brain, *Trends in Neurosciences*, 28: 5: 264–271

As we recall, or create a representation in our minds, we may become aware of a picture, sensations, feelings or sounds first. In NLP this is called our **lead representational system**—the sense that our mind first uses to fish out a representation. Think of an enjoyable holiday experience that you would like to have. You might first feel the warm sun and from there hear the sounds and only finally seeing the place where you were. Each of us will retrieve memories or create future representations using a different starting points (visual, auditory, kinaesthetic, olfactory, gustatory) and this may also depend on the context.

Creating your movie

So if you want an amazing lesson, it starts on the inside by creating a positive internal representation of exactly what you want. By applying NLP concepts we can create strong and powerful internal representations. The more visual, auditory and kinaesthetic information we have in these representations the more powerful and compelling will be the image and the overall movies. Think for a moment about the history of television over the last 50 years. It has been a search for the technology that creates the most realistic representation both in terms of colour, sound and the emotional impact of the movies. In fact, camera techniques are also now skilfully used to simulate the feelings of falling and of movement in our minds.

Exploring the visual, auditory and kinaesthetic elements of your inner representations

As you work through the sections below, have in mind a lesson that you are going to teach sometime in the future.

Visual qualities

Rather than just describing the content of the picture, we are interested in the structural qualities that would be common no matter what the content of the picture. Take a look at this image for a moment.

We could just describe the content of the picture: the skyscrapers, roads, vehicles, sky with clouds.

Instead focus on the qualities of the picture. For a visual representation these include whether it is:

- Colour or black and white
- Bright or dim
- Seen through our own eyes (**associated**), or as if we were an observer, seeing ourselves (**dissociated**)
- Framed or panoramic
- Focused or blurred

Or any other visual distinctions that you can think of.

Whether an image is **associated** or **dissociated** can have a powerful effect on how we feel about the picture. Have a go. Think of something that you really like doing, see it as if you were there doing it through your own eyes. How do you feel? Now imagine a photograph of the same thing but with you in the picture doing it. How do you now feel? When creating an internal representation of a future goal, or outcome, it is really important to pay attention to the details of the image and have as many rich details as you possibly can. The closer to a real image or movie (that you might see through your own eyes) the representation is, the more compelling it is likely to be.

Bring up that representation of the future lesson you know you are going to teach:

- Is it a movie or still?
- Is it colour or black and white?
- Is the image bright, dim or dark?
- Is the image life size, bigger or smaller?
- How close is the image to you?
- Are you in the picture or watching from a distance?
- Does the image have a frame or is it a panorama?
- Is it three-dimensional or two-dimensional?

Auditory qualities

Our inner sense of sound is coded in much the same way and again we can adjust the qualities to improve the experience just as you might change the volume, bass and treble responses on a hi-fi. Words also form part of this process (both the words we say to each other in our representation and the words we say to ourselves as part of our internal dialogue, or self-talk). In addition, the tonal part of the auditory system gives us information about the emotion engaged.

Think about that future lesson and ask:

- Are you saying something to yourself or hearing it from others?
- What specifically do you hear or say?
- How loud is it?
- What is the tonality?
- How fast is it?
- Where is the sound coming from?
- Is there an inflection in the voice?
- How long did the sound last?
- What is unique about the sound?
- What other sounds are there?
- What are those other sounds like?

Kinaesthetic qualities

We often pay little attention to the sensations and feelings in our body, and yet they can be a phenomenal source of information both about the outside world and our internal world giving information on how we are dealing with the challenges on a day-to-day basis.

This system has three parts: the external tactile sensations that we are aware of on our body surface; the internal or visceral sensation that we can feel inside our body (e.g. that sinking feeling or being light-headed); and the movement or psychomotor functions involved in doing. It can be just as important when learning something to have our internal visceral sensations engaged as to be doing an activity that involves movement and tactility.

Bring the experience back and ask yourself:

- Is there a temperature change? Hot or cold?
- Is there a texture change? Rough or smooth?
- Is there a vibration?
- Is there an increase or decrease in pressure?
- Where was the pressure located?
- Is there an increase in tension or relaxation?
- If there was movement, what was the direction and speed?
- What is the quality of your breathing? Where did it start/end?
- Is it heavy or light?
- Are the feelings steady or intermittent?
- Did it change size or shape?
- Were feelings coming into your body and/or going out?

These small distinctions of recall or representation are called **submodalities**. Chapter 8, Memories are made of this, explores the use of submodalities in detail so that you can learn how to deal with and change your experience of negative memories. The same approaches can also be applied to internal future representations. So you may wish to revisit this chapter again later when you have even more inner mind tools in your NLP toolboxes.

You are now ready to explore some NLP Techniques.

Well-formed outcome—bringing it all together to create your movie

Giving our minds a strong and detailed pattern of what we want automatically tunes the mind to bring to your conscious attention those things outside yourself that are similar to your internal representation. The mind is almost saying 'here is one and here is another one'. In NLP we learn how to manage this phenomenon and turn it to our benefit. With practice you will begin to notice how your most motivational internal representations share common visual, auditory or kinaesthetic qualities. For now, as you begin to construct a **well-formed outcome**, just focus on the emotions that you want to experience when you get what you want and let your mind do the rest for you. To really embed your well-formed outcome we suggest you follow the following **seven steps to achievement**.

Step 1: Define your outcome

Think of a class that you teach and from which you want a positive outcome. Remember this is not about your past experience but rather what it would be like if you were to get everything that you want. So stop and become the scriptwriter for this future blockbuster movie.

A great way to explore this for the first time is to get a friend or a colleague to ask you the questions as if they were your personal life coach. You can find a worksheet that is helpful to support this process in Chapter 15, *Instant training day*.

What do you want? Be really clear about want you want. Below are some useful ways to think through your outcome and to collect lots of information about what you want to achieve. You will already be familiar with the acronym SMART. In NLP we add also add PURE to ensure that your outcome is really appropriate to you and makes sense in terms of your values and your whole life. Many people find it helpful to write their outcomes down if they are learning this for the first time. Of course as you grow in confidence and skill so you will learn to do this more quickly and easily.

Specific

Be specific—define what you want for the outcome being addressed. Let yourself work out the details exactly (what will you see, hear and feel).

Milestones

What will the milestones be? How will you know you are on track towards your outcome? What will be happening half way through your successful lesson?

As Now

Outcomes are best written as if you have achieved them, so write them in the present tense as if you are doing it right now.

Results

What will be the effects of achieving your outcome? What will you see, hear and feel when you have the outcome?

Time Based

When will it happen? What is the timescale? Name the date and time.

Now look at your outcome from a different point of view.

Positive

It is important to put what we want in a positive frame. We often think of the issues in our life as being 'problems'. This is why we get stuck, as problems tend to hold us back. We even get into a 'problem state' that becomes an issue in itself.

You can make a problem into an outcome:

'I don't want/don't like'—ask *'What would you like instead?'*

'I can't/won't'—ask *'What would happen if you could?'*

Our minds do not process negatives. Just for a moment, don't think of a blue donkey. Were you able to not think of one?

Under your control

Are you able to take the steps yourself, or engage others, if you need to achieve your outcome?

Right size

Do you always achieve your outcome, in which case you can go for a bigger outcome; or do you just miss your outcome, in which case make it smaller.

Ecological

What will the effects be on the system you work in if you got your outcome?

Example

It is 24 February 2008, I am headteacher of an inner city school in Manchester. I am inspiring staff to create innovative lessons which engage the visual, auditory and kinaesthetic senses of the students who are learning through activities which include investigation and reading.

Step 2: Check your present state

We quite often have every intention of pursuing our outcomes and yet somehow we don't really get started. This is often because there is some activity, thought process or habit in the now (this moment in time) that we have not recognised as also needing to change. Often these are at a lower than conscious level, so until we ask ourselves the right questions we may not be aware of the changes that are needed.

Useful questions to check your present state

- What do you get out of not having your outcome?
- Is there anything you would need to give up or change in order to move towards your outcome?
- Is there any other circumstance that might block your progress?

If you become aware of any of these sorts of things, just allow yourself to move on, knowing that now your mind is aware of these things it will be able to sort and align your inner motivations as you create your movie.

Step 3: Creating a strong internal representation

As we said at the beginning of the chapter, the clearer and more detailed your internal representations are, the easier it is for your mind to bring to your attention those things that will take you towards your outcome.

Imagine how you want your outcome to be, create a representation with pictures, sounds, sensations and the emotion you want. You can spend time doing this. If you like, think of it as a mini meditation. Create the event in a full Technicolor sensorama, real-life movie.

What do you see? Create a movie of the event in full detail.

What do you hear? Both internally (your inner dialogue) and externally (the sounds around you and the words of other people as they too experience your successful outcome).

What do you feel? What are the physical sensations of being there in this place and what positive emotions are there associated with it?

Step 4: Creating well-formedness in your outcome

Here are some questions that will help you form your outcome. When learning this for the first time it is a good idea to get someone to ask you these questions, or to write down your answers clearly and carefully.

- How will you know when you've got your outcome? State in sensory specific terms. Refer to the internal representation you have just created and write down the key features. What will you see, hear, feel?
- Where, when and with whom do you want it?
- Where, when and with whom do you not want it? (Sometimes we want an outcome at work and not at home or vice versa.)
- What resources do you need to get it? Identify your internal needs, help from others, any material requirement, and create a complete list.
- What will happen when you get it? What will be the consequences of reaching your outcome?
- How will getting it benefit you? Find three clear benefits that will occur when you have your outcome.
- Do you want this change in any other situations? Are there any other contexts in your life that would benefit from the outcome you are working on?
- How will making this change affect other aspects of your life? What effects will the outcome have on your life balance? Is this ok, or do you need to make modifications?

Step 5: Integrating your outcome

Now just relax. Close your eyes and play your movie as many times as you need to integrate all the details in your own mind. When you are ready, open your eyes again. Imagine where this outcome might be in the room or space around you. Walk to that place, stand in your outcome and feel all of those positive emotions again. Return to where you started your journey and take the first and next step towards what you want.

NLP Toolbox No. 2

Well-formed outcome 'Quick Start'—Creating future movies mind exercise

You can read this to a tape and then play it back to yourself, have a friend read it to you or read it first and use your imagination.

Find somewhere comfortable where you can be relaxed and undisturbed for 10 minutes or so. Close your eyes and become aware of your breathing. Notice for a few moments (five to six breaths) the coolness of the air as it enters you and the warmth as it leaves ... *Pause* ... Allow yourself to relax and your body to soften as you place your awareness on the muscles around your eyes and let those muscles relax now ... *Pause* ... Allow that sense of relaxation to flow right down your body from the top of your head, down your face, relaxing the face and jaw muscles ... *Pause* ... Down your torso to your legs ... *Pause* ... And feet to the tips of your toes.

As you become totally relaxed bring to mind your outcome. Begin to be aware of what it will be like when you have achieved your outcome. Notice what you will be seeing, where will you be ... *Pause* ... What will you be doing ... *Pause* ... Who will be there. Begin to create it just the way you want it. Make the colours bright and the picture close and large. See it all as if you are there ... *Pause* ... As you are aware of those sights you can notice the sounds around you ... *Pause* ... What are they, how loud are they and from what direction do they come? Are there voices and what are you saying to yourself inside? 'Well done, good job, I am proud of myself'... *Pause* ... As you hear those sounds and words notice the sensations and feelings that you have inside as you know you will get your outcome. How big are they? Can you make them bigger and even more pleasurable right now? That's right you can, can't you?

Just sit back and play that movie over again until you get it just the way that you want it, and it feels good, does it not? ... As you do this you can allow your mind to explore all the questions that will help you to ensure that your outcome is well-formed ... Is it under your control? ... Is it right? ... Play some more ... *Pause* ... Now you can begin to re-orientate yourself back into the room, back into your body, and open your eyes.

Research Zone

Mental rehearsal and internal imagery

A number of studies have demonstrated the effects of positive mental rehearsal on performance in areas including golf and music (e.g. Woolfolk et al., 1985; Pascaul-Leone et al., 1995) Taylor and Shaw, 2002). Similar effects have been demonstrated in relation to the influence of self-talk, mental imagery and 'thought self-leadership' on performance (Neck and Manz, 1992). In particular, a study using the Tennessee Self-Concept Scale, Rosenberg Self-Esteem Scale, and Fishbein and Ajzen-type scale of self-attitude showed that positive imagery significantly affected self-attitude in a positive direction (Patrizi, 1982).

Recently researchers at University College London have shown conclusively that creating internal representations using all sensory modalities is an effective tool for regulating our emotions and specifically anxiety and distress. In a study using fMRI scanning, subjects were taught to identify a safe and relaxing 'special place' and to bring that place into mind as vividly as possible in all sensory modalities (visual, auditory and kinaesthetic). They were then asked to create a self-statement and to give the place a name in order to be able to recall the experience effectively in the future (Kalisch et Al., 2005).

Kalisch, R., Wiech, K., Critchley, H. D., Seymour, B., O'Doherty, J. P., Oakley, D. A, Allen, P. and Dolan, R. J. (2005) Anxiety reduction though detachment: subjective, physiological, and neural effects, *Journal of Cognitive Neuroscience*, 17: 6: 874–883

Neck, C. P. and Manz. C. C. (1992) Thought self-leadership: the influence of self-talk and mental imagery on performance, *Journal of Organizational Behavior*, 13: 7: 681–699

Pascual-Leone, A., Nguyet, D., Cohen, L. G., Brasil-Neto, J. P., Cammarota, A. and Hallett, M. (1995) Modulation of muscle responses evoked by transcranial magnetic stimulation during the acquisition of new fine motor skills, *Journal of Neuroscience*, 74: 3:1037–1045

Patrizi, F.M. (1982) Self-attitude enhancement through positive mental imagery, Paper presented at the 90th annual convention of the American Psychological Association

Taylor, J. A. and Shaw, D. F. (2002) The effects of outcome imagery on golf-putting performance, *Journal of Sports Sciences*, 20: 8: 607–613

Woolfolk, R. L., Parrish, M. W. and Murphy, S. M. (1985) The effects of positive and negative imagery on motor skill performance, *Journal of Cognitive Therapy and Research*, 9: 3: 335–341

NLP Toolbox No. 3

'Stepping stone' your outcome

Once you have a well-formed outcome the stepping stone exercise is a good way to uncover what is stopping you, what the important next steps are and ensuring that you are including in your planning all the things that you need. Answer the questions only as fast as you need to in order to uncover your internal resources and understanding. This is a really effective tool for using with yourself or when coaching others.

1. Make sure that you have thought through your well-formed outcome in detail so that you have lots of sensory information.

2. Uncover the first level of what is stopping you from doing this. Ask yourself, 'What stops me?' Write your answer down.

3. Without dwelling on this issue ask yourself, 'What do I want instead?' Think about what you would rather have happen. Write this down.

4. Now ask yourself, 'What stops me from getting the thing that I would like instead?'

5. Continue this process until you have exhausted all the possible things that might stop you and have explored all the things that you would rather have.

NLP Toolbox continued ...

6. Beginning where you have ended up with the last layer, ask yourself what you would get if you achieved this as an outcome. Write your answer down.

7. Again continue asking this question until you have explored all possibilities.

This is also a great technique for working with children in a counselling context. You could write the questions on cards and then get the children to write on each card. Alternatively have the questions on pieces of paper on the floor and literally walk them through the exercise 'stepping stone' by 'stepping stone'. One teacher does this with her examination classes to help them plan their revision timetable and ensure that they explore and find solutions to the limiting ideas they have about time and opportunities for revision.

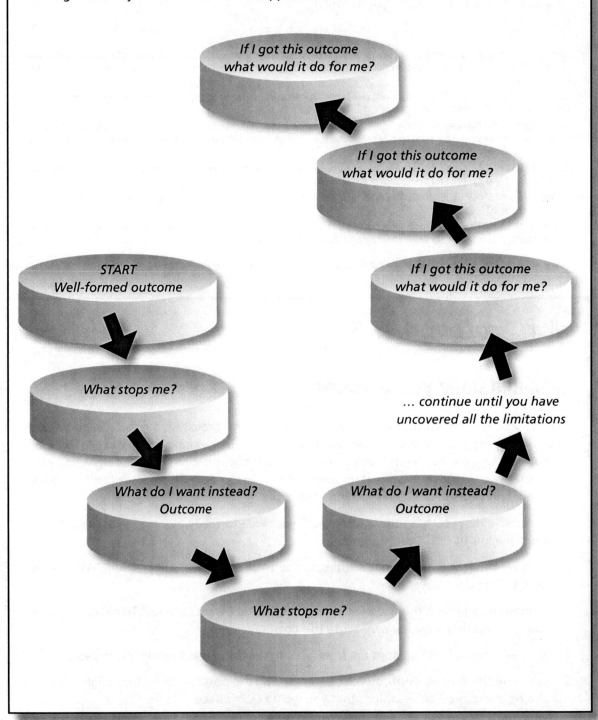

More ways to start improving your classroom practice with NLP

■ Create a detailed well-formed outcome of how you would like a difficult class to be, before you teach them. Then use the stepping stone exercise in the last toolbox to work through the things that stop you. Remember it is you that needs to change, as you can't change other people's behaviour—only your own!

■ Use the well-formed outcome process with one of your examination classes to support them in achieving what they want and to help them become more motivated to revise.

■ Use the 'What will you see, hear and feel?' questions in your classroom conversations to help students become more future-focused when they are stuck in 'problem thinking' mode.

■ When working with colleagues on school improvement and development planning add sensory information about the intended outcome that you are seeking to get to and ensure that there is lots of detail around your strategic goals.

Chapter 3
We like like

How to build rapport and influence others

During their studies of highly effective therapists and excellent communicators, Richard Bandler and John Grinder consistently noticed these people's extraordinary abilities to build rapport and therefore to be able to influence the people that they were working with. From this they modelled a series of strategies and approaches for both building **rapport** and for developing what they termed **sensory acuity** (the ability to read the emotional experience of another by noting small details in their facial expressions and physiology). For many years there was little evidence to support this area of NLP and the techniques that have been taught by NLP trainers for the last 20 years. Today, evidence from neuroimaging supports both the underlying assumptions of rapport and sensory acuity and the strategies and approaches that were developed from their research.

A chance encounter with an ice cream

At a research lab in Italy on a hot summer's day in 1992, a macaque monkey sat in a laboratory chair waiting for researchers to return from their lunch. The researchers, led by Giacomo Rizzolatti, had been plotting the areas of activity in the primate's brain when they engaged in physical activity. Each time the monkey grabbed and moved an object, cells in the monkey's brain would fire and a monitor would sound. A graduate student entered the lab with an ice cream in his hand. Then something extraordinary happened: they noticed that when the animal was watching the student lifting his arm to lick the ice cream the same parts of the monkey's brain were fired as when the monkey was actually lifting its arm. This led to further investigation and to the discovery of mirror neurons. Today we are beginning to understand the importance of mirror neurons. The human brain is thought to have multiple mirror neuron systems that enable us not only to understand the actions of others ,but also their intentions, emotions and the social meaning of their behaviours.

Nearly 20 years earlier Bandler and Grinder had observed Milton Erickson, the hypnotherapist, mirroring his patients' body language and language patterns. Erickson, who as a post-polio patient, was severely restricted in his movements, had become a master at building rapport. In mirroring his patients, he would not directly imitate their movements but would make small gestures and movements that responded to the body movements of his patients.

Communication

In NLP we often say **the meaning of your communication is the response you get**. When we work with teachers in relation to the difficulties they face, the key cause of their difficulties is frequently miscommunication. Teaching is one of those professions where we are constantly at risk of having our communication misunderstood because we are continually communicating. As social beings, communication is vital to our functioning. If you were an alien and heard this you might be mystified; looking in from the outside all humans seem to do is communicate, yet we are not always doing this quite as well as we might.

So what can we do to improve our ability to communicate? Are there some practical ways in which we can enhance what we already do? NLP has some simple answers to this problem and it centres on knowing how to build **rapport**.

Rapport

What happens when we communicate?

When one person pays attention to another, they take in what the other person is saying and doing. They then get in touch with their own internal thoughts and feelings and respond in their own individual way. The other person pays attention to them … and so a communication loop forms.

To communicate more effectively it is essential to develop the skill of rapport. This does not mean that you have to agree with someone but it does mean that you respond to them and give them the experience of feeling understood.

Think about how you communicate. What is it that the other person is receiving, and how are they receiving it? Here we are not talking about the content of the communication, more thinking about the structure—not the words but the way they are said, the gestures and postures. We can think of these as our output channels. You could think about this as an elegant dance in which people respond step by step to and with each other.

Jargon Buster

What happens when we communicate?

A relationship or state of having trust and mutual responsiveness with others.

The Dance of Communication

Output External Behaviour

Generate Internal Response

Observe External Behaviour

Observe External Behaviour

Generate Internal Response

Output External Behaviour

Output Channels

Body	Voice	Words
▦ Gestures	▦ Speed of speech	▦ Common expressions
▦ Posture	▦ Tone of voice	▦ Key words
▦ Facial expression	▦ Volume of voice	▦ Sensory words (known as **predicates**)

These outputs are the way in which we pick up information from, and about, the other person when communicating. Most of the information is outside of our conscious awareness most of the time. By bringing it to our attention and by paying attention to the output from the three channels (visual, auditory and kinaesthetic) we can change our own behaviour and become more like the other person we are communicating with. In NLP this process is called **matching** or **mirroring**. We create rapport by matching or mirroring another person's body language and voice tonality, to literally 'join their dance'. This creates a bridge between our world and theirs. This builds trust and is the basis of effective communication.

> We can create rapport by matching or mirroring another person's body language and voice tonality, by joining their dance. This creates a bridge between our world and theirs. This builds trust and is the basis of effective communication.

How does this work?

You are bombarded by information every second: the light levels in the room, your heart beat, the feeling of your foot in your left shoe, the feeling of the book in your hand, etc. Your mind filters out most of this information from conscious awareness so that you have the feeling that you are paying attention only to that which is important at any one time. If you didn't do this you would go into **overload**. Within this mass of information are the micro patterns and behaviours of other people, including voice tone, gesture, blink rate, breathing rate and depth, and all the many other output patterns of the body. Because we are social creatures one of our unconscious drives is for relationships, so our mind has evolved a way of searching out those people with whom we might build relationships. In order to do this our brain matches incoming data against a pattern. The pattern we are looking for is our own or something similar. Invariably we are sending out a similar pattern in our own body language and language as our inner attention is focused on the pattern that we are searching for. Therefore we are constantly scanning the outside world for people who are like us. To build rapport easily all we need to do is to engage in the art of rapport by creating similarities in our output channels to the person we are with.

There are two basic patterns for creating rapport—**matching** and **mirroring**. Neither of these means mimicking; it means adopting a similar posture, words, rhythmic patterns, etc. You can use either pattern, which gives plenty of room for variation. The aim is similarity, not to be identical; all you want to do is have the other person's unconscious mind recognise that you are someone like them. The term 'matching' is used to describe the exact copying of an aspect of another person's behaviour (e.g. crossing left leg over right when this is what the other person is doing), 'mirroring' is adopting a mirror image of the person you are communicating with (e.g. crossing right leg over left, when they are doing left leg over right).

Examples of things that can be matched

Body	Language	Voice
■ Posture	■ Sensory word preferences	■ Volume
■ Facial expressions		■ Pitch
■ Hand movements	■ Descriptive words	■ Tempo
■ Eye movements	■ Key phrases	■ Vocal qualities (pace, rhythm, tonality)
■ Breathing rate	■ Repetitive phrasing	
■ Movement of feet	■ Exact words	
■ Body shifts		
■ Spine angle		
■ Head tilt		
■ Energy levels		

More advanced rapport techniques

Cross-over matching

The simple rapport-building techniques described above are very effective, particularly in the first stage of building rapport. A more advanced, and more subtle, technique is called cross-over matching. **Cross-over matching** involves matching another person's behaviour with a different behaviour of your own (e.g. matching their breathing rate to your finger movement, or their eye blinks to your foot-taps). This way of building rapport is very difficult for the other person to detect, and yet is still highly effective.

If you have an agitated child in class who is fidgeting, pick up the rhythm of the movement and begin matching with a different behaviour—the movement of a pen for instance. When you have held the rhythm for a while begin to slow down and notice the effect. If there is no change all you need to do is follow the rhythm for a little while longer and repeat—this is called **pacing and leading** (more about this later). We are very sensitive to rhythms and in a group situation we will tend to synchronise with any steady beat, even if it is barely audible. Playing music with such a beat in the classroom can also create rapport across the group.

Research Zone

Mirror neurons—brain cells that can read minds

Mirror neurons fire when we perform an action and when that same action is observed by another, and were first noted in primates in the 1990s (Rizzolatti et al., 1996; Gallese et al., 1996; Fogassi et al, 2005). In doing so the neurons literally mirror the behaviour of the other person. The activities of mirror neurons have been observed in primates and are thought to exist in humans and in some birds. Within the human brain, activity in the premotor cortex and the inferior parietal cortex has been found that is consistent with mirror neuron activity (Gallese et al., 1996). A number of writers consider the discovery of mirror neurons to be one of the most important in the last 10 years (e.g. Ramachandran, 2006). Studies of humans in fact suggest that the mirror neuron system develops in the first year of life and that this system is important in helping infants understand people's actions (Wicker et al. 2003).

Mirror neurons are thought to be particularly involved in the perception and comprehension of motor actions. They may also have a central role in higher order cognitive processing, for example imitation, language, theory of mind and empathy (Rizzolatti et al, 2001, Gallese and Goldman, 1998; Carr et al., 2003). All of these areas are known to be impaired in people with autism. The term 'theory of mind' refers to our ability to infer another person's mental state (e.g. beliefs and desires) from their behaviour or experiences. For this reason dysfunctional mirror neuron activity has also been implicated in cognitive disorders such as autism (Oberman et al., 2005; Dapretto et al., 2006). Children who have autism will also frequently have problems with the interpretation of proverbs and metaphors. This suggests a link between mirror neuron activity and the creation and understanding of metaphor (Ramachandra and Oberman, 2007). As Ramachandra and Oberman put it, mirror neurons may not only help us to reach for peanuts but also may have allowed humans to 'reach for the stars'. Mirror neurons have attracted considerable interest in popular psychology writing in recent years. In particular, Daniel Goleman has coined the phrase 'Neural WiFi' to illustrate the interrelationship of neural networks in social relationships and their importance in what he called 'social intelligence' (Goleman, 2006).

Carr, L., Iacoboni, M., Dubeau, M-C., Mazziotta, J. C. and Lenzi, G. L. (2003) Neural mechanisms of empathy in humans: a relay from neural systems for imitation to limbic areas, *Proceedings of the National Academy of Science*, 100: 5497–5502

Dapretto, M., Davies, M. S., Pfeifer, J. H., Scott, A. A., Sigman, M., Bookheimer, S. Y. and Iacoboni, M. (2006) Understanding emotions in others: mirror neuron dysfunction in children with autism spectrum disorders, *Nature Neuroscience*, 9: 1: 28–30

Fogassi, L., Ferrari, P. F., Gesierich, B., Rozzi, S., Chersi, F. and Rizzolatti, G. (2005) Parietal lobe: from action organization to intention understanding, *Science*, 308: 662–667

Gallese, V., Fadiga, L., Fogassi, L. and Rizzolatti, G. (1996) Action recognition in the premotor cortex, *Brain*, 119: 2: 593–609

Gallese, V. and Goldman, A. (1998) Mirror neurons and the simulation theory of mind-reading, *Trends in Cognitive Science*, 2: 493– 501

Goleman, D. (2006) *Social Intelligence*, London: Hutchinson

Research Zone continued ...

Oberman, L. M., Hubbard, E. M., McCleery, J. P., Altschuler, E. L. Ramachandran, V. S. and Pineda, J. A. (2005) EEG evidence for mirror neuron dysfunction in autism spectrum disorders, *Cognitive Brain Research*, 24: 190–198

Ramachandran, V. S. (2006) Mirror neurons and imitation learning as the driving force behind 'the great leap forward' in human evolution, *Edge Foundation*, <http://www.edge.org> accessed June 2007

Ramachandra, V. S. and Oberman, L. M. (2007) Broken mirrors: a theory of autism, *Scientific American Reports, Special Edition on Child Development*, 17: 2: 20–29

Rizzolatti, G., Fadiga, L., Gallese, L. and Fogassi, L. (1996) Premotor cortex and the recognition of motor actions, *Cognitive Brain Research*, 3: 131–141

Rizzolatti, G., Fogassi, L. and Gallese, V. (2001) Neurophysiological mechanisms underlying the understanding and imitation of action, *Neuroscience*, 2: 661–670

Wicker, B., Keysers, C., Plailly, J., Royet, J-P., Gallese, V., and Rizzolatti, G. (2003) Both of us disgusted in my insula: the common neural basis of seeing and feeling disgust, *Neuron*, 40: 655–664

NLP Toolbox No. 4

Get some practice with rapport

Before you use rapport in an important meeting, or an important context, get some practice. Experiment with matching and mirroring in various circumstances. For example, socially at a party where you could match or mirror someone new you are introduced to and notice how quickly you can build a relationship. Alternatively, use rapport when you are having a disagreement and notice how quickly that common ground appears. Pay particular attention to blink rate and breathing. To notice breathing rate and depth without being obvious look at the top of people's shoulders. Match these with small finger movements or with your own breathing and blinking.

Top tips

- Build rapport fast with difficult pupils by matching small body rhythms.

- Feel confident that you can stand your ground in a difficult situation by paying attention to rapport as well as what is being said.

- Always match parents at the start of a parent conference.

- Use your group rapport skills to create a more purposeful classroom environment. Notice who is the rapport lead in the group and match them. When you are in rapport gradually lead them with something different.

How using our senses can help build rapport

We take in our experiences through our senses. We are then able to use our thought processes to recreate these sensory experiences internally. For example, remembering a pleasant memory will make us smile, an unpleasant one will kindle painful emotions, and the thought of a favourite food or drink will make us salivate.

We represent our experiences to ourselves using our senses. In NLP we use the term **representational systems** to describe the six representational systems.

Representational Systems		
Sight	Visual	V
Hearing	Auditory	A
Speaking	Auditory digital	Ad
Feeling	Kinaesthetic	K
Smell	Olfactory	O
Taste	Gustatory	G

There are subdivisions within the systems. Auditory includes both imaginary hearing of words and sounds, and talking to oneself. Kinaesthetic includes internal bodily feelings, touch and emotions.

A useful metaphor is to see each sensory system as part of a network:

1. Input—the gathering of information internally and externally.
2. Thinking/processing—mapping, learning, decision-making, motivation strategy, storage of information, memory, visualisation of the future.
3. Output—how we express ourselves to others: language, voice, physiology.

As individuals, we have very different preferences in how our senses are used. If you ask someone to describe a fun time, one person might talk about what they saw while experiencing the event (V). A second may talk about the sounds and conversation that they heard (A), whilst a third may express how they felt during the experience and/or what they felt with their hands or their body in a tactile way (K). Noticing the sensory language that people use and matching that language can be a powerful way of influencing others. If you know someone well you can even match the proportions of visual, auditory and kinaesthetic language that they use. You can do this when speaking or when writing. In the world of e-mail this is a particularly useful strategy.

Using sensory preferences in language

In their early writings Bandler and Grinder noted the significance of sensory information within the process of communication. The linguistic evidence suggested that people engage in an initial filtering process based on sensory input preferences. These preferences appeared to be primarily for visual, auditory or kinaesthetic information. However, they also noted the importance of gustatory (taste) and olfactory (smell) information. When they were modelling Milton Erickson (the hypnotherapist), they found that he was not only very sensitive to noticing these preferences when they appeared in people's language, but also used this awareness to influence his clients by matching their **sensory preference** (visual, auditory or kinaesthetic) in his own language. For example, if someone used visual words when talking (e.g. I see what you mean), he would also use visual language when working with them, in order to build rapport.

It is important to note that Bandler and Grinder's research was not, however, about sensory preference and learning. Indeed there is substantial evidence that puts in doubt the existence of stable learning styles (see Research Zone below) and certainly there are no neurological structures that echo this phenomenon. This does not mean that we do not have linguistic preferences for certain words and language (as has been demonstrated by numerous personality type and trait measures in applied psychology—including learning styles inventories). Rather Bandler and Grinder demonstrated that excellent communicators are sensitive to and will often match the sensory language patterns of people they are communicating with in order to build rapport.

The language that we use can often be an indication of the way that we like to think. Most of us seem to demonstrate a linguistic preference for one, or possibly two, senses. If you listen to your own and to other people's language, you will begin to notice what these preferences are. Matching sensory language (or **predicates**) definitely shows that you have been listening to the other person and it is at this level that this sort of matching probably has an effect. Recent research (see the Research Zone above) has also shown an association between language (specifically metaphor) and mirror neuron activation (Ramachandra and Oberman, 2007). The extent to which sensory language as a form of metaphor is involved in this sort of functioning is as yet unresearched. So, as it currently stands, the proof is in the pudding— therefore, we suggest that you just give it a go and see what happens.

Noticing the sensory language that people use and matching that language can be a powerful way of influencing others. If you know someone well you can even match the proportions of visual, auditory and kinaesthetic language that they use.

It is worth noting that some people avoid sensory language and prefer to adopt a neutral non-sensory language. Genie Z. Laborde in her book *Influencing with Integrity* (1983) recognises this as a fourth type of processing that she labels 'cerebral'. Again this style of communication can be matched.

Some more examples …

Visual

I get the picture … I see what you mean … let's get this in perspective … it appears that … show me … the focus of attention … looking closer … it's clear to me … a different angle … this is the outlook … with hindsight … you'll look back on this.

Auditory

That rings a bell … we're on the same wavelength … let's talk about it … who calls the tune … within earshot … let's discuss things … I'm speechless … shout from the hilltops … people will hear you … this silence is deafening … it's music to my ears … word for word … in a manner of speaking.

Kinaesthetic

He's thick skinned ... a cool customer ... I grasp your meaning ... a heated argument ... I will be in touch ... I can't put my finger on it ... we are scratching the surface ... let's dig deeper... hit the nail on the head ... I feel it in my bones.

Cerebral/digital

It is interesting the way in which this might work ... Assuming that we must be objective ... It would be good to map out together the details and ensure that we have something to work to.

Olfactory and gustatory

It's a matter of taste ... let's chew it over ... I smell a rat ... it's a bitter pill ... that's an acid comment ... it's a bit fishy ... it leaves a bad taste.

Pulling it all together

Step 1

Match or mirror the other person's body positions. This is the most powerful way to generate rapport, and remember: similarity not mimicry. Start with the spine and head angles then arm and leg positions. Notice how the person is holding their hands and the types of gesture they use.

Step 2

Be aware of the sensory language they are using. If this proves difficult at first then adjust your language so that you use words from all the senses.

Step 3

Notice some of the body and language clues that are present, and match your language and body to them.

Research Zone

A note on learning styles, sensory preference and learning

Much attention has been paid to learning styles in teaching in the last 10 years. A number of theories have become particularly influential in recent years (e.g. Kolb's Learning Cycle (Kolb, 1995) and sensory preference theories (e.g. Benzwie, 1987)). A learning styles inventory is also available (Dunn et al., 1984) and there is psychological evidence to support the possibility that individual preferences exist regarding how we like to learn. Sensory learning theories tend to classify students into either: visual, auditory, kinaesthetic/tactile, interactive, olfactory or print-orientated (preferring to learn by reading).

The notion of visual, auditory and kinaesthetic preference is one of a number of areas of NLP that have migrated into other areas of life. As in linguistic translation, things can easily be lost in the process. Early NLP research showed evidence for the importance of sensory preference in communication, rapport and in the coding and recoding of memories from a subjective experiential perspective (1975a and b; 1976a and b). However, this research did not show any evidence in relation to learning.

Recent education research shows that there is very little evidence that modifying teaching approach to take into account learning styles has any impact on achievement (Davis, 1988; O'Sullivan et al., 1994; Stahl, 2002) and the use of learning styles in teaching is questioned (Coffield et al., 2004a; b). One study (Knight, 1990) found that the control group in the study, whose lessons had not been adapted to reflect learning style, actually outperformed the group whose learning environment had been adapted to match their learning styles. In relation to Kolb's learning styles Inventory, Garner (2000) found no evidence to support the existence of learning styles. A recent Demos report chaired by David Hargreaves (Hargreaves et al., 2005) concluded that evidence in support of learning styles was 'highly variable' and that researchers and practitioners were 'not by any means frank about the evidence for their work'.

Bandler and Grinder's work would suggest that using a range of sensory learning styles would tend to create better group rapport, as a teacher would then be in a position to motivate more of the learners within the group. There is as yet no research to support this hypothesis, however, we would from our own experience of working with teachers suggest that good group rapport is a significant factor in teacher effectiveness and that using multiple sensory approaches is a way of achieving this. Numerous studies, however, support the importance of teacher-class rapport at a general level.

Bandler, R. and Grinder, J. (1975a) *The Structure of Magic I: A Book About Language and Therapy*, Palo Alto, CA: Science and Behaviour Books

Bandler, R. and Grinder, J. (1975b) *Patterns of the Hypnotic Techniques of Milton H. Erickson, M.D.* vol i, Cupertino, CA: Meta Publications

Bandler, R. and Grinder, J. (1976a) *Patterns of the Hypnotic Techniques of Milton H. Erickson, M.D.* vol ii. Cupertino, CA: Meta Publications

Bandler, R. and Grinder, J. (1976b) *The Structure of Magic II*, Palo Alto, CA: Science and Behaviour Books

Benzwie, T. (1987) *A Moving Experience*, Tuczon, AZ: Zephyr Press

Coffield, F., Moseley, D., Hall, E. and Ecclestone, K. (2004a) Learning Styles and Pedagogy—in Post 16 Learning: *A Systematic and Critical Review*, London: Learning and Skills Research Centre, Institute of Education

Coffield, F., Moseley, D., Hall, E. and Ecclestone, K. (2004b) *Should We Be Using Learning Styles? What Research Has To Say To Practice*, London: Learning and Skills Research

Davis, J. (1988) *On Matching Teaching Approach with Student Learning Style: Are We Asking the Right Question?* Memphis, TN: University of Memphis

Dunn, R., Dunn, K. and Price, G. E. (1984) *Learning Style Inventory*, Lawrence, KS: Price Systems

Garner, I. (2000) Problems and inconsistencies with Kolb's learning styles. Educational Psychology: *An International Journal of Experimental Educational Psychology*, 20: 3: 341–348

Hargreaves, D., et al. (2005) *About Learning: Report of the Learning Working Group*, London: Demos

Knight, K. (1990) Effects of learning style accommodation on achievement of second graders, Paper presented at the meeting of the Mid-South Educational Research Association, New Orleans, November 1990

Kolb, D.A. (1995) The process of experiential learning, in M.Thorpe, R. Edwards and A. Hanson (eds) *Culture and Processes of Adult Learning*, Milton Keynes: Open University

Stahl, S. A. (2002) Different strokes for different folks? in L. Abbeduto (ed.), Taking Sides: *Clashing on Controversial Issues in Educational Psychology*, Guilford, CT: McGraw-Hill, 98–107

Pacing and leading

Pacing and leading is one of the keys to influencing people. It refers to meeting people half way and matching them where they currently are (**pacing**) and then taking them where you want them to go (**leading**). You know if you have rapport because, once you have it, you are then able to lead people. When pacing and leading you should aim for a relationship of at least two to one: **pace, pace, lead**. Once you find yourself in the position to lead, people are much more open to suggestion and influence. Once you are confident in doing this you may like to explore the verbal pacing and leading tool below and incorporate with some hypnotic language patterns from Chapter 5, *Don't think about chocolate cake*. In all this, remember to be subtle; you should not mimic the other person, so similarity and timing are important.

Just do it

Here's how to do simple pacing and leading with physiology

Choose a safe situation to practise matching or mirroring an element of someone else's behaviour. When you have matched or mirrored them for a while, and think you are in rapport with the person, scratch your nose. If they lift their hand to their face within the next minute or so, congratulate yourself—you have led their behaviour!

You can find some exercises that you can use to practise this in Chapter 15, *Instant training Day*.

Group rapport

When leading and teaching a group, creating rapport is critical to generating a learning environment that will be comfortable and relaxed. Whilst up to now we have been focusing on rapport between two people, when working in groups having ways of creating rapport both physically and through language is just as much an essential skill. Applying these skills in the classroom is easy to do and will get you quick results.

Let's look at some of the principles involved. Rather than you as a teacher attempting to create rapport with each individual, there are some strategies that will create synchronisation in the group. The idea is to have everyone doing the same thing—you included. Here are some ideas.

- Ask *universal questions* to which the answer will be yes for everyone and get them to raise their hands by all doing the same, e.g. Has anyone seen a TV programme? This may seem strange, and has a blindingly obvious answer, however what occurs is agreement in the group. So when you raise your hand so will almost everyone else. You can do this in a sequence.

  e.g. Put your hand up if you have ever had a conversation? (hand up)... Have you ever had a conversation and said something wrong? (hand up) ... Have you ever had a conversation, said something wrong and then regretted it? (hand up) ... How would it be to know how to build rapport to avoid this, would that be useful?

  Notice how the pattern also follows the pace, pace, lead structure.

- Use truisms, e.g. "We are all sitting down" and pace, pace, lead statements (see Chapter 5, *Don't think about chocolate cake*).

- Use handouts so that the group is engaged in handing round a resource and working with it, all doing the same thing.

- Any activity that synchronises movement and breathing will create rapport. Laughter, music, song or a sequence of movements (simple 'brain gym' or yoga exercises work very well).

- In any group there will be individuals who are rapport leaders. You can spot these by noticing who moves first and seeing how many follow. Building rapport with a rapport leader will enable you to have rapport with a number of others at the same time.

- Make sure you maintain eye contact throughout the group. Imagining yourself being a lighthouse is a useful metaphor to help to ensure that you connect with each person during the lesson.

NLP Toolbox No. 5

Verbal pacing and leading

We have learned about pacing, to get rapport, and leading towards an outcome by learning to pace voice tone, tempo, volume and timbre; body physiology; visual, auditory, and kinaesthetic sensory language, etc. We can use this same concept for verbal pacing and leading.

So, how does it work?

It works by blurring the distinction between what is absolutely true and undeniable (observable in the person's own experience) and what we want to be believed as true (or has yet to be established as true). We are not saying that what you are suggesting is not true; only that it has yet to be established as being true in their minds.

It's harder to explain than to demonstrate, so let's demonstrate how it works.

We will use the following pattern by gradually moving from pacing to leading …

Pace, pace, pace, lead

Pace, pace, lead, lead

Pace, lead, lead, lead

… and we will then repeat this same pattern over and over.

We will illustrate this by using verbal pacing and leading pattern to **pace** and **lead** you, the reader, (yes **YOU**) into learning to use and actually do the process. Before you begin any influencing process you need to be clear about your outcome. Our outcome in this instance is to use the pattern to pace and lead you into learning to use and actually do the pacing and leading process.

Read the following:

As you look at this skill building exercise and you read each of the words, you have thoughts in your mind about what we are saying and how you can begin to use this material in your everyday school life. And as you have the thoughts and have the feelings that you are having, you know that this is something that really interests you and because of that it will be easy for you to learn. And as you wonder about being able to understand and learn what we are writing here, you begin to think about where else in your teaching you can use this process and what outcome you might want to obtain by using this skill. And you wonder how you can set aside enough time to really learn these skills to improve your results.

Analysis of what we just got you to read

Pace: As you look this skill building exercise

Pace: and you read each of the words

Pace: you have thoughts, in your mind, about what we are saying

Lead: and how you can begin to incorporate this material into your everyday school life.

Pace: And as you have the thoughts

Pace: and have the feelings that you are having,

Lead: you know that this is something that really interests you

Lead: and because of that it will be easy for you to learn.

Pace: And as you wonder about being able to understand and learn what I'm writing here

Lead: you begin to think about where in your life you can use this process

Lead: and what outcome you might want to obtain by using this skill

Lead: and you wonder how you can set aside enough time to really learn these skills to improve your results.

NLP Toolbox No. 5 continued ...

This is a useful and powerful pattern. When you use it correctly it is almost impossible to tell which of the statements you are using are undeniably true and which statements are the ones which you want people to believe as being true. The same applies if you are suggesting activities or actions. These strategies are widely taught as part of sales training and it is well worth spending sometime embedding and integrating them with your other behaviour management strategies.

Research Zone

The simulation theory of empathy

Simulation theory originated as a result of the discovery of the mirror neuron system and is an explanation of how humans understand the emotions and experiences of others. It is believed that observing the experience and actions of others automatically activates shared neural networks. For example people may feel pain when they observe others experiencing pain (Avenanti et al., 2006), sense touching when they see another brushed (Keyser et al., 2004), feel disgusted when they see someone else smell a bad odour (Wicker et al., 2003) or feel sad when they see a sad expression on another's face (Harrison et al., 2006). The understanding of others' emotions and actions is believed to facilitate communication, and evidence from neuro-imaging suggests that empathy is a crucial factor in human communication (de Vignemont and Singer, 2006). Specifically, the mental mirroring of actions and emotions enables communication. Mentally mirroring the actions and emotions enables humans to understand others' actions and their related environment quickly, which helps humans communicate efficiently.

Avenanti, A., Paluello, L. M., Bufalari, I., and Aglioti, S. M. (2006). Stimulus-driven modulation of motor-evoked potentials during observation of others' pain, *Neuroimage*, 32: 1: 316–324

de Vignemont, F. and Singer, T. (2006) The empathic brain: how, when and why? *Trends in Cognitive Sciences*, 10: 10: 435–441

Gallese, V., Keysers, C. and Rizzolatti, G. (2004) A unifying view of the basis of social cognition, *Trends in Cognitive Sciences*, 8: 9: 396–403

Harrison, N. A., Singer, T., Rotshtein, P., Dolan, R. J., and Critchley, H. D. (2006) Pupillary contagion: central mechanisms engaged in sadness processing, *SCAN*, 1: 5–17

Keysers, C., Wicker, B., Gazzola, V., Anton, J. L., Fogassi, L., and Gallese, V. (2004) A touching sight: SII/PV activation during the observation and experience of touch, *Neuron*, 42: 2: 335–346

Wicker, B., Keysers, C., Plailly, J., Royet, J. P., Gallese, V., and Rizzolatti, G. (2003) Both of us disgusted in my insula: the common neural basis of seeing and feeling disgust, *Neuron*, 40: 3: 655–664

Brain waves are affected when matching takes place

In a groundbreaking experiment in Florida, neuroscientists recorded the brain rhythms of two people sitting opposite each other as they carried out a series of up and down finger movements. Two participants were sat opposite each other. When separated by a barrier, so that they could not see each other, there was no evidence of the recently identified Phi brain rhythm (which appears during social interaction). However, when both subjects were able to view each other's movements the Phi rhythm was identifiable originating from brain regions that are associated with mirror neuron activation. The Phi rhythm varied depending on whether the participants maintained independent finger movements or whether they synchronised their movements (Tognoli et al., 2007).

Tognoli, E., Lagarde, J., DeGuzman, G. C. and Scott Kelso, J. A. (2007) The Phi complex as a neuromarker of human social coordination, *Proceedings of the National Academy of Science*, 104: 19: 8190–8195

More ways to start improving your classroom practice with NLP

■ Get into the habit of matching the small rhythmic patterns of your students as you teach them, particularly the difficult students and the ones who are 'rapport leaders' in their group. Do it with all your students every lesson. With skill and practice you can do more than one student at once (e.g. if leading a discussion group you could match the body language of one student by crossing your arms whilst tapping you foot in time to the rhythm of another student's body language).

■ In a confrontational situation remember to pace first by matching before your lead. You can do this very quickly with a finger movement, etc.

■ In a situation where a student has shouted at you, very quickly match their voice volume (not their voice tone or words) for a fraction of a second before lowering your voice and then matching blink rate or other strong signals—then continue to match other physical cues as your carry on talking.

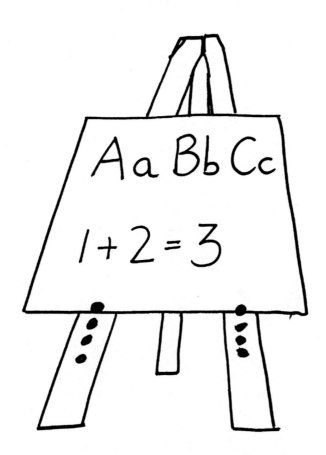

Chapter 4
Dolphin aquarium

How to get the relationships (and therefore the behaviour) you want from the classes you teach

Have you ever known a teacher follow the school's behaviour policy consistently – applying rewards and sanctions in the same way, all the time – and yet still not get the desired behaviour from the students? How can this be? What's going on? How would it be if there were some simple answers to this problem? In fact, how would it be if the answers were so simple that teachers often miss the obvious? Would that be useful? These common experiences tell us that there has to more going on than purely behaviourist psychology has so far explained.

It is often said that the co-founders of NLP were inspired to study how excellent people do what they do as a result of a conversation with Gregory Bateson. Bateson became a sort of mentor to Bandler and Grinder and introduced them to the medical hypnotist Milton Erickson. Bateson is widely recognised as one of the most influential thinkers of the twentieth century. He was a brilliant scientist and biological philosopher. Gregory Bateson was born in England, studied at Cambridge, and was married to the anthropologist Margaret Mead. He carried out pioneering anthropological studies into patterns of behaviour and communication in Bali and New Guinea. He played a major role in defining areas such as cybernetics and other systems thinking. He also carried out research into schizophrenia, learning and psychiatry. His work and writings have inspired many ideas and areas of research into NLP.

What you'd expect from dolphins

In the 1960s Bateson spent a number of years researching the communication and behaviour of dolphins and porpoises at a research centre in Hawaii. This was expensive work and in order to support the research programme that was being undertaken, the scientists would occasionally create live performances for paying audiences. Part of the entertainment involved demonstrating to the audience how they trained the animals to do amazing tricks. It worked like this. A dolphin would be led in front of the watching crowd and the trainer would wait for the animal to do something unusual, for example, moving its head in a particular way. Immediately the trainer would blow a whistle and throw the dolphin a fish. He would then wait for the animal to do the same thing again, following which the whistle would be blown again and another fish would be thrown. Very quickly the dolphins would know what to do to get a fish and, indeed, were soon able to put on an impressive display of single behaviours.

A little later on the dolphins were brought back to the main arena to do a follow-up show. Once again they would begin to do the same tricks and wait for a fish. However, the trainer didn't want them to do the same things but to show how they learnt a second trick, so no fish was awarded. Invariably the animals would spend some time repeating the old trick continuously. Eventually they became frustrated and flipped their tail, or did something similar in disapproval. Straight away the trainer blew the whistle and threw another fish. Once again there would be a period of demonstration where the dolphin was rewarded and then returned to the other tank. Later again a third session was held in the main arena.

This time the animals would demonstrate the second trick that had been learnt and again the trainer would not reward the dolphins because a new trick was required. After a while the animals would eventually do something different and again they would be rewarded with a fish. A display involving the new trick with rewards of fish would follow.

After a while something amazing happened

All of the above is, in itself, is of no great surprise, as Pavlov and Skinner have demonstrated very effectively in their experiments and theories of behaviour. What Bateson and his colleagues discovered, over time, was something fascinating about the nature of learning, as opposed to just behaviour: namely that context is extremely important also and that communication takes place at both a contextual and at a relationship level.

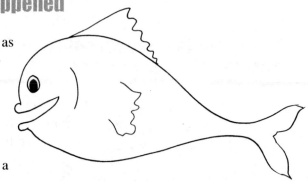

For approximately 14 shows the dolphins would follow the same pattern. The first two thirds of the display would consist of repetitions of unwanted behaviour until eventually, by chance, a new behaviour occurred and the cycle would begin again. By the time they got to around the fourteenth show, however, the dolphins were no longer willing to participate and appeared to have become frustrated by the constant reminder of having got something wrong. They had to some extent begun to become aware of the process. Indeed the trainers were required to start giving the animals fish rewards just to preserve their relationship with the animals. This 'relationship reward' had extraordinary consequences. As a result of the addition of 'relationship rewards' the dolphins would then become very excited and start coming up with a whole suite of new and original tricks and behaviours. On one occasion one animal came up with eight completely new tricks that had never been seen by the trainers before.

What Bateson's research means in relation to behaviourist theories and learning

Bateson suggests that the later novel behaviour indicated learning on a different level, namely that of context. As well as associating behaviours with reward, it appeared that through the process of experiencing repetitions of the context the dolphins had learnt something about the nature of the situation they found themselves in – particularly in terms of their relationship to the trainer and the training. They were 'learning to learn'. For Bateson, the dolphin story demonstrates the distinction between learning 'content' and learning 'context'. Bateson breaks away from the behaviourist tradition by suggesting a consideration of the circumstances in which the reinforcement of behaviour occurred and sees this context as an important level of restriction. In this sense we can see the 'unearned fish' as a form of 'higher level' conditioning in which it acts as communication that reinforces the relational aspects of the context. By inference, sticking too closely to the rules of reward and consequence earlier on in the process may have communicated (at a 'meta' level) that the trainers were unconcerned about their relationship with the dolphins. What Bateson demonstrated was that although the trainers had influence they were not in control as such. The same thing applies in the classroom. You, as a teacher, are part of a context in which although you have influence you are, at the end of the day, an equal participant and are no more in control than anyone else.

Lessons from Bateson's research with dolphins and porpoises

1. The actual behaviours that were exhibited were under the control of the dolphins rather than the trainer. The trainer's input was to use contingent reward to not only ensure repeated behaviour but also to preserve relationships.

2. Contingent reward worked for a time. However, there was always a point where this was not enough to ensure that the dolphins co-operated. At this point they just needed a fish to preserve the relationship. Therefore Bateson concluded that the fish reward was not so much a reinforcement for the behaviour, but rather a message to the dolphin about its relationship with the trainer. The trainers' sensitivity to the relationship with the animals, and consequent actions in giving an extra fish, were critical to the success of the relationship and the experiments.

3. The dolphins had to learn a specific behaviour and not a group of behaviours. In other words, you have to learn each separate behaviour in its context.

4. The whistle was not a stimulus, or trigger, for the behaviour. Rather it was a message about something that had already been done by the dolphin.

5. Giving 'relationship rewards' generated motivation and more learning than had been anticipated or expected.

6. Where learning takes place there is always a 'higher' context. In the case of the dolphins it was the context of 'entertainment by showing how the dolphins learnt'. In the classroom you must consciously decide to train positive behaviours and to train your expectations – if you want them to happen.

7. All dolphin training was done with reward and removal of reward – there were no consequences as such.

In terms of the classroom it is important to remember that there is no such thing as ESP, yet! You have to make your expectations really explicit by always praising the behaviour that you want when you see it. Catch the children doing something right, in other words. Where behaviour and relationships are concerned the watchword is WYTIWYG (What you teach is what you get). With practice in the classroom, you can easily move towards a situation in which you are constantly reminding the group about rules by praising the ones who are doing it. The effect on the others will also be a conditioning one because they are part of the same context.

Where behaviour and relationships are concerned the watchword is WYTIWYG
(What you teach is what you get).

Positive reward management

Like most

Being praised

Being told off

Being ignored

Like least

In the dolphin training there was only the use of praise, or the removal of it. There were no direct negative consequences. An important concept from psychology that can add real depth to our practice in the classroom is the idea of strokes. Eric Berne the founder of transactional analysis, notes in his book, *The Games People Play* (1964), that people need and seek the attention of other people whether that attention is positive or negative. According to Berne, strokes are the recognition, responsiveness or attention that one person gives to another person. Strokes can be positive (warm fuzzies) or negative (cold pricklies). At the heart of this concept is the idea that people hunger for recognition, and that lacking positive strokes they will seek whatever kind of stroke they can, even if that recognition is of a negative kind. Furthermore, as children we are constantly testing out which strategies and behaviours seem to get us strokes, both positive and negative. Consequently, children who are getting few positive strokes in their home life or at school can become essentially addicted to seeking out and achieving the wrong sort of strokes.

Just do it

The inherent need for attention stays with us right into adult life. Think about it for a moment. What's usually worse: being told off or being ignored?

This same process can be seen in the behaviours of the dolphins for whom it was not enough that the rules of the game were maintained – they also needed some attention, although praise is by far the best and most desired stroke. Being aware of this hierarchy of strokes is a powerful tool in the classroom and can be used to create a really effective **positive reward management framework**. Obviously you may, of course, need to use punishments and consequences from time to time. Do so, however, with an awareness that you may be creating the opposite to what you really want to achieve. Make sure that these are between you and the child responsible and that you are not simply giving negative strokes. Applied effectively not only should you rarely need to give negative strokes but also you will find that you take your class's learning beyond the basics of stimulus and response and get a lot more that just compliance out of all the children that you teach.

NLP Toolbox No. 6

Peripheral praise in the classroom

Peripheral praise is one of those great classroom tools. It combines the best of our understanding about praise and strokes. It is particularly effective because it not only reinforces rules but also gives rewards to those doing the right thing. At the same time it reduces the possibility of getting any form of answering back from the person that it is directed at and therefore reduces the risk of giving escalating negative strokes to a student who is addicted to negative strokes.

Here's an example of how it works. Imagine you are teaching a class and you notice one person who is off-task or doing something that you didn't ask the class to do. Move over to the student and, when you know that they are aware of your presence, give praise to both students on either side of the person for doing the correct thing. End by looking at the person who is not doing the right thing, look briefly at them, then continue to give other instructions to the class.

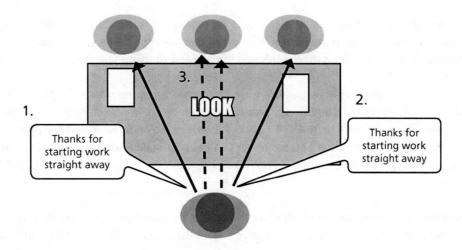

You can extend the approach to the whole class if everyone is doing the right thing apart from one person. For example, you might thank the whole class for being on time when one person arrives late. I (Richard) came across the power of this strategy by accident. In my very first lesson in a very challenging inner city school a child (who I didn't even know the name of) flung a chair in anger in the direction of someone else in the room. The whole class looked stunned and I hardly knew what to say, so I just said, 'Thank you to everyone who is ready to learn, I really appreciate that.' The boy who had flung the chair immediately sat down and apologised. He worked well after that and I made sure that I praised him every time I saw him doing something that followed my expectations. He was and remained one of the best students that I taught and yet continued to misbehave in nearly everyone else's lessons.

In Bateson's research, the dolphins had to learn a specific behaviour in itself and in its context. In a school, just because a child has learnt to be good about one element of expected behaviour, it does not follow that they will do the same in all areas. Each element of expectation has to be taught as a separate behaviour and within its specific context. In our experience, understanding this process, and its consequences, is a liberating experience for many teachers who have become demoralised by struggling with the behaviour of individuals and classes when they appear to be doing the same as everyone else in the school. A little observation of the 'right things' reveals an additional layer of reward interaction between the successful teachers and those who are struggling. In particular, these teachers go beyond the basics of contingent reward and provide rewards as part of the process of developing a positive relationship with the students, whilst at the same time ensuring that they do not compromise their rules and expectations. An easy way to achieve this is to praise as many children as you can every time you see someone doing what you expect – even if it is something that you know they already know how to do.

> An easy way to achieve this is to praise as many children as you can every time you see someone doing what you expect – even if it is something that you know they already know how to do.

It works like this.

1. Take every opportunity to praise good behaviour whenever you see it. In other words, catch the children doing something right.

2. Wherever possible, correct unwanted behaviours by rewarding those that are doing the right thing but avoiding giving a stroke to the person who is not complying. Three great strategies for doing this are **peripheral praise**, the **power look** and **embedded naming** (see NLP Toolboxes 6 and 8).

3. Take some lessons from Pavlov by conditioning classroom group responses to more than just the words you use. Always do certain things from certain places in the classroom so that the children already know what is coming before you say it. Include some anchoring in these places (see Chapter 9, Anchors away) so that you are always in the best state to deliver the particular message. With practice and repetition, even the gestures you use can form a 'metamessage' like the whistle to the dolphin.

4. If you have to give a negative stroke make sure that it is followed by lots of positive rewards and praise for those students who are doing what you want them to do. The more fish, the more tricks.

5. When you have corrected the behaviour of a child always 'give a fish' later on. Make an effort to catch the same child doing something right later on in the lesson.

Reinforcing positive behaviours that are already learnt by children in the classroom will affect other children in the group and help them to understand what it is that you want and what you give rewards for. In a very short time you will find other students following your rules and expectations in order to also get positive reward. As soon as you see this praise them too! We call this compliance by a thousand praises (see Toolbox 7 on the following page).

Top tips

1. When using rewards to develop positive behaviours remember that each desired behaviour will need to be taught and 'trained' in itself and in its context (and with each individual teacher).

2. Sometimes you just need to give rewards to preserve the relationship; just giving purely contingent rewards and consequences has a limited life span in relation to motivation to learn.

3. Praise as often as possible to reinforce relationships and behaviours that are already in place.

4. Poorly behaved children may be responding to the negative strokes that you are giving them and may have become conditioned to behave to get a stroke – use positive reward management strategies such as **peripheral praise** (see toolbox on previous page) as often as possible to avoid this.

5. Focusing on the negatives can often bring these things into existence by reminding the children of the possibility of poor behaviour or rule breaking. Be particularly careful with words like 'don't' – see Chapter 5, *Don't think about chocolate cake*. It is much better and more effective to focus on the desired behaviours by rewarding that behaviour every time you see it than to dwell on the behaviours you don't want.

Bateson's experiments show clearly how the trainer was as much part of the context as was the dolphin. It is important to realise that the purpose of giving positive feedback to the learners about their behaviour and your relationship with them is to encourage them to develop more and more positive behaviours in response to the evolving context. In this sense the objective is to draw out the children's natural abilities to achieve positive strokes through a process of encouragement and effective feedback.

NLP Toolbox No. 7

Compliance by a thousand praises – how to give praise well

Giving praise well is a real skill, but an easy one to grasp once you understand it. Below are some top tips for how to do this really effectively.

■ **Look for the opportunity** to point out those students who have followed an instruction immediately, even if it is only a small group in the class. Give your instructions to the whole group; look for a group who have complied; immediately point out to the whole class that the group have done what they were asked and give them a positive stroke. Invariably other groups will come into line.

■ **Make your praise specific.** Don't just thank people with generalisations: instead of saying 'Thank you for working well', say something like 'Susan I really like the way that you have underlined all of the titles in the piece of work.' Make sure that the praise is heard by others in the group.

■ Continue to **circulate** the room while the students are on task giving positive reward and recognition for the work that is being done in the way that you asked.

NLP Toolbox No. 7 continued ...

- When you are working with a small group or an individual take the time to keep the rest of the class in your peripheral vision and stop to **praise a group from a distance** now and then.

- **At the start of the year you need to put greater emphasis on teaching behaviour and expectations** therefore you will need to give more praise. Actively teach your classroom rules and spend time explaining them right from the start.

- **Make a list of 40 things that you could praise** students for that you normally would ignore, but which are really important in your ideal classroom. For example: listening carefully, being on time, taking turns, asking questions, starting quickly, etc.

- **Always aim to give praise in at least the proportions 5 to 1**. In other words, if you have had to say something negative give five more praises about correct behaviour.

- **When in doubt praise** someone else who is doing the right thing.

NLP Toolbox No. 8

The power look and embedded naming

Below are two other really effective ways of helping to ensure that your expectations are achieved without creating the opportunity for a negative stroke exchange.

The power look - Sometimes just a look can say 'I have seen what you are doing and I am not happy with your behaviour.' This form of non-stroke re-direction can be highly effective particularly with off-task behaviours that are not confrontational. When you notice something like this, instead of saying something, make direct eye contact with the student while accessing a calm and assertive internal state. It is great to combine this with an anchor (see Chapter 9, Anchors away). Keep eye contact until the behaviour has changed then praise something else that you do approve of. As with all of these strategies it is important to catch the person who was denied a stroke doing something right later on in the lesson.

Embedded naming – This strategy works by drawing a child's attention to the fact that you have noticed them without actually speaking to them directly. For example if you noticed that someone in the lesson was not paying attention you might include his/her name in an example that you were giving. Like this:

So if Susan wanted to go to the Great Wall of China she would have the following ways to get there. She could ... or ...

Research Zone

Positive reinforcement and consistency

Research into behaviour management has shown that effectiveness is dependent on praise being delivered contingently (Brophy, 1981) and school-wide consistency (Reynolds, 1992). In particular, changes in behaviour are likely to have a positive impact on learning if there is a continuous 'schedule' of positive reinforcement (Muijis and Reynolds, 2005). Classical conditioning (Pavlov, 1927) and behavioural or operant conditioning (Skinner, 1974) are well established elements of our understanding of learning and still have a strong influence on education practice and theory. You can find more on classical and operant conditioning in Chapter 9, *Anchors away*. What Bateson's experiments (Bateson, 1972) and work in this area add to these ideas is the importance of praise in itself as a motivational force and as a message about relationships. Although consistency and reinforcement are of absolute importance when teaching positive behaviours to children, sometimes you also have to throw them a fish to demonstrate the positive intent of your relationship with them. This dynamic is the same one that you encounter when there are consistent rules and consequences across a school and yet within individual lessons and with different teachers the children interpret or respond to those rules inconsistently. Every interaction has the potential to be a received stroke, whether your intention is to be positive or negative (Berne, 1964), therefore be aware of the potential unintended consequencies of applying sanctions and punishments, particularly with children who have been starved of positive strokes and interactions in their home life.

Bateson, G. (1972) *Steps to an Ecology of Mind*, London: Paladin, Granada

Berne, E. (1964) *Games People Play*, New York: Grove Press

Brophy, J. (1981) Teacher praise: a functional analysis, *Review of Educational Research*, Spring, 5-32

Muijis, D. and Reynold, D (2005, 2nd) *Effective Teaching, Evidence and Practice*, London: Sage

Pavlov, I. (1927) *Conditioned Reflexes*, London: Oxford University Press

Reynolds (1992) School effectiveness and school improvement: an updated review of the British literature, in D. Reynolds and P. Cuttance (eds) *School Effectiveness: Research, Policy and Practice*, London: Cassell

Skinner, B. F. (1974) *About Behaviourism*, New York: Longman

Context markers and levels of learning

Bateson's view of learning is essentially a 'cybernetic' one. Rather than seeing the world as a series of cause and effect relationships, cybernetic thinking looks at the restrictions that are in place that limit the number of possibilities. You can think of the movement of a billiard ball bouncing off a billiard table cushion as the effect of the cue striking it or you can see its movement as a result of the restrictions of the table holding the ball up, the cushion being in the way, etc. Bateson's work applied this principle to behavioural science (Bateson, 1972) and took ideas from basic Pavlovian conditioning, to another level by taking into account the context of the learning. Bateson observed that the stimuli that were being used by the trainers were not so much triggers for the behaviour as in classical conditioning but were rather markers that defined the context, which Bateson called **context markers**. Context markers are in a sense messages that place restrictions on the possible choices that can follow a stimulus. In the case of the dolphins they had moved from *Learning I* where they were essentially having their behaviour corrected from within a set of alternatives, to *Learning II* where they were beginning to notice the context within which the stimulus was taking place. In essence a context

Research Zone continued ...

marker is contextual information that enables an animal to interpret a stimulus in a particular way. Examples of context markers:

■ The Pope's throne from which he makes announcements ex cathedra. These announcements are thereby endowed with a special order of validity.

■ The placebo, by which the doctor sets the stage for a change in the patient's subjective experience.

■ The shining object used by some hypnotists in 'inducing trance'.

■ The air raid-siren and the 'all clear'.

■ The handshake of boxers before the fight.

■ The observances of etiquette. (Bateson, 1972, p. 290)

Once a context marker is established, the number of possible behaviours is **restricted** as is the interpretation of any behaviours that follow. For a full discussion of Bateson's levels of learning see *Steps to an Ecology of Mind* (Bateson, 1972). As we develop our classroom practice and relationships with the children we teach we are constantly putting in place context markers, some of which may be helpful, others that are not. If we want the context to be full of the positive behaviours that we want then we need to set context markers that relate to the desired state rather than the one that is undesirable.

Bateson, G. (1972) *Steps to an Ecology of Mind*, London: Paladin, Granada
Wiener, N. (1961) *Cybernetics*, New York: John Wiley and Sons

More ways to start improving your classroom practice with NLP

■ Catch every child doing something right at least once every single lesson

■ If you have had to phone a parent about a child's poor behaviour, always phone back the next week to praise what has improved

■ If a child has turned a corner behaviour-wise don't wait until the next parents' evening to reward the child by telling the parents. Send a note home or phone up. Be specific about what you now are seeing that is good

■ Avoid generalised waffly praise – be specific about what you see that you like

Chapter 5
Don't think about chocolate cake

How to use your language to get what you want

Imagine for a moment that someone you were to meet in a bar, restaurant or in the street later today were to say to you, 'just by saying a few words in the right way you can send people into wonderful places, influence the way they think or help them to find their own solutions to any problem they face.' That would be good, wouldn't it?

In the introduction we mentioned how the founders of NLP had 'modelled' a number of extraordinary figures at the leading edge of therapy in the 1970s. One person they studied in great detail was Milton Erickson, the world famous hypnotherapist. Erickson, who died in 1980, is widely considered to have been one of the most important leaders in his field. He was so impressed with Bandler and Grinder's work that he wrote forewords for some of their books. In one of these he describes suffering from polio early in his life. During his long periods of treatment and recovery he began to develop his sensory perception in relation to non-verbal communication to a very advanced level (you can learn more about this in Chapter 3, *We like like*).

As well as 'modelling' Erickson's extraordinary ability to build rapport rapidly and deeply with his clients, Bandler and Grinder mapped his language and identified many different patterns that he regularly used to influence, make suggestions and induce trance. So effective was Erickson's use of language that he was able to create change in clients without formally creating a sleep-like hypnotic state. He was also able to dramatically change people by just having a conversation or telling a story. This 'waking-state' form hypnosis was a technique that Bandler and Grinder took forward into their work and their training of NLP.

One of Milton Erickson's greatest skills was the ability to be artfully vague. In other words he would often talk in generalised or ambiguous ways. Vague language is effective because it gets people into an altered state of mind and distracts their attention from, and with, the external world. Putting people into this state makes it easier to connect with them and to create rapport, even with people you do not know well. It also helps to ensure that suggestions and commands are more easily accepted. **Hypnotic language** (sometimes referred to as **soft language**) is very effective in a coaching context, particularly when you want someone to search inside to find their own solutions, rather than impose or directly suggest ideas. Milton Erickson believed that people have all the internal resources they need to solve any problem that they face.

Hypnotic language patterns are powerful tools, both for use in the classroom and in life in general. By the way, should your ethical button have just been pushed a little, listen more carefully the next time a salesperson talks to you, as these things are standard practice in sales and are well worth knowing about! Although this is quite a technical chapter, spending time exploring these ideas and practising the tools will be well worth it in the long run.

Jargon Buster

Milton model

The term 'Milton model' is used in NLP to describe the set of language patterns that can be used to create a trance state, or altered state of consciousness. The Milton model is named after Milton Erickson and is first described in detail in *Patterns of the Hypnotic Techniques of Milton Erickson, vol. i* (Bandler and Grinder, 1975).

Bandler and Grinder noticed that Erickson consistently 'chunked up' out of the details that we might usually include in language, removing the details and creating **generalisations, distortions** and **deletions**. Because information is missing we are forced to go 'inside' (in what is sometimes called a **transderivational search (TDS)**) for meaning. It is this internal search for meaning that places the person's attention on internal representations rather than the external world and which 'induces' trance and suggestibility. Having used vague language to create an altered state Erickson would then make a suggestion or embed a command.

Presuppositions

A key concept to grasp, before you begin to explore a few of these patterns, is the notion of presupposition. Presuppositions are the hidden meanings in sentences, phrases or individual words and work covertly or indirectly. It works like this. If we were to say:

Either now or in the next few seconds you can think of a time when using the right words, at the right time, would have been more useful to you

you are quite likely to do just that.

This is because the first part of the sentence presupposes that you are going to do what we have suggested.

This particular pattern is called a **double bind** and is very useful when you want to limit the number of possibilities that the person you are talking to will have. For example, in the classroom you might say:

John, would you like to start by doing the questions or do the diagram first?

The presupposition is that John will start work now, whichever way he chooses to do it.

John Grinder was a professor of linguistics and in his, and Bandler's writing explains how this process of presupposition works by referring to Chomsky's notions of transformational grammar. In essence the idea is that there are two levels of language structure: a **surface structure** and a **deep structure**. The surface structure contains the basic information, for example:

> *My best friend is trying to get pregnant*

The deep structure contains all the other implicit information that has been passed on but which is not stated, for example, the fact that my best friend is female. In effect, instructions can be hidden within the deep structure of a sentence and do not necessarily need to be said.

Top tips for the classroom

Useful sentences with positive presuppositions:

> *Tomorrow you will be able to learn even more*—presupposes that a lot has already been learnt

> *Starting is just the beginning*—presupposes that there is more to learn

> *This first bit you have learned is the hardest part*—presupposes that the next bit will be easier

> *Knowing this you can realise that you have more resources than ever before*—presupposes infinite internal resources

---

So … how ready are you to read on?

Jargon Buster

Deep and surface structure and transformational grammar

The term surface structure refers to the actual words or phrases that are being used (the syntactic structure of a sentence). Deep structure applies to the actual meaning of the sentence. Chomsky suggested that language is much more complex and less predictable than had previously been believed. He argued that when we hear a sentence we don't actually process or retain the surface structure; rather we transform it into its deep structure. Transformational grammar is the 'know how' of translating a sentence's meaning into the words that make it up and vice versa.

Covering all bases

Have you ever had the experience of not being included in something? How did that make you feel? Well, the same feelings can be easily created in audiences and in classrooms if you are not careful with your language. One approach that can avoid this is to apply a really useful language pattern called **cover all bases**. The pattern is very effective when you want to build rapport with a group. It works by making sure that all people are included.

I know that some of you have already done some work on this with your last teacher, others are coming to this new and some of you have already developed your own interest in this area ...

Many of you could find language patterns like these useful whether you work in a primary, secondary or special school, are in management, an AST, subject co-ordinator or teaching assistant ...

Cover all bases is very influential as a language pattern because it provides us with too much information to deal with in one go and therefore also induces a transderivational search. It also allows you to talk personally to each person in a single hit. This is particularly obvious in the last example above which contains a long list of people who we are suggesting might benefit from the language patterns.

Yes sets and yes tags

Have you ever noticed salespeople in shops, garages or other locations saying things that are obviously true before they move on to directly selling their product. Then, having got you to agree, they begin to offer other things as well? Next time this happens take a moment or two to step outside of the content and notice the processes that are being used. At the heart of this process is likely to be a **yes set**. This was also a key technique used by Milton Erickson.

The yes set pattern is commonly used by public speakers and politicians. By receiving three undeniable facts one after another we are much more likely to take the next statement as true also.

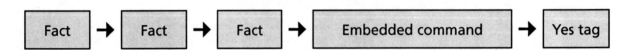

*Its 10am, we have finished the first task, we have **30 minutes left** so now would be a good time to think of some good questions that we can discuss, **wouldn't it**?*

Note the pattern at the end of the sentence **wouldn't it**. This is called a **yes tag** and is very difficult to say no to when placed at the end of a sentence, that's right, **isn't it**?

Top tip

If you nod while you say a yes tag this increases its effectiveness dramatically.

Types of yes tags include:

Isn't it?
Couldn't you?

Can't you?

And you can, can you not?

Haven't you? or Have you?

That's right?

These can be particularly effective after explaining rules, in order to reinforce the point and gain agreement.

John, I've explained what my expectations are to you now, haven't I? Now it should be easy for you to get this right in the future, shouldn't it?

Research Zone

Evidence that supports the effectiveness of yes sets

Psychologists have been aware for many years of the tendency for people who have first agreed to a small request to comply later with a larger one. This is sometimes called the 'foot-in-the-door' technique. In one famous experiment in the United States, Freedman and Fraser (1966) asked people if they would let them put a huge 'DRIVE CAREFULLY' sign outside the front of their house. Only a small number (17%) agreed. Other homeowners, however, were first approached with a smaller (easier to accept) request. These people were asked if they would put a three-inch 'BE A SAFE DRIVER' sign in their window. Nearly all immediately agreed to this request. When the same people were approached a few weeks later they were asked if they would place the gigantic sign outside their house, 76% agreed.

Freedman, J. L. and Fraser, S. C. (1966) Compliance without pressure: the foot-in-the-door-technique, *Journal of Personality and Social Psychology*, 4: 2: 195–202

NLP Toolbox No. 9

Frame setting

Framing is, in some ways, one of the simplest and yet most powerful of NLP tools. Bandler and Grinder noticed that one of the skills of excellent and effective communicators was that they established early on how the communication was to take place and not just what the communication was to be about. In other words, they set a frame for the process and the context. (A form of conditioning and influence at a contextual level was also observed by Gregory Bateson, see Chapter 4, *Dolphin aquarium*.) In the classroom this translates as being clear about the way in which a task is to be done and not just the learning outcome of the task (including the nature of the relationships).

Next time you are going into a situation where you want to influence others or ensure that things go your way, think about the process that is involved and state this upfront with the

NLP Toolbox No. 9 continued ...

children, parents, other teachers or the group that you are working with. Be specific—you will be amazed about what happens. Frames are like creating folders for the mind; just like a really well-organised filing cabinet with files inside files.

In NLP we say that 'the person who sets the frame controls the communication'. In other words, whoever sets the context for the communication at the start, will have more influence over everything that follows. Some key examples of this are:

- Outcome frame—state the outcome that you want in the context.

- 'As if ' frame—e.g. *just imagine, let's suppose*. This is particularly useful in creative problem solving or in creating curiosity at the start of learning (as at the start of this chapter).

- Open frame—state that anything can be discussed (however, be prepared for what may happen). It is useful to close a frame to limit questions/discussions, e.g., 'What questions do you have about the last part of the lesson?'

- Discovery frame—for example, giving people an opportunity to learn things through an activity or process.

- Relevancy frame—use this when you want to save time at a meeting. Make sure that you have already defined and stated the outcome.

Before you begin a section of your lesson, a team meeting, lead a training session or sit down to discuss something one-to-one, decide which sort of frame you wish to set and make sure that the language that you use is in line with it.

Pacing and leading with language and making transitions

In NLP, and hypnosis, the process of gradually increasing compliance using small steps is often referred to as pacing and leading. The core concept is the idea that if you want to influence someone then you need to **pace** their current experience before you seek to lead them. The more you pace first, the more likely you are to be able to influence. This can be particularly effective if you gradually move the balance from **pacing** to **leading**.

Classically in hypnosis you might hear:

As you sit there **[pacing current experience]**, *listening to my voice,* **[pacing current experience]**, *and feeling your weight on the chair* **[pacing/leading]** *you could begin to* **[leading]** *notice your breathing* **[embedded command that includes an element of pacing]**, *and the muscles around your eyes* **[pacing]** *and become aware of how relaxed they could become right now* **[leading]** … *as you do that you could just allow yourself to double that relaxation, right now* **[leading]**.

In the classroom you might say

As you read the sections in the book, noticing the diagrams and the instructions, you could begin to become aware of all the ways in which this learning could be useful to you … **etc.**

There is more on verbal pacing and leading in Chapter 3, *We like like.*

You may also have begun to notice another key element in the language patterns above that enables the linking of the pacing and leading elements. Words, such as 'and' and 'because', provide transitions and links between the various patterns and suggestions. Having transitions make the process of suggestion more easy to accept. These sorts of linguistic links are often referred to as **linkage language** or **transitions**. Words that can be used to make transitions between suggestions and statements of fact also include:

as   and   when   while   because

In essence, transition words are used to make things sound like they have a meaningful relationship when in fact there isn't one at all. Transition words are particularly effective when linked to words like: could, might, can, may, etc. These are referred to as modal operators. There are four easy-to-use types of **modal operator** that will increase your language flexibility: possibility, probability, impossibility and improbability.

So as you read this sentence you could begin to notice all the ways that these language patterns will be useful to you, couldn't you?

Possibility	Probability
Can	Could
Will	Might
	May
Impossibility	**Improbability**
Can't	Couldn't
Won't	Wouldn't

Words to use with care

Some single words have a presupposition already built into them and therefore should be used with caution as it is possible to interpret them to mean the opposite of what is intended.

Examples of this include:

'If ' always implies the possibility of choice, so avoid it—unless you want to allow choice.

'Try' to has the presupposition built into it that you might possibly fail. So, if success is what you want from someone else, use another word. In sales someone might say 'try and find a better deal …'

'But' always negates what has just been said. So if you don't want your last thing to be forgotten, or discounted, use another word. Note, in particular, that beginning a sentence with **but**—when you follow on from what someone else says—invariably puts the other person on the defensive. It is much more influential to begin your sentence with something else, even if you are contradicting them. And works really well! (e.g. and another way of looking at it would be to …)

Another interesting command is **'don't'**. The truth is **we cannot not think of something**.

So when we use 'not' we may be accidentally getting people to think of what we actually wish them to avoid thinking about.

Don't think about chocolate cake right now!

This has all sorts of implications for us as teachers when it comes to reinforcing and expressing rules. It is extraordinary the number of times we say don't, isn't it?

OUR SCHOOL RULES

DON'T RUN

DON'T TALK

DON'T BE LATE

Just do it

Think of a goal or an outcome that you want to achieve. Write it out. Now re-write it in several ways using 'try', 'if' and 'don't'. Write it negatively and positively and see what happens when you use different modal operators: could, would, might, should. Pay particular attention to the deep structure of what you write and what is hidden and not said.

What is different about your own internal motivation depending on what words you use?

NLP Toolbox No. 10

Ambiguity

As well as using generalisation and deletions to influence and make suggestions Erickson also used distortion. In particular he would deliberately create **ambiguity**. As well as generalisations such as **all, many, most**, ambiguities also overload the conscious mind and force us inside to find the answer or to find meaning.

Erickson would use a number of different kinds of ambiguity. Again these are often used prior to the command, suggestion or instruction.

Phonological ambiguity

When words sound alike but have potentially a different meaning:

> *here/hear, right/write, I/eye, red/read, know/no*

> *It's right to write that right (write) now … and begin to* **[embedded command]**

You know how to say no, and knowing that ... you could begin to **[embedded command]**

Scope ambiguity

When it is unclear how much of the sentence an adjective, verb, or adverb applies to,

I don't know when you will fully realise ...

Top tips for learning to use hypnotic language

- Take it slow at first and keep it simple

- Begin by noticing the deep structure (real meaning) of what people say

- Start by removing those loaded words: try, but and if

- Script some of the things that you are planning to say first so that you can get the pre-suppositions right

- When scripting first decide on the embedded commands

- Have fun with yes sets—they are easy to use

- Here's a great pattern to begin with: As you ... (mention something that the person is doing or something that is happening) ... you could ... (add embedded command)

e.g. As you finish reading this top tips box you could begin to think about the next opportunity you are going to have to influence someone.

Opportunities to influence and use hypnotic language:

- With difficult pupils

- With awkward parents

- Making others more accountable

- Gently influencing other members of staff without conflict

- Setting up lessons effectively so that they go the way you want them to

- Encouraging learning

- Rewarding the behaviours that you want to see

- Keeping children on track and motivated

- Elegantly saying no by not even having to use the word!

Chunking up and chunking down

NLP draws from a wide range of influences. Grinder was an expert in transformational grammar and adapted many of Chomsky's notions of language. In particular, they suggest that we are constantly filtering our experience, making deletions, distortions and generalisations. In NLP we call the two directions of this process chunking up and chunking down. **Chunking up** is when we move out of the detail into increasingly abstract or generalised language (or 'big picture ideas'), and **chunking down** is used to describe the process of talking more and more specifically.

Chunking up

Creating generalisations, distortions and deletions (using Milton model language, from Milton Erickson) is a powerful way of influencing people to search inside themselves for meaning. Such language is particularly powerful when combined with an embedded commands.

> *Just imagine* **all** *the possible ways* **this could be useful to you!**

The generalisations at the start of the sentence sends people inside to find the missing information; the command is, in this case, added afterwards. The way it works is that our conscious mind can only process a small number of things at once. Therefore any single word, set of words or phrases that invoke more items than this (e.g. 'all') distracts the conscious mind, during which time we are more open to suggestion or influence). In Chapter 14, *The magic number 7*, we talk about George Miller's research that demonstrated conclusively that the conscious mind can only process seven plus or minus two chunks of information at any one time. Words like all automatically overload the capacity of our consciousness. Words which make a universal generalisation, like *all, every, always* and *never*, are referred to in the Milton model as **universal quantifiers**.

Next time you are talking to someone one-to-one, take a few moments to notice when they go inside themselves to find meaning. Their eye movements will often give this away. You can easily create this altered state of consciousness by using a universal quantifier or one of the other language patterns that are explained in this chapter. As you begin to notice these things you will also begin to notice that trance states are everywhere and that people are dropping in and out of them all the time while talking, listening, reading, watching television and even driving a car. Have you ever noticed yourself arrive somewhere, having driven there, and found that you could remember your internal thoughts about something completely unconnected on the journey but could not remember actually driving there? Becoming aware of, and developing, your awareness of trance states in yourself and others is the first step towards mastering the power of hypnotic language.

NLP Toolbox No. 11

Chunking up

Chunking up is a really great way of helping people to resolve things in their own mind without imposing a solution and by helping them to explore what it is that they really want. One way to do this is separate behaviour from intention and to work up out of the details. This is a powerful tool to use with colleagues who need your support in a line management or coaching context, or with children whom you may need to counsel or help overcome blocks. If you are going to use this tool it is best used in a one-to-one setting where you have time to explore the responses and to respect where the other person is coming from.

You can do this for yourself as well, to help you work through a problem or an issue. Ask the questions that seem appropriate at each stage. By chunking up to the higher purpose of intention you will often help the person to see that there are other more positive ways of achieving their outcomes.

Step 1: Begin by establishing the behaviour

Step 2: Establish the intention behind the behaviour

What is the positive intention behind doing ...?

What does doing ... do for you?

What do you get out of ...?

Step 3: Establish what is important about the behaviour to the person

What is the positive intention behind doing ...?

What does doing ... do for you?

What do you get out of ...?

Step 4: Continue to ask the Step 3 questions until the higher purpose or intention is established

Step 5: Reframe by asking

What other more positive things could you do to achieve the same thing?

Chunking down (meta-model language) and across

Asking questions that restore the details that have been temporarily erased by the 'filtering process' can help people to see these generalisations. For example, if someone were to say, 'She always makes me cross when she does that,' the response might be, 'What, always?' or 'Exactly how does she make you cross?' More about the **meta model** and how to use it can be found in Chapter 10, *Verbal ju-jitsu*.

A further way of creating influence is to 'chunk' just above the actual situation by telling a story that mirrors the situation that you are seeking to influence someone about.

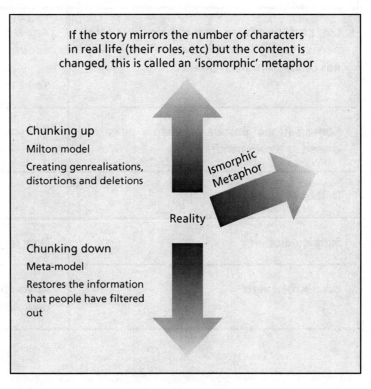

If the story mirrors the number of characters in real life (their roles, etc) but the content is changed, this is called an 'isomorphic' metaphor

Chunking up
Milton model
Creating genreralisations, distortions and deletions

Ismorphic Metaphor

Reality

Chunking down
Meta-model
Restores the information that people have filtered out

For example:

Imagine for a moment if someone you were to meet in a bar, restaurant or in the street later today, were to say to you that ... (see the opening of this chapter!)

Part of Erickson's therapeutic approach was to create teaching stories or tales. These were used to help people explore their problems from a metaphorical perspective rather than through direct confrontation with their problems (Rosen, 1982). Often the stories would contain the suggested solution to the problem, embedded as a metaphor. In NLP, if the story mirrors the exact number of characters in real life (their roles, etc.), but the content is changed, this is called an 'isomorphic' metaphor.

NLP Toolbox No. 12

Milton model language patterns

Generalisations	
Universal quantifiers	*There are **many** ways to begin to approach this* *You already have **all** the skills you need to ...*
Modal operators	*Now that you have finished section 1 you **could** begin to think of what you **would** like to really enjoy doing for your individual study*
Lost performatives (when the identity of the person saying something important or **values** related has been deleted	*And it's a good thing to begin to wonder about ...* *You can always find that ...*
Conversational postulate (when a question is used as a command)	*Can you **see yourself doing this**?*
Deletions	
Simple deletion	*Now that you are ready to listen*
Unspecified verb	*As you begin to make sense of this in your own time ...*

Distortions	
Extended quotes (embedding a command, suggestion or idea within a story)	*I was talking to someone the other day who said that when they were at school they had had to overcome exactly the same problem …*
Phonological ambiguity	*After all you have learned from today's lesson*
Syntactic ambiguity	*Great learning*
Mind reading	*I know that as you become more interested in this topic you will …*
Cause and effect	*As you finish this section you can begin to think about how …*
Complex equivalence	*Having understood this means that you are now ready to …*

You have read this chapter, learned some of the basic principles of influential language and know the names of some key patterns, so either now or in the next few days would be a good time to either practise some of these, or to find some opportunities to learn more … wouldn't it?

Research Zone

Mind your language! Hypnosis—fact or fiction?

As a result of their modelling of Milton Erickson, and their own development of the NLP model, Bandler and Grinder argued that the effects of hypnotic language patterns and processes can be replicated when applied to people in a 'waking state' as effectively as when they are in a deep trance (Grinder and Bandler, 1981). This notion is supported by Kirsch (1977) who, as a result of neurophysiological research, notes that the majority of hypnotic phenomena can be suggested successfully without the application of a formal hypnotic induction.

Recent research in the fields of neurophysiology and clinical psychology, using positron-emission tomography (PET) and magnetic resonance imaging (fMRI) to describe the effects of hypnosis on the brain, have demonstrated conclusively that hypnosis is more than a simple parlour trick (e.g. Brown and Oakley, 2004; Gruzelier, 2006). Furthermore, studies have demonstrated the relative deactivation of the precuneus (Maquet, 1999; Faymonville et al., 2006), an area of the brain that is believed to have a role in consciousness, self-related mental representations and

Research Zone continued ...

non-self-referential goal-directed actions (see Cavana and Trimble, 2006). In other studies, hypnosis has been shown to result in the suppression or disconnection of certain frontal functions (Gruzelier et al., 1988). These include effects on the anterior cingulate's conflict monitoring capabilities leading to people becoming more open to suggestion. Gruzelier (2006) proposes that it is the triggering of similar suppressions and disconnections that results in hypnotically suggestible subjects responding without embarrassment during stage hypnosis.

Brown and Oakley (2004) propose that suggestion effects can occur as a result of a variety of external inputs: hypnotic induction (the key mechanism for which is hypnotic language), context, role, expectancy and task. Their groundbreaking theory unifies previously contradictory theories about hypnosis by explaining how hypnosis can be seen as both a product of contextual influence and as something that has a real effect on brain function. So it does seem that all communication may be hypnosis, as Bandler and Grinder suggested.

Brown, R. J. and Oakley, D. A. (2004) An integrative cognitive theory of hypnosis and high hypnotisability, in M. Heap, R. J. Brown and D. A Oakley (eds), *The Highly Hypnotizable Person: Theoretical, Experimental and Clinical Issues*, London: Routledge

Cavanna, A. E. and Trimble, M. R. (2006) The precuneus: a review of its functional anatomy and behavioural correlates, *Brain*, 129: 564–583

Faymonville, M. E., Boly, M. and Laueys, S. (2006) Functional neuroanatomy of the hypnotic state, *Journal of Physiology*, 99: 463–469

Grinder, J. and Bandler, R (1981) *Trace-formations*, Utah: Real People Press

Gruzelier, J. (1998) A working model of the neurophysiology of hypnosis: a review of evidence, *Contemporary Hypnosis*, 15: 1: 9–21

Gruzelier, J. H. (2006) Frontal functions, connectivity and neural efficiency underpinning hypnosis and hypnotic susceptibility, *Contemporary Hypnosis*, 23: 1: 15–32

Heap, M., Brown, R. J. and Oakley, D. A. (2004) *The Highly Hypnotizable Person: Theoretical, Experimental and Clinical Issues*, London: Routledge

Kirsch, I. (1977) Suggestibility or hypnosis: what do our scales really measure? *International Journal of Clinical and Experimental Hypnosis*, 45: 212–225

Maquet, P., Faymonville, M. A., Degueldre, C., Delfiore, G., Franck, G., Luxen, A. and Lamy, M. (1999) Functional neuroanatomy of hypnotic state, *Biological Psychiatry*, 45: 327–333

More ways to start improving your classroom practice with NLP

- Script your opening words for a new class you are going to teach. Think about the presuppositions in the language you choose and set some good frames

- Encourage learning with presuppositions of success and achievements

- Develop a set of useful yes sets and embedded commands for use when moving from one part of a lesson to the next

- Remember the caveats about *don't* and *try*!

- As you speak, imagine yourself to be a skilled craftsperson able to craft the right language in the right way at the right time—like an elegantly carved antique table or chair. Make your language fit for purpose by thinking about what you want to achieve and making sure your language **always** presupposes your outcome

Chapter 6
Streetwise body language

How to use body language to influence others in the classroom and in life in general

In *The Structure of Magic I* and *II*, Richard Bandler and John Grinder outline in detail their modelling of Virginia Satir and her approach to family therapy. Virginia Satir (1916–1988) was renowned in her lifetime as one of the world's leading family therapists. In particular, she is famous for having developed *conjoint family therapy*. When Satir first applied this approach it was quite revolutionary for a therapist to meet several, or all members of the family group at the same time (hence the use of the term *conjoint*). This approach had the advantage that it made explicit the differences in the ways in which members of the family perceived each others' relationships. Patterns which emerged in the group therapy usually mirrored typical interactions within the home, despite the presence of the therapist. Conjoint family therapy took our understanding of group interrelations beyond the areas of the unconscious mind and early childhood experience which would have been the focus of Freudian-derived therapy. Satir's best-known books are *Conjoint Family Therapy* (1967), *Peoplemaking* (1972), and *The New Peoplemaking* (1988).

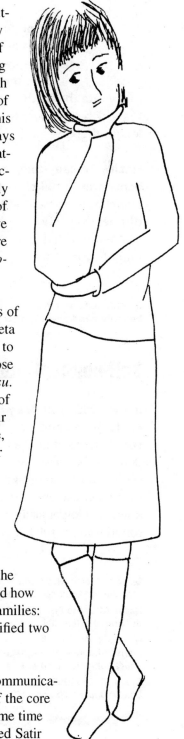

From working with and modelling Virginia Satir and others, two key areas of the NLP model emerged: the **meta model** and **Satir categories**. The meta model is a framework for understanding how language works and helps us to get behind the words that people use to explore the experience behind those words. The meta-model is explored in detail in Chapter 10, *Verbal ju-jitsu*. From studying Satir's sessions, it was noted how Satir was both aware of and made use of a number of broader communication categories, the Satir categories. These categories not only have an effect on the language we use, but also on the person we are communicating with, our external behaviour and our own internal emotional state.

Earlier in the book we talked about how our internal state, external behaviour and internal processing are all interrelated and have a symbiotic relationship—change one and you change the other. The body postures of the various Satir categories appear to have an archetypal significance on all of these areas. They not only have an effect on the giver but also on the receiver of the communication. Initially, in 1975, Bandler and Grinder noted how Satir had identified four communication categories from her work with families: **Placater**, **Blamer**, **Computer** and **Distracter**. Later modelling has identified two further categories: **Leveler** and **Sequencer**.

Children, parents and teachers will usually use a mixture of these in communication. However, Satir noted that we all have preferences for one or more of the core communication styles and may rarely or never use others. If you spend some time working with someone you will begin to get a sense of what their preferred Satir category is. Awareness of these different styles and their effect on other people gives us flexibility to communicate in different ways and be more effective in one-to-one interactions, groups meetings, classroom situations or presentation and training environments.

Research Zone

How quickly do students make decisions about you just on body language?

Nalini Ambady conducted an extraordinary experiment in the US. Initially Ambady showed students three short videotapes of around 10 seconds each. These showed footage of a teacher in the processes of teaching. In each of the tapes the sound had been turned off. The students found it very easy to accurately rate the teacher's effectiveness. Ambady cut these clips down to five seconds and found that the results were the same. Even when the video clips were reduced to only two seconds in length there was a significant amount of consistency.

Finally, Ambady compared the instant judgements of teacher effectiveness made by the students after a full term of lessons. The judgements initially made were consistent with those made later. Therefore it would appear that someone who is shown a silent short video clip of a teacher, who they have not met before, will make a decision about the effectiveness of that teacher that is not changed by the passage of time, or by the experience of actually being taught by that person.

Rosenthal, R. and Ambady, N. (1993) Half a minute: predicting teacher evaluations from thin slices of nonverbal behaviour and physical attractiveness, *Journal of Personality and Social Psychology*, 64: 3: 443–441

Self-concept and learning

In the 1980s a study by Harris and Rosenthal (1985) into the effect of teacher expectations on kindergarten and second grade students found that (alongside a teacher's orientation towards certain types of task) a teacher's non-verbal warmth was a significant predictor of students' academic self-concept. Research in recent years has confirmed that there is a relationship between self-concept and self-esteem and achievement in the classroom, particularly in relation to academic self-esteem. Self-concept affects achievement and achievement affects self-concept and a sense of lower achievement is more likely to affect academic self-concept than the other way round (Muijis, 1998, Marsh et al., 2002, Guay et al., 2003).

Guay, F., Marsh, H. W. and Bovin, M. (2003) Academic self-concept and academic achievement: developmental perspectives on their causal ordering, *Journal of Educational Psychology*, 95; 1: 124–136

Harris, M. J. and Rosenthal, R. (1985) Mediation of interpersonal expectancy effects: 31 meta-analyses, *Psychological Bulletin*, 97: 363–386

Marsh, H. W., Hau, K.-T. and Kong, C.-K. (2002) Multilevel causal ordering of academic self-concept and achievement: influence of language of instruction (English Compared with Chinese) for Hong Kong Students, *American Educational Research Journal*, 39: 3: 727–763

Muijis, R. D. (1998) The reciprocal relationship between self-concept and school achievement, *British Journal of Educational Psychology*, 67: 3: 263–277

Blaming

The Blaming person tends to want to shift responsibility. They will often point their finger and use stiff gestures. Their language will be full of generalisations. They use phrases which include 'all', refer to only part of an experience or make value judgements that omit to mention the speaker (e.g. 'Boys shouldn't cry'— the response to which might be 'who says that?'). Blamer communications from both the receiver and the giver will invariably result in some form of conflict or disagreement despite the words that are actually used.

Words: Tend towards disagreement.

Body language: The impact of this sort of body posture is to imply fault in the receiver, to dictate or imply a superior position.

Internal state: The internal state that we adopt when using Blamer is not a positive one and is rarely received positively. In someone who has this posture as a preference the internal state may be one of loneliness, lacking a positive self-concept or feelings of unsuccessfulness. As with other Satir categories these inner states are not necessarily the way in which the posture is received. In fact, irrespective of the words used the impact on the receiver will often be to create feelings of defensiveness and the need to respond accordingly. In this sense the gesture is predominantly aggressive rather than assertive. Ask someone to point at you and say something positive about you and notice how you actually feel inside.

Placating

The Placating person is the Blamer's counterpart. They seek sympathy and they may even accept the blame for just about everything. Their body language is not forceful and will often include the palms up 'placater' position. They will express themselves by talking about how they 'should' or 'can't' do something to trigger a guilt response in others. They may use verbs in a way that is vague (e.g. 'If only you knew …'). The palms up position makes the communicator look as if they are literally making a gift to the receiver.

Words: Tend towards agreement and pleasing others.

Body language: Placates, communicates giving in.

Internal state: I am not your equal. Despite the fact that this posture communicates a sense of weakness this can be used to great advantage to create a deliberately contradictory message. It works like this. If you have a difficult message to communicate or wish to complain, adopt Placater body position whilst giving the words to the person. Because the message is now ambiguous the dominant communication element, body language, will carry the message (see Research Zone). This will then affect the recipient by literally making them feel that they are receiving a gift. This works particularly if you end the communication by adopting Leveler position—a sign of accuracy and truth. In the classroom, Placating should be used with caution as it can communicate weakness. However, is very powerful for reinforcing rules with very difficult children, providing that (as described above) it is reinforced by the Leveler position.

Computing

The Computing person uses language and body postures that hide emotions. They are dissociated from the situation and can appear cold or unfeeling. In their language they will talk much of 'you' and 'one'. They often say things that are value judgements without indicating who could have made the judgment—the effect of which is to imply that everyone would agree (e.g. 'It's not good to be strict' or 'One must agree that …'). The Computing person is correct and reasonable with no indication of internal feelings. To help yourself to really get into the role of this type of communicator imagine that your spine is a long straight and stiff rod from the base of your spine right though to your neck. Keep everything about yourself as still as possible, including your facial expressions and mouth.

Words: Ultra-reasonable, removed from the situation and dissociated.

Body language: Communicates thinking and being collected and calm/computing or thinking things through logically.

Internal state: Can be dissociated or logical or can be accompanied by a sense of vulnerability. Despite this, Computing is a powerful posture to adopt when you want others to think things through. Allowing yourself to be a little vulnerable and open to others communicates that you are willing to listen to their point of view. This posture is particularly effective in the classroom or the training room when you want people to respond to a question you have asked or to think things through. Just by adopting the posture prompts thought in others.

Distracting

The Distracter will switch quickly between the three positions above. They may be seeking to cause confusion to distract attention from themselves or could be internally confused. In their language they will often fail to refer clearly to what they are talking about (e.g. 'Nobody knows what's going on') or use other generalisations.

Words: Generally come across as making no sense or as irrelevant (even if they are not).

Body language: Angular as if the person is off somewhere else.

Internal state: I really don't want to be here. This is one Satir category internal state that is definitely picked up by external observers. Because of this it is probably one to avoid—however, it can be very effective if used for humour as part of a presentation.

Leveling

The Leveler will use grounded positions that allow them to come across as 'on the level', centred and factual. Their body posture communicates the idea that they are being true to what they think (palms pressing down at mid-body height). This posture has a calming effect on the physiology of not only the Leveler, but also those that see it. Even one-handed, this position holds people's attention. There are few negative things to say about this posture. However, people who do not want to hear the truth may challenge it. Over-used it can lead to disinterest and boredom.

Language: Gently assertive and very influential.

Body language: Communicates honesty, accuracy and factualness.

Internal state: Adopting this body posture or simply the gesture of palms down can be a very powerful way to influence people as it sets up a very adult sort of person-to-person interaction. This is a very good posture to adopt when stating facts that you want to be accepted as the truth or for reinforcing your position in a calm and positive way.

Sequencing

The Sequencer uses measured sequential movements in line with the middle of their body. Often their hands will be positioned vertically and move in steps horizontally from the sides to the centre of their body. They will use similar language to the Computer person, and appear unemotional and thoughtful, yet logical. Although this is not one of Satir's original categories, it is a useful additional tool, particularly for teachers, trainers and leaders.

Making sequential movements when you are talking seems to affect people by communicating notions of time passing and of planning ahead.

Just do it

Next time you tell a joke become aware of what Satir categories you are using and discover what the impact is on your own internal state and how others are affected. Alternatively, have a go at saying the same thing and notice how the sense of what is communicated changes with each change in style. Also, notice how the sense of what is communicated changes as each Satir category is used. A good phrase to try out is 'How do you know?' Think about what the impact might be on other people.

Jargon Buster

Congruence and metamessages

In NLP the term congruence is applied to a person who is communicating consistent messages in relation to the words they say, their voice tone and their body language. Often people who are congruent will be seen as having personal presence and will be perceived as knowing what they are talking about. The term incongruent is used to describe inconsistencies in these messages. Although incongruence can be a bad thing, used well it can be a powerful tool for use when influencing others, particularly, if a softer form of body language is adopted when giving difficult messages.

The term metamessaging is used to describe when more than one message is expressed simultaneously though different 'output channels' (e.g. body language and voice tone). Metamessages can be congruent or incongruent. For example, if someone were to say *I am angry* with a voice tone that is soft and gentle the messages would be said to be incongruent metamessages.

Building rapport with body language—and using Satir categories

In Chapter 5, *Don't think about chocolate cake*, we talked about **pacing** and **leading** with language. You can do the same thing with body language. When people are in rapport they will adopt similar body positions and gestures. By 'matching' or 'mirroring' another person you can build rapport. In matching you do exactly the same as the other person (i.e. both people have right leg crossed over left). In mirroring you are just that, a mirror. Matching the type of sensory words that people use (e.g. visual, auditory, kinaesthetic) also builds rapport. You can learn much more about this in Chapter 3, *We like like*.

When pacing or mirroring the body language of someone who is using a specific Satir category there are some subtle things to be aware of:

- if you match a Blaming person you will tend to get an argument
- if you match a Placating person you may end up in a whingeing contest

When dealing with an angry Blamer it may be effective to match their physiology and the volume of their voice—however, avoid matching their threatening voice tone and the words that they use. Matching a Distracter tends to lead to disorganisation and a lack of focus, whilst matching a Computer can lead to a very unproductive and stale conversation.

With groups (presentations or teaching)

Have you ever been to a presentation, or been a learner, watching a trainer or a teacher and found that although what they said seemed to make sense the whole thing just didn't seem to gel together? Because each of the Satir categories appears to have strong cultural associations we can find ourselves very confused or put out if there is a mismatch in the communication—particularly when we are watching a trainer or a speaker. The same also applies in the classroom. Adopting Satir categories in front of an audience, a group or a class not only affects your internal state but also that of your audience (see the Research Zone on mirror neurons on page (27) for an explanation of why this happens).

To build group rapport, get the whole audience to do the same thing (i.e. raise their hands, laugh, etc.).

Use Satir positions with groups in the following ways

- using all of the categories will help you to establish rapport with the whole audience
- use Blaming sparingly and only to make a strong point (avoid pointing at the audience—point at the ceiling, floor, whiteboard or self)
- use Placating for sympathy or to weigh up possibilities
- use Distracter for fun
- use Leveling when being frank or to convince
- use Computing to suggest dissociated logic or encourage thinking and questioning; Computing tends to say *I'm thinking about what you said*

For an advanced approach to using Satir categories combine them with a specific spotlight state (see Chapter 9, *Anchors away*).

Jargon Buster

Dissociated

Seeing the world from the perspective of a dispassion-ate observer, as if you were watching other people doing something without actually being part of the action yourself. When we adopt this perspective there is a sense of emotionless detachment. This can be a helpful place to be when making logical decisions or dealing with conflict and challenges. The choosing of internal representations and physiologies that evoke dissociation may be mechanisms by which we are able to 'con-sciously' affect the prefrontal cortex to limit inappropriate amygdala reactions, such as anger and rage. The opposite term, **associated**, is applied to the perspective of seeing the world though your own eyes. From this point of view you are fully aware of yourself, including all of your personal values, emotions and feeling. As with most things in life flexibility seems to be the key, and highly effective people appear able to balance dissociation and association and use these at appropriate times.

NLP Toolbox No. 13

Managing your internal state with Satir categories

You can train your brain really easily to be aware of the effects of the different Satir categories on yourself and on others.

NLP Toolbox No. 13 continued ...

- Take each one of the categories: **Blamer**, **Placater**, **Computer**, **Distracter**, **Leveler** and **Sequencer**.

- Hold the position for about a minute and notice what happens to you

Paying attention to your internal state at the same time as your physiology can be a new experience for many people. Initially it is not unusual to be so busy thinking about what you are doing that you do not notice your internal feelings and emotional state. If you stick with it you will gradually become aware of the presence of these feelings when you are adopting a Satir category. Increasing your awareness will help you to choose the appropriate category in any situation and will help you to communicate much more effectively.

Finding ourselves in a stressful situation will often prevent us from accessing Leveler and force us to adopt one of the other strongly emotional categories, particularly Blamer, Placater or Distracter. Often we will be forced into our most preferred category. This can limit our flexibility and consequently our ability to communicate. It can also often make things worse, particularly if our preferred Satir category is not appropriate at that particular time. When in this place, the words we use can often be overridden by the metamessages in our body language resulting in more stress and difficultly.

Knowing that you have Leveler as a ground place and a resource to which you can go can be very helpful in difficult situations and can have a calming effect on both yourself and on others.

NLP Toolbox No. 14

Sequencing Satir categories

- If you do not know what to do, or are unsure then begin with Computing. The computing person tends to avoid taking risks—however, they do not tend to say much of any note. Adopting this position gives you time to think and consider what to do next. Also, you will be in the best internal state to do just that.

- As a general rule always avoid using Distracter. Adopting a distracting body posture and body language tends to make people think that you have nothing useful to say or add to the conversation. In its extreme form it can lead people to think of you as slightly unbalanced.

For a powerful end to any sequence of categories use Leveler. This will tend to make your words more acceptable and believable.

NLP Toolbox No. 15

Puppet Master's parents' evening

Here's a fun activity to do on an inset or training day with your colleagues or other teachers.

- Firstly, do a little bit of upfront teaching so people understand a bit about the theory of Satir categories and where they come from.

- Divide the group into threes. Two people need to sit facing each other as if at a parents' evening. One person takes the role of a parent, the other of the teacher. The third person (or Puppet Master) stands behind the person who is being the parent so that the parent cannot see what they are doing.

- Ask the teachers to think back to a time when they had to give a difficult message to a parent.

- As the teachers explain the difficult message to the parent, the Puppet Master chooses a Satir category and displays it. The teacher then has to use that category.

- The Puppet Master should then randomly work their way through the different categories whilst the poor teacher is forced to follow their lead.

- The parent can choose to match a category or to mismatch one. Blamer, in particular, usually creates some really interesting interactions.

This exercise, if prepared well, usually results in a lot of fun and learning about how our body language has an effect on others. Make sure that you debrief the session afterward (ideally to flipchart) and ask people what they have learnt.

Alternatively, do the same exercise in the context of dealing with a difficult student.

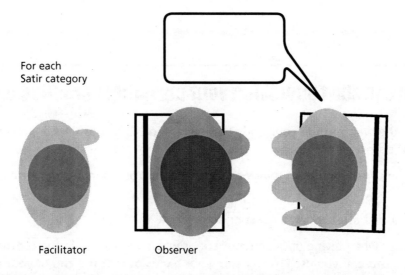

For each
Satir category

Facilitator   Observer

Research Zone

It ain't what you say, it's the way that you say it— the 7% + 38% + 55% Rule

As a result of research in the late 1960s and early 1970s Albert Mehrabian, currently Professor Emeritus of Psychology at UCLA, came to two conclusions regarding face-to-face communication (Mehrabian, 1971; 1972; 1981). Firstly that communication contains three basic elements: words, voice tone and body language. Secondly, that these distinct elements make different contributions to what is understood and communicated. Specifically, Meharabian concluded that actual words used generally account for only 7% of the message, voice tone for 38%, whilst body language can account for up to 55% of the meaning that is communicated.

Merahbian suggests that effective communication, in relation to emotions, feelings and attitudes, required all three of these elements to support each other and be **congruent**. Consequently **incongruence** between the elements can result in a mis-message. For example, a verbal communication could state That's OK and fine with me whilst non-verbal cues (avoiding eye contact etc.) could have an opposing effect. Furthermore, Merhabian's work suggests that if there is incongruence then the receiver of the communication is most likely to accept the dominant elements—non-verbal (body language, 55% and voice tone, 38%). Earlier work by Ray Birdwhistell (1970) also suggested that no more than 30 to 35% of the social meaning of a conversation or an interaction is carried by the words.

Birdwhistell, R. L. (1970) *Kinetics and Context: Essays on Bodily-Motion Communication*, Philadelphia: University of Pennsylvania Press

Mehrabian, A. (1971) *Silent Messages*, Belmont, CA: Wadsworth

Mehrabian, A. (1972) *Nonverbal Communication*, Chicago, IL: Aldine-Atherton

Mehrabian, A. (1981) *Silent Messages: Implicit Communication of Emotions and Attitudes*, Belmont, CA: Wadsworth

More ways to start improving your classroom practice with NLP

Think about the way you use your body language and which postures are most suitable for what sorts of classroom presenting:

- Use Leveling when you want things to appear factual or when dealing with rule explanation

- Use Computing after asking a question to promote thinking

- Use Placater when giving difficult feedback or messages and avoid the confrontational blaming posture. If you use Placater turn your hands over at the end of your point and go into Leveler to avoid ending in a submissive stance

- For an advanced strategy adopt suitable postures in any spotlight spaces that you have created in your classroom—see Chapter 9, *Anchors away* for how to do this

Chapter 7
Knowing me, knowing you ... a ha!

How to increase your personal and interpersonal effectiveness by just seeing the world differently

Have you ever had the experience of seeing the world through the eyes of someone else? Or have you ever found yourself being an observer, detached and rational looking at a situation as if you were not part of it? We all know how very different a school can seem from the perspectives of a headteacher, a teacher, a student or parents. Understanding other points of view adds to our ability to be highly effective communicators and supports us in developing flexibility. The notion that we have the flexibility to adopt different perceptual positions was inspired by Gregory Bateson's idea of double description. The idea that two or more descriptions of a situation are inherently

better than one was developed into a toolkit of approaches that you can train yourself to use and adopt. In developing these ideas they were also influenced by gestalt therapy, an approach developed by Fritz Perls whose work they studied, and by techniques that Virginia Satir was using in her family therapy. Satir used to hold what became known as 'parts parties'. In these, clients were asked to 'stand in the shoes' of everyone involved in the situation until they gained enough information to deeply understand what was going on. All of these concepts came together in the idea of **perceptual position**. Initially they worked with three perceptual positions. Later, Robert Dilts (an early colleague of Bandler and Grinder) identified a fourth position during his modelling of highly effective leaders. In the 1990s, ways of using a fifth perceptual position were first identified by Marylin Atkinson. Learning to move between perceptual positions can help you to see a problem in new ways and with more emotional detachment.

First position

The self-perspective: seeing the world completely through one's own eyes.

Second position

The other-perspective: seeing the world through the eyes of and from the point of view of someone else. Being completely referenced from their world, their values and their perspective and adopting their physiology.

Third position

The observer position: looking at the situation as an external observer, dissociated and unconnected to the situation emotionally.

Fourth position

The system viewpoint: looking at the situation from the perspective of the whole system, associated in the process as if you were the system.

Fifth position

Taking a universal perspective: seeing the whole perspective and taking on multiple perceptual positions.

Accessing fourth and fifth position can feel like a spiritual experience for many people and can create a sense of 'we-ness' and of being part of something much larger than oneself.

How many times have you had the experience of seeming to be the only person in a particular situation? In this sort of position we can be very limited and cannot see what others might see. By consciously developing our ability to adopt different perceptual positions we can develop new choices and ways of responding to others. These tools and techniques are useful, and highly effective, in a range of contexts: motivation, conflict, communication, understanding others, influencing, goal achievement and coaching, amongst other things. As with many NLP techniques some people find that they have a preference for one position or another (particularly when it comes to the first three). Spending time developing your flexibility in your least preferred position can bring huge rewards. Learning to move between perceptual positions helps you to see a problem in new ways and with more emotional detachment. In this chapter we will focus on how to use and develop your skills in the first three positions: **self, other** and **observer**.

Just do it

In this visualisation you may find it easier to work with your eyes closed. Read the instructions carefully first then find a quiet moment to explore the process. Can you remember being in conflict with a particular person or a student in class?

Take a moment to recall all of the details (what you saw, what was said and how you were feeling). Allow yourself to feel the same things you felt then and the same negative emotions. Visualise yourself moving out of your own body and floating up and into the body of the person that you were in conflict with. Now imagine yourself looking through their eyes across at you. Pay attention to all the details of what you looked like to them when you were in this emotional state. What did you look like? How did you stand? What was your voice tone like? Now reposition yourself in your own mind to the side of the conflict and look at the conflict as observer, as if you were watching a video of both yourself and the other person. What is different? What would you like to say to yourself?

Making effective use of perceptual positions

First position

Use first position when you want to be clear about what is important to you and do an inner check on your own personal values and beliefs. This is a good place to be when you need to stand up for yourself. However, always remember to do a health check by visiting the other positions. You will be much more influential and effective if you can understand the other person's position and at the same time be an observer of the process—so that you get it right and don't miss important information.

Second position

Use second position to enter the other person's shoes and really get a sense of where they are coming from. Using this position will help you to gather essential information and even predict what strategies, language or approaches will be effective.

Third position

Adopting third position gives you a different perspective and will help you to ensure a balance in your approach. Make an effort to have third position as your default perspective in potentially emotionally charged situations, like dealing with a disruptive student. Once you have a clear head you can then use the other positions to elegantly resolve the situation, maintaining your own calm perspective when you need to by returning to third position. This type of approach is sometimes referred to as dissociation (see Jargon Buster on page 69). In the Toolbox No. 16, below, you can learn an excellent technique (double dissociation). This will allow you to deal with the most challenging of situations and feedback. In the dissociated third position state we are able to monitor what we are doing as we do it. Some people believe that this perceptual position allows us to manage our emotions more effectively by ensuring that our prefrontal cortex is engaged in a logical and rational way, as opposed to being at the mercy of our amygdala with all the associated risks of emotional excess.

NLP Toolbox No. 16

Take a look in the meta mirror

This toolbox will help you to learn how to use the three core perceptual positions. With practice you will easily find yourself adopting the positions in your own mind as you work with other teachers, children or parents, one-to-one, in groups, in the classroom or when problem-solving. For the moment, however, find some quiet time and some space to work through the exercise below.

A good way to rehearse this before you use it is to set out three chairs in a triangle (facing

NLP Toolbox No. 16 continued ...

each other) or decide on three positions on the floor. If you want to you could mark these with three pieces of paper with the words **First position**, **Second position** and **Third position**. You may find it helpful to work through this with someone else coaching you. This technique is just as effective if it is done content free. In other words you do not have to say anything out loud. It can all be worked through in the privacy of your own mind. If you are running this in a coaching context it is preferable to mark the positions on the floor with pieces of paper rather than to use chairs as this can help people to change their physiology more easily to be like the person they are becoming in second position.

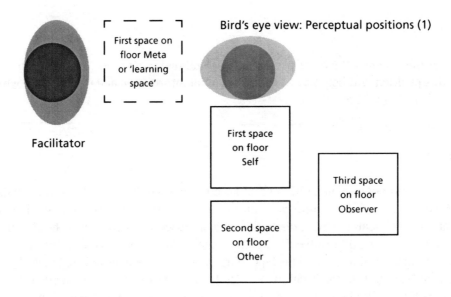

Facilitator

First space on floor Meta or 'learning space'

Bird's eye view: Perceptual positions (1)

First space on floor Self

Second space on floor Other

Third space on floor Observer

1. Think of a situation in which you have difficulty dealing with someone and would like that situation to change for the better. Stand in first position and look across at the person as if they were stood in the second position. Tell the person what it is that you find difficult about their behaviour.

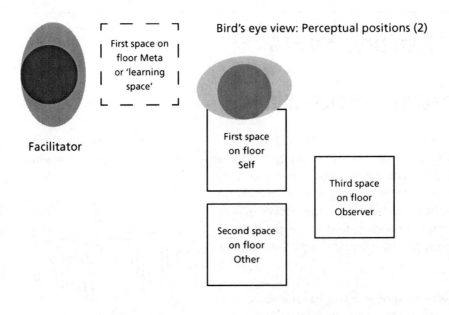

Facilitator

First space on floor Meta or 'learning space'

Bird's eye view: Perceptual positions (2)

First space on floor Self

Second space on floor Other

Third space on floor Observer

2. When you are sure that you have said everything that you need to move to the second position location. As you enter second position you need to become the other person, step into their shoes, adopt their body language and posture and become them. Now, as closely as possible, give the point of view of the other person looking across to where you would be sat in first position. Say what they would say and respond to some of the things that you said in first position

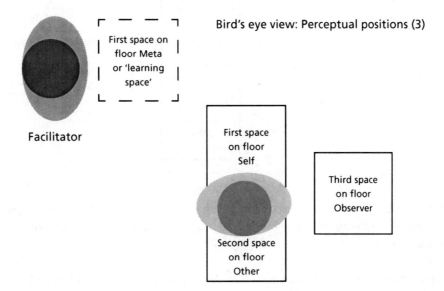

Facilitator

First space on floor Meta or 'learning space'

Bird's eye view: Perceptual positions (3)

First space on floor Self

Second space on floor Other

Third space on floor Observer

3. When you have finished move to the third position and imagine yourself as a detached and impartial observer who has heard everything that has been said for the first time. In this position give some words of advice to the first position on how your own behaviour could be modified to improve the situation.

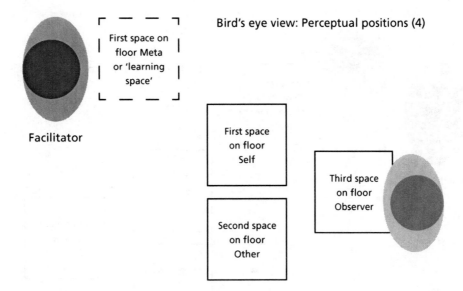

Facilitator

First space on floor Meta or 'learning space'

Bird's eye view: Perceptual positions (4)

First space on floor Self

Second space on floor Other

Third space on floor Observer

4. Finally, stand in first position again and notice what has changed. If you want to return to any of the different perceptual positions, to collect more information, you can.

NLP Toolbox No. 16 continued ...

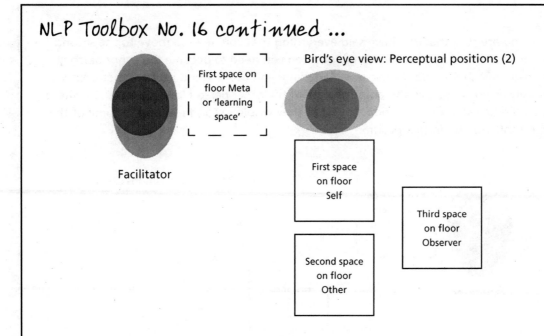

Bird's eye view: Perceptual positions (2)

First space on floor Meta or 'learning space'

Facilitator

First space on floor Self

Second space on floor Other

Third space on floor Observer

This exercise has been used to great effect in a number of schools recently as part of anti-bullying strategies. In many cases the bullies themselves have been taken through the exercise with significant results.

To gain even more information you can move outside of the triangle before returning to first position. In this fourth position reflect on how what you said and thought in third position compared to first position. Switch them around. If your felt cross in first position but thoughtful in third swap these feelings so that you experience in your own mind how it would have been to feel cross in third but thoughtful in first. When this additional step is added into the exercise this is known as the **meta mirror**. Using the four-step process above is also highly effective and is a good place to start your learning journey.

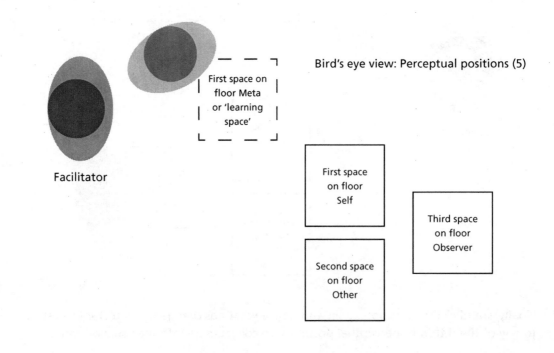

Bird's eye view: Perceptual positions (5)

First space on floor Meta or 'learning space'

Facilitator

First space on floor Self

Second space on floor Other

Third space on floor Observer

Top tips

Bullying

Use the meta mirror in Toolbox 16 above as part of a whole school strategy on bullying. Run the bully through the process to help them understand the consequences of their behaviour and to develop their empathy for others.

Parents' evenings

Run through the perceptual positions for yourself before you meet a parent that you know is going to be a bit challenging. This will enhance your flexibility and give you more communication options.

Asking senior management for something

Running perceptual positions for yourself before that critical meeting when you are seeking to influence is a powerful way of getting more information and preparing yourself to influence in the most effective way.

When you just can't make your mind up what to do

The meta mirror exercise is a great way to give yourself feedback particularly if you are not sure how something you are planning to do will come over in the future.

You can have too much of a good thing

Our preferred perceptual position is not always the best one to be in. Indeed as with many areas of life you can have too much of a good thing. If we spend too much time in one preferred preference to the exclusion of all the others, this can become an **overdone strength** and we can get what didn't really intend. For example, spending too much time in first position can lead us to become over emotional, self-centred or lacking in empathy, whilst finding ourselves trapped in second position can result in an overemphasis in helping others to the detriment of our own well-being. Being inflexible and staying in first position can lead us into two unhelpful psychological traps: **transference** and **projection**.

Transference occurs when we see a current relationship, or situation, only through the lens of a past relationship or situation. In a sense we are filtering our current understanding through something that is not actually happening now.

Projection occurs when we have not come to terms with a past traumatic experience and cut ourselves off from it (in other words we no longer recognise that it is affecting us). In this trap we can end up seeing the emotional response we had in other people's behaviour when it is not actually there. We have seen this happen on occasions with teachers who have had a bad experience with a class and never detach from the expectation of bad behaviour occurring again. In doing so they will often make the error of assuming the class does not like them, when in fact this is their own hidden emotion being projected. In our experience children rarely hate teachers and always respond well to consistency, structure and praise, irrespective of a past experience with a teacher (see Chapter 4, *Dolphin aquarium*, for a whole toolbox of practical approaches).

Finally spending all of our time in third position can make us cold and uncaring about others; always do a health check by visiting another position and you will quickly begin to gain flexibility.

NLP Toolbox No. 17

Double dissociation

This is quite an advanced tool. Many people find that they get it first time. If you don't get it first time you can just return to it after you have worked through the rest of the book, at which point your visualisation skills will be well developed.

The double dissociation tool is an extension of third position and is very useful in difficult situations (such as dealing with criticism, confrontation and situations where you need emotional protection of some sort). It is all done in the mind. Once you have trained your mind to do it you will be amazed how easily and effortlessly you can find yourself doing it. In fact as you experience how much easier it is to deal with challenging students, parents or just that awkward soul in the staffroom, your brain will soon find more possibilities for double dissociation.

Top tip

Learning to double dissociate is a great tool for learning to take things less personally and for managing confrontation.

1. Adopt third position in your mind. Imagine yourself looking at yourself in the situation that you are in, as if you were watching a movie or being an observer.

2. To help you maintain the dissociated position imagine a sheet of bullet proof glass between yourself and the scene you are observing.

3. Double dissociate. Now step back again and imagine yourself watching yourself in the scene or situation.

With practice, double dissociating can easily become second nature.

Research Zone

Understanding others—a neurological perspective

Neurological research had shown that when someone observes another person's emotional state, this activates part of the same network of neurons that is involved in the processing of the same state in themselves (e.g. Wicker et al., 2003). These studies were inspired by the discovery of mirror neurons (see Chapter 3, We like like) which suggest the existence of a neurological mechanism for mapping the feelings of others onto our own nervous systems. It has also been suggested that mirror neurons may effect our awareness of goal-directed actions (Fogassi et al., 2005) and that they may be responsible for understanding the intention behind the actions of other people (Nakahara and Miyashita, 2005).

In the philosophy of mind the phrase **theory of mind** is applied to our ability to infer the mental state of another person from their behaviour. Mirror neuron activity is now seen by many as the mechanism by which we are able to understand other people and to simulate their behaviour. Although there is currently no evidence that mental rehearsal directly stimulates the firing of mirror neurons, it is a reasonable hypothesis. Researchers (Gentili et al., 1995) have shown that when people imagine a motor task they demonstrate an improvement in the task when tested later.

Bower, B. (2005) Goal-oriented brain cells: neurons may track action as a prelude to empathy, *Science News*, April 30, 2005

Fogassi, L., Ferrari, P. F., Gesierich, B., Rozzi, S., Chersi, F. and Rizzolatti, G. (2005) Parietal lobe: from action organization to intention understanding, *Science*, 308: 662–667

Gallese, V. and Goldman, A. (1998) Mirror neurons and the simulation theory of mindreading, *Trends in Cognitive Sciences*, 2: 493–501

Gentili, R., Papaxanthis, C. and Pozzo, T. (2005) Improvement and generalisation of arm motor performance through motor imaginary practice, *Neuroscience*, 137: 3: 761–772

Nakahara, K. and Miyashita, Y. (2005) Understanding intentions: through the looking glass, *Science*, 308: 644–645

Wicker, B., Keysers, C., Plailly, J., Royet, J-P., Gallese, V. and Rizzolatti, G. (2003) Both of us disgusted in my insula: the common neural basis of seeing and feeling disgust, *Neuron*: 40: 655–644

Other people are mirrors of ourselves

One of the presuppositions, or fundamental concepts in NLP, is the idea that **the meaning of your communication is the response you get**. This can be quite a challenging concept to embrace, however, spending some time reflecting on this idea and then making it a core part of how you interact with the world can be hugely beneficial. What it says is that we are all to a large extent responsible for the behaviour of the other people that we interact with. If you think about this it makes sense. At the end of the day there is nothing I can really do to change someone else's behaviour as they will always be reacting to something that I have done or initiated. Therefore, if you want someone else to change how they behave you need to do something different yourself. This is a particularly important concept when planning how to deal with a difficult class. Remember that **if something isn't working do something different**. Take a moment to find someone else who is making it happen and model what they are doing.

> If you want someone else to change how they behave, you need to do something different yourself.

Internal perspectives and how to use them

How many times have you heard people say, 'You know there is something missing but I just can't put my finger on it'? Being aware that things just aren't aligned correctly, or that you are missing some important detail or perspective is a common experience. Think for a moment about the last time this happened to you. Did you ever figure it out or is it unresolved? As well as perceptual positions, there are a number of other NLP tools that can help you to explore different ways of thinking about a problem, an issue or just life in general.

Robert Dilts identified a really useful model which he refers to as neurological levels of change. Others have confusingly applied the terms logical levels of thinking or neuro-logical levels. Dilts suggested that there were layers of thinking that make up our experience and that bringing these into alignment with each other can really help us to understand what we really want, what behaviours we need to adopt to achieve this and where we are out of balance in our life. Although the title of this tool has come in for a lot of debate in the world of NLP, it remains a very useful and practical way of exploring the 'ecology' of an experience, or the whole context. The levels represent increases in the extent to which they are psychologically impactful and encompassing, as you move through the levels from environment to purpose and purpose/spirituality.

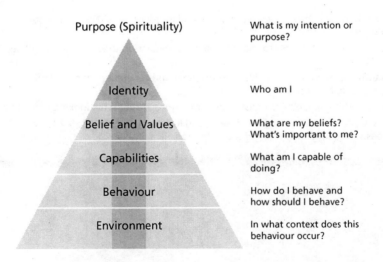

Purpose (Spirituality)	What is my intention or purpose?
Identity	Who am I
Belief and Values	What are my beliefs? What's important to me?
Capabilities	What am I capable of doing?
Behaviour	How do I behave and how should I behave?
Environment	In what context does this behaviour occur?

You will sometimes see this represented as an iceberg with behaviours and environment shown above the water line and our more hidden personal characteristics represented as being under the surface. Each level of self is progressively deeper and more hidden until we reach our deep anchor (our essence, purpose or spiritual connection to the universe). This metaphor emphasises the importance of having clarity of purpose and intention.

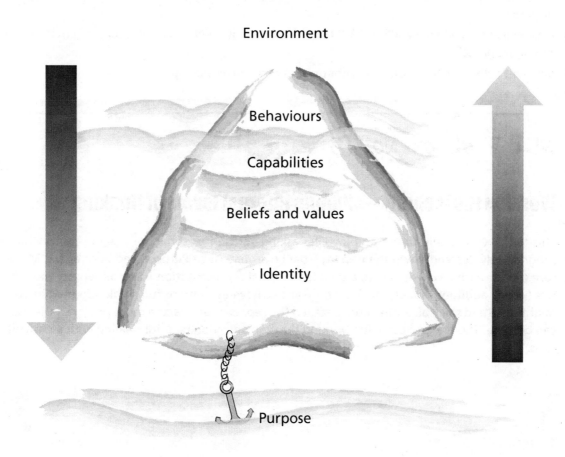

Ways to use this model

■ Coaching
■ Exploring all aspects of a change
■ Thinking through and exploring change
■ Planning your career
■ School improvement planning
■ Personal alignment (see Tool 3 in Toolkit 18 on the following page)
■ Planning schemes of work

Using the model above as a brainstorming tool for departmental, subject or whole school development or improvement planning can be very powerful. Begin by clarifying what your school's core purpose is and work up through the levels to ensure that each level is in alignment with all the other levels. You can also use this model when planning a scheme of work or a series of lessons that have never taught before. We have found it particularly helpful for PGCE students and other trainee teachers. In this context ask yourself or the trainee you are supporting to think through the following questions:

■ What is my core purpose in teaching this? What do I want the children to have learnt at the end of the unit?

■ Who will I be when I am teaching this if I am to be true to myself?

■ What are my values and beliefs about this area of knowledge?

■ What capabilities do I bring and what areas do I need to develop to be more effective to teach to my purpose?

■ What behaviours will the children see? How will I teach it? What types of teaching activity are most appropriate?

■ How will I structure the learning environment to best deliver the topic?

NLP Toolbox No. 18

Working the iceberg—aligning internal levels of thinking

This tool is very simple to use and involves asking yourself or someone else questions which progressively descend down the iceberg from Environment to Purpose and back again. Make sure that at each level you create a detailed internal representation using all sensory modalities (visual, auditory, kinaesthetic). If you want to have even more fun think about what you might taste and smell also. The more detailed the representations, the more powerful the tool can become. This is a great tool for working through an action plan for dealing with a difficult class.

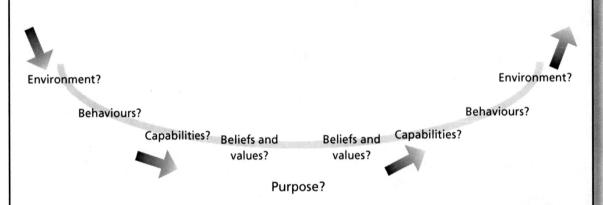

1. Begin by identifying a situation in which you feel out of alignment. You know this is the case when you get that uncomfortable feeling. Think about the environment that this happens in. Make sure that you elicit lots of sensory detail. What do you see? What do you hear (both external sounds and internal dialogue)? What do you feel (physiologically and emotionally)? How are you standing?

2. Explore what behaviours you are using. Again draw out as much sensory detail as you can. What do you see, hear and feel? Include your internal dialogue (self-talk) as well as the environmental sounds around you. Also notice your physical feelings as well as your emotions.

3. Follow the same process for Capabilities and Beliefs and Values in this context.

4. What, at the deepest and most spiritual level, are you about? What are you here in the universe to do? Take some time to experience this deeper aspect of yourself. Think of a symbol or a metaphor that you can take back through the levels.

5. Begin to re-explore the levels that you came back through. At each level in turn—Beliefs and Values, Capabilities, Behaviours and Environment—ask yourself what you need to do to ensure alignment with your purpose. Collect all the sensory information you need to see, hear and feel yourself doing what you need to. As you do this pay particular attention to whether any of the levels are out of alignment with your purpose or with each other. If any are out of alignment, rest there a while and allow your unconscious mind to identify what you need to do.

6. At the final level of Environment take a moment to do a final internal check to feel how you are now aligned at all levels.

Metaprograms

Metaprograms is another area to pay attention to in order to understand where other people are coming from. These have a parallel with personality traits and types in applied psychology and indeed several of them have direct parallels with measures within established psychometric instruments (e.g. the preference for big picture thinking versus detail, which parallels the intuition verses sensing dichotomy in the Myers-Briggs Type Indicator (Myers, 1995)). Over the last 30 years a large number of metaprogram have been noted by NLP writers with some writers pointing to as many as 51 (Hall and Boddenhamer, 2003b). Several small-scale attempts have been made to design personality instruments to assess people's metaprogram preferences and we believe that it will only be a matter of time before a valid and reliable instrument is constructed and accepted within the world of applied psychology.

Key metaprogram patterns

Take a few moments during your conversations with others, during meetings or when working with children in the classroom, to tune in to the processes that underlie what people are saying rather than simply the content. As you do that you will begin to notice some of the metaprograms below. Once you have done that orientate the content of what you have got to say to the tasks that you initiate so that they begin to match the metaprogram preferences of the children, parents and other teachers that you are working with. You will quickly find that your level of rapport increases and that you more often are able to easily achieve what you want. The seven metaprograms listed below are all 'either/ors', in other words people tend to prefer to do one or the other.

1. General or specific

Some people like the big picture first before they are required to work through to the detail; others need the detail before they can be chunked up to see the big picture.

2. Towards or away from

This pattern is about motivation. People who are towards motivated tend to be drawn to and focus on the end goal in order to be motivated. People who are away from motivated tend to need to have something negative to move away from in order to be motivated and energised to act.

3. Options or procedure

Some people like procedures that are clear and structured so that they know exactly what to do; others prefer things to be flexible and for options to be kept open so that they can improvise.

4. Internal or external

This metaprogram is about where you draw your values and internal standards from. For some people their locus of control is internal and they make all decisions and act according to their own internal benchmarks. Others need to be given external standards and frameworks in order to make decisions and to feel comfortable taking action.

5. Proactive or reactive

This metaprogram is about action. People have a tendency to either jump in to initiate action or to wait for others to initiate before following.

6. Match or mismatch

Take a look at the illustration below and describe what you see:

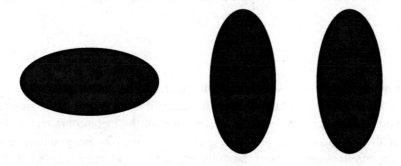

Some people notice similarities first; others notice the differences. In other words, some people have a preference for noticing when things are the same, others for when there are differences.

7. Self or others

People have a tendency to view the world from a self-perspective, or from the point of view of others. This is a very powerful metaprogram, particularly when seeking to influence. Explaining something to someone who is focused on self from the perspective of the personal benefits to them works extremely well. Doing the same for someone who is focused on others is less effective. This filter correlates very strongly to McClelland's notions of motivation. McClelland noted that there are three key types of motivation: power, achievement and affiliation. All people respond to all of these depending on the context; however, any individual will have a preferred hierarchy. For example, someone with the preferences: (1) affiliation, (2) achievement, (3) power, will usually put the quality of their relationships ahead of their own achievement and well ahead of being in charge or having control over others.

NLP Toolbox No. 19

Influencing with metaprograms

There are a number of key metaprograms that appear to be particularly important when seeking to understand the skills and strategies of excellent achievers and which appeared to be particularly useful when seeking to influence others. The process is a simple one: (1) Notice the preferred metaprogram by listening to language and observing behaviour; (2) Use the same metaprogram to build rapport and demonstrate like-mindedness; (3) Suggest what you are seeking to influence through the lens of that metaprogram.

1. Notice the preferred metaprogram
Listen to language and observe behaviour

2. Use the same metaprogram
Build rapport and demonstrate like-mindedness

3. Suggest what you are seeking to influence
Through the lens of that metaprogram

For example, in the classroom:

Teacher: *John, have you finished that work yet?*

Student: *No, because I don't want any mistakes I'm going over it again. I have finished it.* (**'Away from' motivation**)

Teacher: *Making mistakes is OK because that way we learn to work accurately* (**teacher used the same metaprogram**)

Teacher: *Why not hand it in now and I can help you to know where your mistakes are?*

Research Zone

Emotional intelligence and empathy

The idea that empathy (seeing the world from another's point of view) is important for effective communication and relationships has long been accepted (see e.g. Rogers, 1959). In recent years ideas about empathy have taken on a new lease of life as a result of the popularisation of the concept of emotional intelligence. Daniel Goleman, in particular, has proposed that emotional intelligence may matter more than IQ in relation to success in career and life in general (Goleman, 1995; 1996). The exact definition of emotional intelligence is in dispute, as indeed is its existence (Eysenck, 2000) and its effect (Antonakis, 2003). Some writers suggest that what may be being measured is, in fact, social conformity (Roberts et al., 2001). Generally EI or emotional quotient (EQ) is defined in terms of a person's capacity or ability to perceive and manage their own emotions and those of others. Whether emotional intelligence can be improved is also a contentious issue. However, even early researchers like John 'Jack' Mayer, who suggests that emotional intelligence is unlikely to be something that can be raised, accept that emotional knowledge and social and emotional functioning can be enhanced, and indeed that it is probably desirable to do so (Mayer, 2005). Within most concepts of emotional intelligence (e.g. Goleman, 2001; Bar-On, 1997; 2000) empathy figures strongly as a core area of emotional competence.

Antonakis, J. (2003) Why 'emotional intelligence' does not predict leadership effectiveness: a comment on Prati, Douglas, Ferris, Ammeter, and Buckley, *International Journal of Organizational Analysis*, 11: 4: 355–361

Bar-On, R. (1997) *Bar-On Emotional Quotient Inventory (EQ-I): Technical Manual*. Toronto, Canada: Multi-Health Systems

Bar-On, R. (2000) Emotional and social intelligence: insights from the emotion quotient inventory, in R. Bar-On and J. Parker (eds), *The Handbook of Emotional Intelligence*, San Francisco: Jossey-Bass

Eysenck, H. (2000) *Intelligence: A New Look*, Brunswick, NJ, Transaction Publishers

Goleman, D. (1995) *Emotional Intelligence*, New York: Bantam Books

Goleman, D. (1996) *Emotional Intelligence: Why It Can Matter More Than IQ*, London: Bloomsbury

Goleman, D. (2001) Emotional intelligence: Issues in paradigm building, in C. Cherniss and D. Goleman (eds), *The Emotionally Intelligence Workplace*, San Francisco: Jossey-Bass

Mayer, J. (2005) *Can Emotional Knowledge Be Improved? Can You Raise Emotional Intelligence?* University of New Hampshire <http://www.unh.edu/emotional_intelligence/> accessed 2 January 2006

Roberts, R. D., Zeidner, M., and Matthews, G. (2001) Does emotional intelligence meet traditional standards for an intelligence? Some new data and conclusions, *Emotion*, 1: 3: 196–231

Rogers, C. R. (1959) A theory of therapy, personality and interpersonal relationships, as developed in the client-centered framework, in S. Koch (ed.), *Psychology: A Study of Science*, 3: 210–211

More ways to start improving your classroom practice with NLP

- Be in **third position** in your mind when dealing with behaviour issues

- Adopt **second position** when planning lessons, explaining concepts or asking questions

- Choose **first position** when giving praise or rewards

- With practice you will also be able to maintain a monitoring position in your classroom using **fourth position** so that you become associated in the process of your lesson

■ Have a classroom rule for each of Dilts' levels: Purpose, Values and Beliefs, Capabilities, Behaviour and Environment. Display these in your classroom. You can also agree the rules with the children or get them to design them

■ Use Dilts' levels as an analytical tool when covering topics that require children to understand where people are, or were, coming from. This is particularly effective with historical concepts and where there is conflict between people. Ask at what level were these people in conflict? What could they have done?

■ Influence groups by ensuring that in your classroom explanations and planning you cater for children with different metaprograms. When giving context pay particular attention to whether you start with general or specific information. Plan activities to cater for both options or procedure preferences. When working one-to-one make sure that you give information according to the preferred metaprogram first and then work round to the less preferred metaprogram

■ Make the children aware of their preferences and encourage them to learn to use their less preferred style of thinking to encourage development and flexibility

■ If a child just doesn't immediately understand something that you have explained, think about which metaprogram you used to explain it and re-explain in the alternative way.

Chapter 8
Memories are made of this

How to use your inner resources effectively

Have you ever had a bad experience in the classroom with an individual child, or with a group of children, and found that the memory comes back every now and then? Have you noticed how when this happens you get the same feelings as before? You may even have experienced this past event influencing your behaviour even though you really wish that it wouldn't. Feels silly, doesn't it, that a memory could evoke past negative emotions when you are well past the situation that caused these original feelings? How useful would it be to be able to change this so that negative past experiences could be experienced from a detached position as if you were an observer rather than a participant?

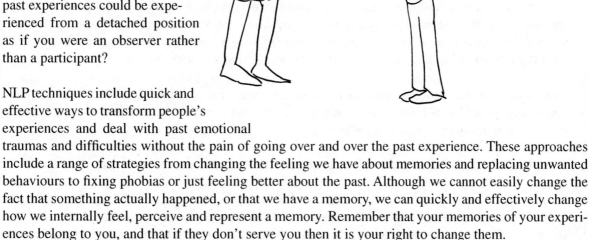

NLP techniques include quick and effective ways to transform people's experiences and deal with past emotional traumas and difficulties without the pain of going over and over the past experience. These approaches include a range of strategies from changing the feeling we have about memories and replacing unwanted behaviours to fixing phobias or just feeling better about the past. Although we cannot easily change the fact that something actually happened, or that we have a memory, we can quickly and effectively change how we internally feel, perceive and represent a memory. Remember that your memories of your experiences belong to you, and that if they don't serve you then it is your right to change them.

> Remember that your memories of your experiences belong to you, and that if they don't serve you then it is your right to change them.

Let's go inside and explore—internal representations and submodalities

Take a moment to think about a really enjoyable experience that you had once. It's OK, no one else is going to know what you are thinking about; it's all going to be in your own mind, so let yourself go. As you recall that experience what happens? Have you got a picture, or feelings, can you hear the words or sounds?

In NLP we call inner experiences like this internal representations. **Internal representations** can be memories or they can be projections of future events, and can be pictures, sounds, feelings or a combination of all three. As discussed earlier, we use the terms visual, auditory and kinaesthetic to refer to these differences.

One of NLP's unique contributions to the fields of personal development and therapy is the recognition of the importance of the small details that are part of our internal imagery or internal representation (such as colour, brightness, movement). These sorts of details are called **submodalities**. If you have already worked through Chapter 2, *Blockbuster movies*, you will already have some skill and experience of using internal imagery to help you become more motivated to achieve future goals. NLP practitioners have also modelled a range of strategies for playing around with details of memories so that we can change the emotional experience associated with a particular memory when recalled later.

Just do it

First make sure that you are in the right place to pay attention to your inner world.

Now think of a very happy and satisfying experience that you have had in the past. As you did before, think of something that gives you joy when you think about it, or recall it. Allow yourself to have that experience again. Let the experience become much closer and more vivid. Turn the brightness up and notice how you feel about that experience now.

Next allow the experience to become more distant, less clear and a little smaller. Now check inside and notice what feelings you have now and what is different. Turn the dial back and return the memory to how it was before.

What happened when you changed the representation of your past experience in your mind?

Most people find that the emotions and experiences become stronger when the experience is made to appear closer, and that the emotions and the experience become less vivid when the experience is seen as farther away or more distant. Some people find that noticing their internal images and processes is a fairly new experience, that's OK. Just allow yourself to relax and run the experience again, knowing that the more you do this the easier it will become. Your brain learns fast and with practice you will be able to easily manipulate your internal representations at will.

In the 'Just do it' above we focused on the effect of several **submodalities**, and in particular distance. Can you begin to see how this might be useful? If you want to experience positive experiences more intensely then move your inner representations of those experiences closer. If you want those times that have been negative to have less emotional intensity for you, then you can move them further away.

This can be done with any aspect of life, at work, when working with children or other adults, or at home. If you are have had an experience of working with a difficult child you can send that experience further away, so that you can deal with it in a more detached way. If there is some sort of career progress you want to achieve or a goal that you want to achieve with a class or a student, you can bring that representation nearer so that you feel more motivated to achieve the goal and become clearer about what it will look like when you get there. This is just one of a number of ways in which you can work with your internal representations and images to feel more comfortable in the work that you do. Four specific techniques (**Pump up the Volume, Art Gallery, the Swish Pattern and the Godiva Chocolate Pattern**) are given at the end of the chapter. You will get the most out of this learning if you work through the whole of this chapter first and then find some dedicated quiet time to work through the techniques at the end.

Using these powerful techniques you can work your way through your past experiences **re-coding** them to increase the intensity of past positive experience and reducing, or removing, the negative feeling from those experiences that are unhelpful to you now—like recovering and re-ordering the books in a library: upgrading the bindings for some books and re-locating them nearby, or putting others onto microfilm and storing them right away.

Research Zone

Memory reconsolidation

The term **memory consolidation** has been applied to the process by which memories become 'crystallized' into long-term memories. It refers to two different levels of activity. **Molecular consolidation** is the molecular process during which the long-term conductivity of synapses (the chemical junctions between neurons) is affected. Consolidation of this type occurs as a result of training or exposure to any stimulus-response process. Molecular consolidation increases with repetition. The term **network consolidation** is applied by a number of researchers who take the view that episodic memories (memories of time, place, events and associated memories) are initially stored in the hippocampus and then are slowly moved or consolidated into the neocortex. This was originally thought to happen during dreaming (Marr, 1971). More recent research indicates that it is the NREM phase of sleep that is associated with this process (Stickgold et al., 2001).

Research Zone continued ...

In recent years there has been growing evidence to suggest that memory is more complex than we thought and that memories are subject to change each time they are activated—what is called **memory reconsolidation** (see e.g. Lopez, 2000; Miller and Matzel, 2000). Furthermore, it is also likely that memories never reach a completely stable 'cast in stone' state. Original representations are open to modification in line with new associations each time they are recalled. The plasticity of memory is also supported by evidence that suggests that memories 'move' location in the brain, which again casts doubt on the idea of memories becoming 'crystallized' with time (Wirth et al., 2003; Gluck et al., 2003).

Gluck, M. A., Meeter, M. and Myers, C. E. (2003) Computational models of the hippocampal region: linking incremental learning and episodic memory, *Trends in Cognitive Sciences*, 7: 6: 269–276

Lopez, J. C. (2000) Shaky memories in indelible ink, *Nature Reviews Neuroscience*, 1: 6–7

Marr, D. (1971) Simple memory: a theory for archicortex, *Philosophical Transactions of the Royal Society of London*, Series B, Biological Sciences, 262: 841: 23–81

Miller, R. R. and Matzel, L. D. (2000) Memory involves far more than 'consolidation', *Neuroscience*: 1: 214–216

Stickgold, R., Hobson, J. A., Fosse, R. and Fosse, M. (2001) Sleep, learning and dreams: off-line memory reprocessing, *Science*, 294: 5544: 1053–1057

Wirth, S., Yanike, M., Frank, L. M., Smith, A. C., Brown, E. N. and Suzuki, W. A. (2003) Single neurons in the monkey hippocampus and learning of new associations, *Science*, 300: 1578–1581

Zeineh, M. M., Engel, S. A., Thompson, P. M. and Bookheimer, S. Y. (2003) Dynamics of the hippocampus during encoding and retrieval of face-name pairs, *Science*, 299: 577_580

Exploring visual, auditory and kinaesthetic submodalities

As discussed above, internal representations are have numerous qualities (or submodalities). For example a visual representation can have the qualities of brightness, size, colour or black and white, etc. As you will have noticed in the 'Just do it' on page 92, it is the submodalities hold in place the quality of the experience and the emotions associated with that experience, rather than there being any particular inherent emotion in the memory itself. As with any new skill, many people find that they need to practise to gain flexibility, whilst others can grasp the basics quite quickly. Whichever camp you fit into you should work through this chapter carefully so that you can train your mind to work with the ideas and techniques that have been included.

Where are you at the moment as you read this book? If you are standing in a bookshop you were probably completely unaware of the feeling of the floor under your feet, or if you were sitting down to read the book, of the feeling of the chair underneath you—until we mentioned this to you. Likewise we are not always aware of the details of our memories as they flash in and out of our conscious experience. Take some time to explore the list of submodalities below. Bring back the positive memory that you thought of earlier and ask yourself the questions below to help you to **elicit** the details, or submodalities, of the experience.

As with many things in life, we all have preferences, and that means some of these submodalities will be easier for you to notice and make use of than others. Imagine that you are in charge of a mixing desk, a set of video editing tools, or a theatre lighting board and have a go at turning up or down the intensity of any submodalities that seem particularly important for you. Or, if they seem to have a location, imagine being able to move them around like panning from one speaker to another. Some submodalities work like they have an on-off switch (they are either one thing or another—e.g. something is either moving or still), whilst others you can gradually increase or decrease, like the volume on your television. To go back to your original memory just give it a name now, before you start. Recalling that name can act as a reset button. Of course, if you are looking to change something permanently you would not need to do this.

Visual submodalities

Is your internal image large or small?	**Size**
Is your internal picture bright or dim?	**Brightness**
Are you seeing a colour or a black and white image?	**Colour**
Where in the space around you is the image located? Is it in front, to the left or right, or behind you?	**Location**
Does your image have movement or is it still like a photograph?	**Motion**
Are you seeing the picture as if through your own eyes or can you see yourself in the picture as if you were an observer?	**Association and dissociation**
How in focus is the picture?	**Focus**
Does the image appear panoramic with no edge or border, or does it seem to have an edge like a photograph?	**Panoramic or framed**

Auditory submodalities	
Are any sounds quiet or loud?	Size
Are sounds high pitched or low	Pitch
Where in the space around you are the sounds coming from?	Location
Is there a rhythm to the sounds?	Rhythm
Are the sounds fast or slow?	Speed
	You may also be able to identify tone qualities and even a tune associated with the memory

Kinaesthetic submodalities	
Is the memory hot or cold, or something in between?	Temperature
Is the memory located somewhere in your body, if so where?	Location
Does it feel light or heavy?	Weight
Can you feel movement or stillness?	Movement
Does the memory seem to exert any physical pressure?	Pressure
	You may also be able to feel shape, physical size or texture

Driver submodalities

The effect of changing submodalities will be different for everyone. Changing one submodality may make a huge difference for some people, whereas, for others, making a similar change will have little effect. You need to explore your own submodalities to uncover which ones have the greatest effect for you personally. With practice you will find two or three that make a significant difference when you change them. These are called **driver submodalities** because they are able to drive significant changes in your feelings or emotions. Commonly, people respond most significantly to changes in colour, brightness, distance, location, temperature and shifts from association to dissociation and vice versa.

Association and dissociation

A really important thing to notice is whether you are experiencing the internal representation through your own eyes (**associated**) or from the position of an observer seeing yourself doing something (**dissociated**).

Switching between these two perceptual positions is likely to affect how you feel emotionally. Go inside your mind and remember a time when things weren't going quite as well as you might have wanted—nothing too heavy, just an average problem that felt irritating. What submodalities do you notice? What are you feeling? Are you associated or dissociated? Now imagine the picture as if you were seeing yourself in the moment as an observer, perhaps as if you were holding a photograph of yourself taking part. What's changed? What do you feel now? If you were already dissociated, pull back as if you are zooming away with a camera so that you look small in the distance. What is different now?

Learning to use clusters of submodalities

Once you have practised eliciting and exploring your submodalities you will begin to notice common patterns for each type of emotional experience. For example, all of your confident memories may be bright, coloured, sharp focused, warm feeling, panoramic and close up. In contrast, your uncomfortable experiences might be recorded as dim, black and white, slightly cold and distant. Once you have mapped the structure of different types of memories you can transfer these patterns to any other memory that you would rather experience in a similar way. We call this **mapping across submodalities.**

In the case of the example above the process would look like this:

Unconfident memory	
Dim	Change to bright
Black and white	Change to colour
Slightly cold	Turn the thermostat up so that the memory is warm
Distant	Bring the memory closer

Remember everyone codes their memories differently, so you will need to explore your own internal representations carefully to work out what is effective for you.

Just do it

Contrasting clusters of submodalities and mapping them across

Think about something at school that makes you cross and perhaps even angry. Notice what sort of picture you recall when you think of this. Is the picture colour or black and white? Do you see yourself in the picture or are you seeing it through your own eyes? Is it close up or distant? Is it panoramic or does the image have an edge? Now write down the things that you notice and explore other submodalities from the lists above.

Take a quick break and notice something in the space around you that you hadn't seen before.

Now imagine something that makes you feel comfortable, warm and relaxed. Really associate into the experience and notice the submodalities. Is the picture colour or black and white? Do you see yourself in the picture or are you seeing it through your own eyes? Is it close up or distant? Is it panoramic or does the image have an edge? Again write down what you notice.

Circle or underline those submodalities that are different between the two experiences. What do you notice? Now recall the image of something that makes you cross. One by one adjust the submodalities so that this representation has the same cluster of submodalities and the memory of warm relaxation.

Once you have done this, take a quick break.

Now recall the first memory again. What's changed?

NLP Toolbox No. 20

Pump up the Volume and Art Gallery

These techniques are really effective for dealing with those everyday experiences that have caused us distress, or which still have unwanted negative emotions associated with them. There are other NLP techniques for serious traumas and phobias and an NLP practitioner will be able to help you if you need to deal with something more substantial.

Two approaches are given below. You may find either the auditory strategy (**Pump up the Volume**) or the visual strategy (**Art Gallery**) more effective for you. You may even want to use both with some past experiences. Just relax, experience and enjoy the changes. Choose a real event that took place in the past. For example, dealing with a difficult member of staff, a difficult parent, a lesson that just didn't go very well, etc.

Pump up the Volume

1. Find somewhere comfortable where you will not be disturbed. Now recall the details of that experience. Notice what you see, hear and feel—pay attention to the images and sounds that are present.

2. Allow yourself to travel to the very beginning of what happened.

3. As you watch the experience play out again, listen to some music (something silly, like circus music, the Monty Python theme, or something that you know always makes you laugh). Turn the volume right up. Let the music play all the way through the experience as you recall the experience in a different way. Let your mind react in the way that it would if you were dancing and allow the position of the memory to swirl around you until it finds a new place to rest. Take as long as you need and repeat the process if it feels right to do so.

4. Rewind the experience back to beginning and this time play it again without the music. Take a moment to notice what's different, however small or big that change is.

NLP Toolbox No. 20 continued ...

Art Gallery

You can use this strategy immediately after Pump up the Volume if you still feel that you would like to create more change, or just use on its own if visual representations come easier to you.

This time pick one still image from the experience that sums up for you the whole event and what it meant to you, like taking a still from the movie.

1. Are you in the picture? Or are you looking at the scene as if it is through your own eyes?

2. If you are looking at the scene through your own eyes begin to zoom back until you see yourself in the picture, as it you were watching yourself in a movie as if an observer of what happened to you.

3. What kind of frame would you like for your picture? Gilded or modern? Dramatic or understated? Or maybe something silly?

4. Once you have decided on the frame include some lighting—like the lights you get in art galleries or museums. You could even see your picture as if it had been painted by a famous artist.

5. Take a moment to think of the incident that you used to feel unhappy about. Notice how it has changed. It can stay changed.

6. Let the picture drift down the corridor of the art gallery and see it hanging on a wall far away at the end of a room.

You now have a simple and easy technique to use that you can apply quickly and effectively. Many of the teachers we have worked with have also applied these sorts of *strategies* to help children with exam nerves deal with experiences that keep coming back to influence their behaviour.

Research Zone

An important skill for teachers and trainee teachers

There is much evidence to suggest that teacher expectations are one of the most significant factors affecting both the climate of individual classrooms and school improvement (Reynolds and Muijis, 2005; Mortimore et al., 1988). Research has demonstrated that unwanted negative beliefs and biases can exist with or without teachers being aware of them, in many areas, particularly ethnicity, gender, class (see e.g. Brophy and Good, 1986). In psychology and cognitive science it is widely recognised that **memory bias** either enhances or impairs the recall of a memory and can effect the chances that the memory will be recalled at all and/or the time that it takes for it to be recalled or the actual content of a reported memory. Evidence has shown that this sort of cognitive bias can effect the way in which we perceive the world and therefore affect the way in which we respond when we encounter similar situations (e.g. Baron, 2000; Gilovich, 1993; Mather et al., 2000; Craik and Lockhart, 1972; Von Restorff, 1933). In our practical experience helping teachers gain flexibility over their memories of past classroom experiences can help them to overcome the effects of inherent biases.

Baron, J. (2000) *Thinking and Deciding*, New York: Cambridge University Press

Craik, F. I. M. and Lockhart, R. S. (1972) Levels of processing: a framework for memory research, *Journal of Verbal Learning and Verbal Behavior*, 11: 671–684

Gilovich, T. (1993) *How We Know What Isn't So: The Fallibility of Human Reason in Everyday Life*, New York: The Free Press

Mather, M., Shafir, E. and Johnson, M. K. (2000) Misrememberance of options past: source monitoring and choice, *Psychological Science*, 11: 132–138

Mortimore, P., Sammons, P., Stoll, L., Lewis, D. and Ecob, R. (1988) *School Matters*, Somerset Wells: Open Books

Muijis, D. and Reynolds, D. (2005) (2nd edn) *Effective Teaching: Evidence and Practice*, London: Sage Publications

Von Restorff, H. (1933). Über die wirkung von bereichsbildungen im spurenfeld (The effects of field formation in the trace field), *Psychologie Forschung*, 18: 299–34

NLP Toolbox No. 21

The Swish Pattern

The Swish Pattern makes use of both past memories and future representations in a pattern that is very effective for removing and replacing negative experiences. It has also proved to be very effective for generating more positive behaviours. In the example below it has been given in the latter form. However, once you know how to do this in your own mind you will be able to apply the approach to memories and past experiences alone.

1. Identify a behaviour or a pattern that you want to change.

2. What is it that triggers that behaviour? Take some time to identify the trigger. Find the earliest memory you can of the thing that triggers the behaviour.

3. Create a picture of the trigger or cue. Make sure that this picture is **associated**. In other words, it is an image as if seen through your eyes, as if you were actually there. Emphasise the submodalities to make the picture more compelling. Increase the size of the image, its brightness and the vividness of the colour.

4. Think of something different and take a moment out to clear your mind.

5. Create an image of the person that you want to become when you have stopped that old habit or behaviour. Create a picture of this outcome. This time make sure that the picture is **dissociated**. In other words you can see yourself in the picture doing the things that you want yourself to achieve.

6. Take a moment to ask yourself whether this is really what you want. What's important about this new behaviour? Imagine a time in the future when you have got what you wanted and think about what that now means for you.

7. In your mind's eye take the cue or trigger picture—make it really big and bright.

NLP Toolbox No. 21 continued ...

8. Next place the outcome picture in one corner of the other picture—small and dark.

9. Quickly, whilst you say the word **swish**, swap the two pictures over so that the outcome picture becomes large and bright and the cue picture becomes small and dark in the corner.

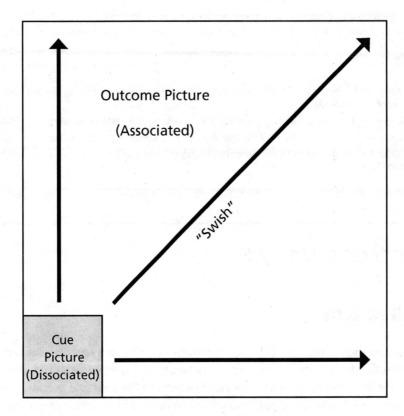

10. Clear the screen in your mind and repeat the exercise about five times getting quicker and quicker.

11. Notice what has changed by trying to get back the original cue picture of the old behaviour. Notice how you feel about the change.

You can also do this pattern with distance if that is more effective for you. To do this simply place the outcome picture in the distance behind the cue or trigger picture. Then imagine the picture rushing towards you until it breaks through the cue picture and occupies all the space. Again repeat this as many times as you need to make the change effective. Again, finish by paying attention to what has changed.

NLP Toolbox No. 22

The Godiva Chocolate Pattern

Ever had one of those days when you just don't feel motivated to do what you really want to do—teaching a difficult class, phoning a parent, just getting on with the things you need to do for tomorrow before you go home? Richard Bandler developed a really effective change pattern that he called the Godiva Chocolate Pattern. It works by making use of an internal representation of something that you already have great enthusiasm for and 'mapping across' the submodalities so that these same feelings can be experienced in relation to the activity that you are currently less enthused about.

1. Think of something that you do that you really desire, are enthusiastic about doing, and/ or feel completely compelled to do if you could do it right now. You can use a memory for this or, if you want to, you can imagine something that you have not actually done yet, but that drives you wild with excitement at the thought of doing it. Remember that you are doing this in your own mind so feel free to let your imagination run wild. Make sure that the image you have really excites you. Imagine in rich detail what you will see, hear and feel when you are doing it. Make sure that the feelings are emotional as well as physical and notice what words you hear yourself saying internally as well as the sounds around you. Make sure that the image is big, bright and vivid. See this image through your own eyes fully **associated** in the experience. We will call this image *Picture 1*.

2. Take a short break and notice something around you.

3. Now think of the thing that you have to do that you are currently not so enthusiastic about. Change the image, if you need to, to make it **dissociated**, as if you were seeing yourself doing it as an observer. This is what we will call *Picture 2*.

4. Check inside that this is what you really want.

5. Now imagine that *Picture 2* (the less desirable activity) is behind *Picture 1*

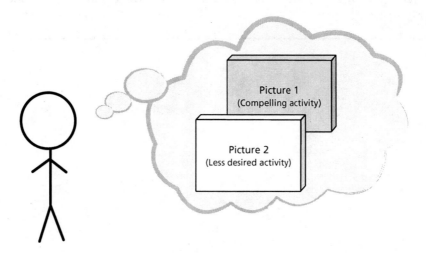

6. Imagine a connection between the two images. As you do this open up a small hole in the centre of *Picture 2* so that you can just see *Picture 1* through that hole.

NLP Toolbox No. 21 continued ...

7. Now very quickly allow all the feelings and images from *Picture 1* to tear through the hole in *Picture 2* so that *Picture 1* rapidly covers *Picture 2* and allow yourself to experience all the wild excitement and desire of *Picture 1.*

8. Now, keeping all the positive emotions in place, close up the hole as quickly as possible.

9. Repeat the process as often as you need to in order to experience the compelling feeling of desire as completely associated with the activity you need to do.

More ways of improving your classroom practice with NLP

Use submodalities exercises to change your emotional responses in the classroom and help you to manage your internal state:

■ Recode the submodalities in your memories of positive classroom experiences to enhance the positive feeling that you have about these and your skills as a teacher

■ Dissociate your worst classroom experiences

■ If you have any students with whom you repeatedly have difficulties, and negative associated feelings, pay particular attention to recoding your memories of these experiences. Use Art Gallery or Pump up the Volume in Toolbox 20 above to do this

■ Run the Godiva Chocolate Pattern for those tasks that you know you have to do but just don't feel motivated about yet (marking, planning, etc.)

■ When working with children who are upset, or troubled by something, simply getting them to think of the memory (or experience) and sending it further away in their mind's eye can be a really quick and effective intervention. Alternatively, get them to imagine where the image of the memory is in the space around them and get them to move it somewhere else. Use presuppositional language to support this (e.g. where would you like to put this memory ... as you move it you could begin to notice what changes about how you feel ... what's different now?). Add a change from colour to black and white as you do this etc.

Chapter 9
Anchors away!

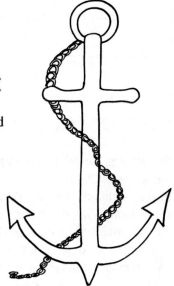

How to harness your internal mental resources within yourself and in your learning environment

Have you ever wondered why that comfy old sofa feels just so good and relaxing and why, as you sit there reading this, those same good feelings could come over you right now?

In NLP we call this anchoring. Anchoring happens when an emotional state, or process, is so strongly associated with a word, touch, place, sound, smell, taste or image that your current internal state is changed to match the remembered one.

Convinced? Do the thought experience to explore this further …

Just do it

This exercise is about your inner world and how it can connect to your feelings, emotions and behaviour. All you need to do is relax and go inside.

Stop for a moment, and recall a time when you were really happy, and allow yourself to be there once more … that's right … and as you do that, you can notice how those same feelings are here again with you, right now …

Notice what you see, hear and feel in that moment.

Imagine a dial like the volume control on an old record player and notice what number the feelings are set at. Turn the dial up (move your hand if it helps) and notice how the feelings change as you turn up the dial.

Now think of a word for the feelings you now have—something unusual that you would rarely say.

Take a break and then say the word to yourself again. Notice the extent to which you are able to return to the state of mind that you have anchored. Now that you know how to do this you will find that this resource is accessible to you whenever you need it.

In NLP we learn not only to access internal resources and states of mind but also to literally **anchor** them to a specific stimulus. In a way **anchoring** is a form of Pavlovian conditioning for people. The amazing thing is that with skill (and consistency), anchors can not only affect you, but also the children, parents and other teachers around you. There are many ways to anchor positive states of mind. In this chapter we are going to look at a variety of techniques that can help you create positive learning and motivational states, and organise your classroom environment from your inner mind out—rather like a director on a film set.

In a way, anchoring is a form of Pavlovian conditioning for people.
The amazing thing is that with skill, (and consistency) anchors can not only affect you, but also the children, parents and other teachers around you.

Pavlovian conditioning

The Russian scientist Ivan Petrovich Pavlov was born in 1849 in Ryazan, where his father worked as a village priest. In 1870 Ivan Pavlov abandoned the religious career for which he had been preparing, and instead went into science. There he had a great impact on the field of physiology by studying the mechanisms underlying the digestive system in mammals. While Ivan Pavlov worked to unveil the secrets of the digestive system, he also studied what signals triggered related phenomena, such as the secretion of saliva. When a dog encounters food, saliva starts to pour from the salivary glands located in the back of its oral cavity. This saliva is needed in order to make the food easier to swallow and digest. Saliva also contains enzymes that break down certain compounds in the food.

Pavlov became interested in studying reflexes when he saw that the dogs drooled without the proper stimulus. Although no food was in sight, their saliva still dribbled. It turned out that the dogs were reacting to lab coats. Every time the dogs were served food, the person who served the food was wearing a lab coat. Therefore, the dogs reacted as if food was on its way whenever they saw a lab coat. In a series of experiments, Pavlov then tried to figure out how these phenomena were linked. For example, he struck a bell when the dogs were fed. If the bell was sounded in close association with their meal, the dogs learned to associate the sound of the bell with food. After a while, at the mere sound of the bell, they responded by drooling.

Different kinds of reflexes

Reflexes make us react in a certain way. When a light beam hits our eyes, our pupils shrink in response to the light stimulus; when the doctor taps you below the knee cap, your leg swings out. These are called unconditioned, unlearned, or built-in, reflexes. The body responds in the same fashion every time the stimulus (the light or the tap) is applied. Pavlov's discovery was that environmental events that previously were not related to a given reflex (such as the sound of a bell) could, through experience, trigger a reflex (salivation). This kind of learnt response is called conditioned reflex, and the process whereby dogs or humans learn to connect a stimulus to a reflex is called conditioning. The thing is that you are creating anchors all the time. Most people, however, are not systematic in the way they do it.

In NLP, we understand that we can create a conditioned response not only to a reflex but also to an emotional state (such as confidence, enthusiasm and calmness). How useful would it be to be able to instantly call upon a particular emotional state to aid you in teaching?

The thing is that you are creating anchors all the time. Most people, however,
are not systematic in the way they do it.

Anchoring resourceful states

Anchoring is one of the most useful of NLP techniques. Anchoring is the process by which a memory, a feeling or some other response is associated with (or 'anchored' to) something else.

> Anchoring is the process by which a memory, a feeling or some other response is associated with (or 'anchored' to) something else.

Anchoring is a natural process that usually occurs without our awareness. For example, when you were young, you undoubtedly participated in family activities that gave you great pleasure. The pleasure was associated with the activity itself, so when you think of the activity, or are reminded of it, you will tend to re-experience some pleasurable feelings. It is by the same process of associated memory that anchors are reactivated or triggered.

NLP Toolbox No. 23

Simple kinaesthetic anchoring

1. Select a feeling that you would like to have in a particular situation.
   (For example, you might want to feel motivated and energised when you sit down at your desk to work on your marking.)

2. Take a few moments to remember a time when you had that feeling. Be sure to choose a strong example. If you don't have one in your past, imagine what it would be like to feel this way. Your mind will be unable to tell the difference.

3. Close your eyes and remember that feeling in vivid detail.

4. Put yourself back there now and re-live it in all its intensity—be associated (see it through your own eyes).
   To enhance the experience you can experiment with the following:
   - make the image sharper
   - make the colours brighter
   - bring the image closer
   - shift the image position on your mental screen
   - make the sounds clearer
   - choose a word that enhances the feeling
     (for example, 'Yes!', 'Brilliant!' etc.)

5. As the feeling begins to grow create a physical association by making a single unique gesture (for example, you might touch a knuckle, squeeze your thumb, make a fist, press your middle finger and thumb together or pull your earlobe, etc.).

6. When the feeling is reaching its peak of intensity set off your 'anchor'.

7. Open your eyes, do something else (e.g. count down from 10, think about your journey to work, etc.). This is called breaking state.

NLP Toolbox No. 23 continued ...

8. Repeat the steps above several times, each time making the memory more vivid. Do this until the anchor is as strong and intense as you need it to be. With practice you will be able to do this on many occasions first time— depending on the intensity of the experience you are using.

Anchors Away! Timing

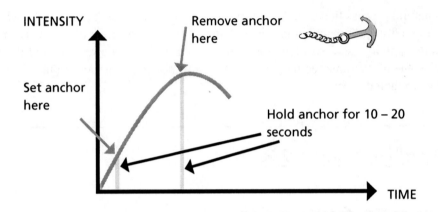

9. Think about a time in the future when you will be able to use this desired state. Fire the anchor to check that it creates a sufficiently resourced state to work in that situation.

10. Check the anchor the next day to ensure it is a permanent anchor.

To anchor an experience effectively there are **four steps** and **four keys** to success:

The four steps

1. Recall a past vivid experience
2. Provide specific stimulus near the peak
3. Break state
4. Set off anchor to test

The four keys

1. The **intensity** of the experience used
2. The **timing** of the anchor
3. The **uniqueness** of the stimulus
4. The **replication** of the stimulus

Top tips for anchoring

■ The anchor should be fired in exactly the same way every time you link them to the resourceful experience.

- Anchor just before the high point of the experience containing the resourceful state.

- If you do not experience the positive state when future pacing (imagining the use of it in the future) simply repeat the process.

- There is a knowingness that makes anchoring work that is established by the unconscious mind, so avoid over analysing—just do it.

- You can strengthen the anchor by repeating the above process over several days.

- If you are in a situation where you experience the desired state in reality, then you can reinforce the anchor to that situation.

Anchoring happens around and within us all the time, whether we are aware of it or not. Most of the time we are not aware of it and this makes it a powerful force in our lives. Understanding the process and how we can use it with ourselves and to influence others is a critical life skill for anyone who works with groups or with people. Every experience that we have includes some, or all, of our sensory inputs—visual, auditory, kinaesthetic, olfactory and gustatory. The process of anchoring draws on our mind's tendency to bring back the whole of the experience when only one or more elements are present. Smells, in particular, have the power to bring back vivid recollections.

Anchoring is used by skilful film makers and film music composers to evoke suspense in their audiences. A camera angle, musical sequence or particular shot can easily be associated with an emotion or experience—with the result that when this stimulus reappears it can immediately evoke the feelings, or associations, even if only referred to in passing.

In everyday life as teachers, when we are with a child and they experience a strong emotion (as a result of what we have done), whatever we were doing or saying can become associated for them with that emotion. Usually this process occurs at the unconscious level. Subsequently, whenever we do or say the same thing in the same way in their presence we will tend to re-stimulate for them some portion of the previous feeling.

Being aware of this phenomenon enables us to recognise the kinds of responses we are anchoring in others, how we are doing it, and conversely, what kinds of responses are being anchored in others. It is also useful to get to know your personal anchors. Some will be resourceful—perhaps walking through your classroom door, being in front of a particular class, putting on work clothes. Some anchors will put you into an unresourceful state— perhaps meeting a certain person, going into a particular room, hearing a particular phrase. Once you know these anchors you can decide whether to respond or not. Think about the power of the routine that a professional golfer develops before teeing off or taking a putt. Without exception they will have a set of behaviours that triggers the right mindset and internal state before they act. The same thing can be seen in professional tennis players as they set up to make a serve. Have you noticed how, if they don't do it exactly the same, they stop and reset?

Spotlighting

A spotlight is a place in your learning space where you have a positive association with a particular internal state or personal strength. If you have already read about, or studied NLP, you may have come across this technique as the **Circle of Excellence** or **spatial anchoring**. Associating that space on the floor with these positive states will allow you to return to chosen feelings and a state of being whenever you want to, just like the comfy old armchair we mentioned at the start of this chapter. For example, you could have an anchored state for relaxation, one for feeling energised and one for dealing with behaviour calmly and effectively.

A spotlight is a place in your learning space where you have a positive association with a particular internal state or personal strength. If you have already read about, or studied NLP, you may have come across this technique as the Circle of Excellence or spatial anchoring.

Having spotlights also affects your learners. It works like this. By consistently adopting a particular behaviour or approach when you stand or sit in one place, your learners will begin to associate that space with what you are about to do and what will happen next. Your learners' own internal state will change in anticipation for what they know from experience will come next. As their internal state changes so will their behaviour. This works for adult learners in a training environment just as well as it does with children in the classroom. Other useful spotlight states could include:

- the place where you always ask questions (with an internal state of curiosity, openness and interest)
- the place that says: this is going to be the plenary when I draw the lesson to a close or set homework (with an internal state of confidence and business-like certainty). When Richard was an AST, he used to like to do this sitting on the edge of his desk—sitting there always said, 'Time for homework!'

Another good idea would be to have a behaviour management space (calm, congruent, confident and in charge). Having a place like this can be particularly effective for both your own state management and also as a signal to students. If well marked out, through experience, just going to that place, pausing and looking at the students can have a significant impact! Remember that it is important to keep the spaces separate and unique and to make sure that you apply the approach consistently.

By consistently adopting a particular behaviour or approach when you stand or sit in one place, your learners will begin to associate that space with what you are about to do and what will happen next.

NLP Toolbox No. 24

Creating spotlight states (spatial anchoring)

1. In your mind create an imaginary circle on the floor in front of you. Give it a colour.

2. Remember experiences where you felt powerful, creative, composed or any other resourceful state where you were balanced and centred.

3. Re-access one of your powerful positive memories. Notice as the sensory elements (visual, auditory, kinaesthetic) of the memory build inside you. Step into the circle just before you reach the peak of the experience.

   See what you saw through your own eyes, within the actual experience … hear the sounds and language used and get in touch with your posture, breathing and emotions when inside the desirable resourceful memory. Note that an observer would see changes in your physiology such as a better posture, deeper breathing and skin colour changes.

   If there is no noticeable change in your physiology the resource state is either poorly accessed or low intensity. If it is low intensity, choose another resourceful state that is more powerful.

4. Repeat Step 4, adding the other different resourceful states if you like. When you step back into the space you will be able re-access the positive feelings and states of being that you anchored there.

5. You can take this imaginary spotlight and use it whenever you need to, or you can set up spotlights in specific places in your classroom. Imagine doing it right now—what differences do you notice?

Remember you can choose to build spotlights with any number of different internal states and for any positive purpose!

From a theoretical point of view, spotlighting in the classroom can be seen as the practical use of classical conditioning and mirror neuron activation (see Research Zones on pages 27 and 115). The diagrams below illustrate the basics of the combined processes in action.

Jargon Buster

Stacked anchors

In the spotlighting tool above we learned to anchor more than one state to a single stimulus. This is called a stacked anchor. You can do the same thing with kinaesthetic anchoring.

Spotlighting (applying classical conditioning and mirror neuron activation in the classroom)

Step 1: Condition yourself

Stage 1 (before learning)	Time when rules need to be explained effectively (Unconditioned Stimulus) UCS →	Desired emotions (e.g. calm, focused, successfully assertive) Including visual representations of success and appropriate body language (e.g. Leveler) (Unconditioned Response) UR
Stage 2 (during learning)	Create spotlight [Specific place to stand in classroom] (Conditioned Stimulus) CS **+** Time when rules need to be explained effectively (Unconditioned Stimulus) UCS →	Desired emotions and internal representations (Unconditioned Response) UCR
Stage 3 (after learning)	Spotlight [specific place in classroom] (Conditioned Stimulus) CR →	Desired emotions and internal representations (Conditioned Response)

In Charge   Calm
Confident

Step 2: Condition the children

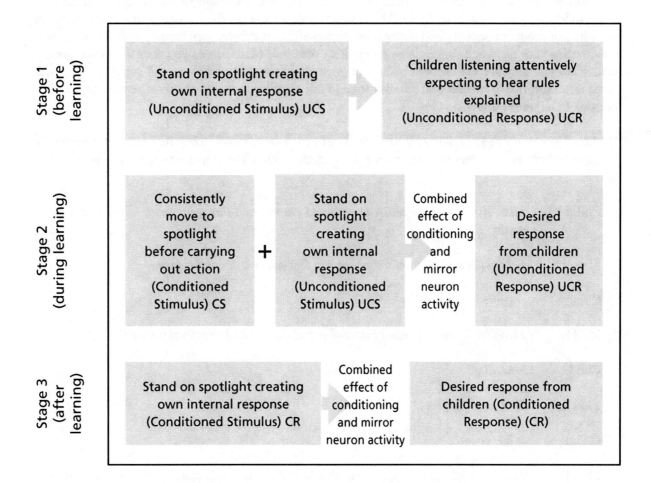

Directing your classroom experience like a film set

Spotlights are just part of a stage performance—the set and direction are just as important. In earlier chapters (*Don't think about chocolate cake* (Chapter 5) and *Streetwise body language* (Chapter 6)), we explored influential language patterns and other aspects of communication, including body language. When teaching or training, non-verbal communication extends beyond our gestures and body posture to our environment (including the space in which we are teaching). All non-verbal information is also recorded by students as part of the learning experience. A useful metaphor would be to think of yourself as a film or theatre director, whose outcome is to create the most memorable performance you can (you are, of course, the leading actor).

When we watch a film we like to make sense of what is going on. If the plot is too complicated, unstructured or full of irrelevant detail, we can get confused and switch off. A film director pays as much attention to the big picture as to the smallest detail. Teachers can use the same principle in the classroom to create a cinema of the mind for students.

Using anchors in conversation with others

The process of eliciting and re-eliciting desired resourceful states and feelings is a fairly simple one. If you are working with someone else simply ask them to recall a past experience that is likely to contain the desired response. For example, if you want the other person to experience a pleasurable response ask them to recall a pleasant incident. In doing so, the person will bring up, with that memory, many of the feelings felt at the time of the incident.

The purpose of eliciting certain responses is to establish a more favourable and receptive ground for communicating your ideas effectively. The person's state of mind—their feelings, the things they are attending to (both consciously and unconsciously)—will be of critical significance with regard to how they receive your ideas and suggestions. By eliciting the kinds of responses you want when you present your idea, you increase the chances of having your idea favourably received and acted on. This will come as no surprise to anyone who has ever tried to sell anything, but even the most sophisticated sales-person often ignores this basic fact.

We know a primary headteacher who has a really effective strategy for doing this when children come to her to talk about a conflict they are having with another child. The conversation goes something like this.

Child: *Miss, Eric makes me really angry and I am worried I'm going to hit him if he does it again.*

Miss R: *Eric, what sort of creature makes you feel really calm and relaxed?*

Child: *A white butterfly, Miss.*

Miss R: *I wonder if you can reach inside and find that white butterfly right now?*

Child: *Yes, Miss.*

Miss R: *How does that feel?*

Child: *It feels good.*

Miss R: *Do you think that the next time this happens you could reach inside and find that white butterfly again?*

Child: *Yes, Miss.*

Miss R usually touches the child on the shoulder as the child accesses the state again for the first time and by doing so has another way of re-eliciting the state on another occasion. To make use of either touch or verbal anchoring make sure that you are in rapport before you start (see Chapter 3, *We like like*) and that it's OK to touch.

Research Zone

The feeling of consciousness

There has been a tendency for writers on the 'mind brain' debate to focus on reasoning and logical faculties and to regard the emotions as a separate compli-cation and of no real importance to our understanding of how the mind works. Even if emotion is considered, it has often been seen as something separate from intellectual activity. More recently neuroscientists like Antonio Damasio have demonstrated that this is incorrect (Damasio, 1994; Bechara et al., 1996; Bechara et al., 1999; Bechara et al., 2000). Famously Damasio refers to this as 'Descartes' error', in other words rather than reason like Descartes and say 'I think therefore I am', we should see it the other way round (Damasio, 1994). In fact, all consciousness involves feelings and it would be more accurate to say that human consciousness is the consciousness of feeling. More specifically feeling is the product of low-level cognitive processes, the content of which we typically have no awareness of. The fact is you cannot separate the process of thinking from emotions, feeling and the body (Damasio, 2000).

Bechara A., Damasio H. and Damasio, A. R. (2000) Emotion, decision making and the orbitofrontal cortex, *Cerebral Cortex*, 10: 295–307

Bechara A., Damasio H., Damasio, A. R. and Lee, G. P. (1999) Different contributions of the human amygdala and ventromedial prefrontal cortex to decision-making, *Journal of Neuroscience*, 19: 5473–5481

Bechara A., Tranel D., Damasio H. and Damasio A. (1996) Failure to respond automatically to anticipated future outcomes following damage to prefrontal cortex, *Cerebral Cortex*, 6: 215–225

Damasio, A. R. (1994) *Descartes' Error: Emotion, Rationality and the Human Brain*, New York: Putnam

Damasio, A. (2000) *The Feeling of What Happens: Body, Emotion and the Making of Consciousness*, London: Vintage

Classical and operant conditioning

Classical (or Pavlovian conditioning) has attracted a wide array of research since it was first described in 1927. Pavlov put hungry dogs on a stand and following the sounding of a tone gave food powder to the animals. Initially only the food presentation resulted in salivation. After repetition of the tone-food pairing, several times Pavlov noted that the dogs began to salivate prior to the food being delivered. This form of classical conditioning is known as excitatory conditioning. Pavlov (1927) noted that in terms of acquisition the 'conditioned response' increased in magnitude and frequency—in other words the more you did it the greater the effect—and that where a previously functioning response has become extinct it can be renewed with a novel stimulus. Pavlov also noted a temporal effect in conditioning, namely that peak conditioned response occurs at the end of a long stimulus, a finding that was supported and expanded on by further research (Smith, 1968). Later researchers have noted that inhibition can be conditioned (Rescorla, 1969), that conditioning works less effectively if the stimulus had been presented on a previous occasion, prior to the experiments talking place (Lubow and Moore, 1959), and that conditioning depends not on the number of presentations of the experience but rather the quality (intensity) of the stimulus (Wagner et al.,1968). All of which supports the approaches to anchoring presented by Bandler and Grinder (1979). In relation to the NLP concept of **collapsing anchors**, the ability to replace one anchor with a stronger new anchor, there is also evidence that the conditioning of one stimulus will block another when these are trained simultaneously (Kamin, 1968).

The term operant conditioning (see e.g. Thorndike, 1901; Skinner, 1974) is distinguished from classical conditioning in that operant conditioning describes the use of consequences (positive or negative) to modify the occurrence and form of a behaviour. Classical conditioning occurs when behaviour is conditioned to a stimulus outside of the context of reward. The core components of operant conditioning are reinforcement and punishment, both of which can be positive or negative. Recently the notion that there is a neurological relationship between cognition and both classical and operant conditioning (Kirsch et al., 2004) has been demonstrated and a number of studies support the existence of automatic conditioning without awareness (e.g. Öhman and Soares, 1994; Dijksterhuis and Smith, 2002) and higher order cognitive mediation as a process within both classical and operant conditioning (see Kirsch et al., 2004).

Research Zone continued ...

Bandler, R. and Grinder, J. (1979) *Frogs Into Princes*, Moab, UT: Real People Press

Dijksterhuis, A. and Smith, P (2002) Affective habituation: subliminal exposure to extreme stimuli decreases their extremity, *Emotion*, 2: 203–214

Kamin, L. J. (1968) 'Attention-like' processes in classical conditioning, in M. R.Jones (eds), *Miami Symposium on the Prediction of Behavior: Aversive Stimulation*, Miami: University of Miami Press, 9–33

Kirsch, I., Lynn, S.J., Vigorito, M. and Miller, R. R. (2004) The role of cognition in classical and operant conditioning, *Journal of Clinical Psychology*, 60: 369–392

Lubow, R.E. and Moore, A. U. (1959) Latent inhibition: the effect of non-reinforced preexposure to the conditional stimulus, *Journal of Comparative and Physiological Psychology*, 52: 415–419

Öhman, A. and Soares, J. J. F. (1994) Unconscious anxiety: phobic responses to masked stimuli, *Journal of Abnormal Psychology*, 103: 231–240

Pavlov, I. (1927) *Conditioned Reflexes*, London: Oxford University Press

Rescorla, R. A. (1969) Conditioned inhibition of fear resulting from negative CS-US contingencies, *Journal of Comparative and Physiological Psychology*, 67: 504–509

Skinner, B. F. (1974) *About Behaviourism*, New York: Longman

Smith, M. C. (1968) CS-US interval and US intensity in classical conditioning of the rabbit's nictitating membrane response, *Journal of Comparative and Physiological Psychology*, 66: 679–687

Thorndike, E. L. (1901) Animal intelligence: An experimental study of the associative processes in animals, *Psychological Review Monograph Supplement*, 2: 1–109

Wagner, A. R., Logan, F. A., Haberlandt, K., and Price, T. (1968) Stimulus selection in animal discrimination learning, *Journal of Experimental Psychology*, 76: 171–180

More ways to start improving your classroom practice with NLP

- Create a series of spotlight states in your classroom for: reinforcing rules (confident, in charge, assertive); questioning (curiosity, interest, open to possibilities); a time to move on space (where you go to end a section of the lesson or when it's time to pack up. Choose some appropriate internal states and perhaps have an attention signal linked to it, for example, tapping a coin twice on a desk). Make sure that these are in distinctly different locations

- Have a kinaesthetic anchor set on a knuckle to help you relax at the end of the day

- Take your well-formed outcome (see Chapter 2, *Blockbuster movies*) of confident effective teaching to the next level and have an auditory anchor that can help you re-associate into the feelings and fire the representations. Simply visualise your outcome and when it is nearly at it most powerful think of an unusual word that you can associate with the feelings

- Teach the spotlighting (circle of excellence) strategy to your examination classes, or to pupils who are about to take their SATs, so that they can access a good state before the test or examination

- Prepare yourself for a difficult parent–teacher conference by anchoring the states you will need

- Start each day by anchoring an 'emotional state for the day'. Choose something that will help you with the sorts of things that you know are coming up

Chapter 10
Verbal ju-jitsu

How to be elegant with language

Have you ever had the experience of having thought that you understood what someone had said only later to find out that they meant something completely different? What if asking the right questions not only helped you to get people to give you the answers you want, but could also change the way they think and even influence them? In the classroom with students, in the staff room with colleagues and when working with parents, the ability to ask that 'killer question' or just turn a person's language around can make a real difference. We constantly filter the world around us and create **distortions**, **generalisations** and **deletions**. The process of filtering information takes place on many levels. In relation to language we do this all the time.

Take a moment to describe your last holiday to yourself …

What happened to all the really specific details (getting up in the morning, what you had for breakfast before you left the house, what were you wearing, etc.)? Communication would be impossible if we didn't filter out some of the details. As you begin to listen more carefully to the language that people use, you will begin to realise that no one ever talks in a way that provides a totally complete description of an idea or a thought. One way to think of this is to think of the ocean. There is a *surface structure* to the ocean and the patterns of the waves can often be influenced by what lies beneath (rocks that are just under the surface, the depth of the water, passing sea creatures and so on); *the deep structure* is, however, hidden under the surface.

Research Zone

Higher order questioning

Effective questioning and interaction in the classroom has been consistently shown to have a positive impact on learning (Rosenshine and Furst, 1973; Brophy and Good, 1986; Gagne et al., 1993). In particular, the use of frequent questioning, communicating and specifically the use of 'higher order' questions has been shown to have a positive impact (Mortimore et al., 1988), as has the frequency of questioning, the use of open-ended questions and the process of asking students to explain their answers in more detail (Muijis and Reynolds, 1999). High order questioning involves asking questions that prompt more complex thinking rather than the repetition of basic facts and simple answers.

Brophy, J. E. and Good, T. L. (1986) Teacher behaviour and student achievement, in M. C. Wittock (ed.), *Handbook of Research on Teaching*, New York: Macmillan, 328–375

Gagne, R.M., Yekovick, C.W. and Yekovich, F.R. (1993) *The Cognitive Psychology of School Learning*, New York, HarperCollins

Mortimore, P., Sammons, P., Stoll, L., Lewis, D. and Ecob, R. (1988) *School Matters*, Somerset Wells: Open Books

Muijis, R. D. and Reynolds, D. (1999) School effectiveness and teacher effectiveness: some preliminary findings from the evaluation of the mathematics enhancement programme, Presented at the American Education Research Association Conference, Quebec: Montreal, 9 April 1999

Rosenshine, B. and Furst, N. (1973) The use of direct observation to study teaching, in R. W. M. Travers (ed.), *Second Handbook of Research on Teaching*, Chicago: Rand McNally

This chapter will give you an introduction to how to take further the understanding of language that you developed in Chapter 5, *Don't think about chocolate cake*. Specifically we cover two areas of NLP, the **meta model** and **reframing**. In this chapter the core concepts that we introduced to you in Chapter 5 are revisited and more details are added.

In essence, the meta model is the opposite of the Milton model. The Milton model 'chunks up' out of the detail to bigger picture ideas and notions, whereas the meta model 'chunks down' into the details. Becoming a master of meta model language will give you all the tools you need to work with the energy of communication. Like the most skilled practitioner of ju-jitsu, with practice, you will be able to use the energy in others' communication and turn it around with elegance and skill.

Key concept

We use the Milton model to 'chunk up' out of the detail to create change through suggestibility. Meta model questions are used to 'chunk down' to create change by restoring the details that have been filtered out by a speaker.

In essence the Milton model is the process of deliberately creating *distortions*, *generalisations* and *deletions*, whereas the meta model is the process of restoring the details that have been missed out by other people.

The language patterns in the Milton model and meta model share similar descriptive names (e.g. nominalisation, cause_–effect, etc.) because they refer to the same linguistic phenomena seen from two different perspectives. In defining these patterns Bandler and Grinder were influenced by the work of Lauri Karttunnen, who researched natural language presuppositions in the 1970s.

Bandler and Grinder based the notion of the meta model on Chomsky's transformational grammar (Chomsky, 1957; Grinder and Elgin, 1973). Although, inspired by Chomsky, Bandler and Grinder developed a unique and practical linguistic model that still has application today.

The power of collecting more specific language

One of the first things that Richard Bandler and John Grinder noticed when they began their modelling of therapists in the early 1970s, was that people automatically engage in three distinct processes when they are speaking. These processes they called—distortion, generalisation and deletion—happen all the time. They help us to communicate more effectively, by removing unnecessary detail. These processes can also have a negative effect by leading to miscommunication, not only with others but also with ourselves. Because the language we use affects our internal processing it can also have an effect on our internal emotional state and therefore our behaviour.

Distortion: the process of changing reality so that what is said, seen or remembered is not the same as what happened

Generalisation: the process of describing things at a level where experiences are seen as being in common. When we do this we can ignore special situations or possible exceptions. Often generalisations include words like: all, every, always and never

Deletion: the process of removing some of the detail and not giving the whole picture

At times we can all be guilty of over-generalising, over-distorting or over-deleting elements of our experience. In NLP the words we use are viewed as a map of our reality rather than the reality itself. Bandler and Grinder were particularly interested in seeing if there were any patterns or rules that could be associated with the types of language that people use, how they use them, and what effect an awareness of this sort of language can offer. The result of their studies was the meta model. The model provides a collection of questions that can give you the tools to deal effectively with the distortions, generalisations and deletions that people create for themselves and for others. As you begin to notice the different types of language patterns that people use, and explore using the questioning tools, you will find yourself more and more able to deal effectively and respond appropriately.

Just do it

Find a few people to work with on this one. First decide on a topic. It can be fun to ask people if they would like to think about 'sex or education'. This usually gets a laugh. Then ask people to write down five words that are the meaning of the topic for them. Then see how many words the people in the group wrote down that are the same.

Just do it continued ...

Even in large groups you will very rarely find many similar words. Have a go yourself and see what you find.

If you do this as part of a training session you can debrief it by getting the group to think about the implications of this for communication in general. Because of our extraordinary ability to see the world differently from each other we often say in NLP that **the meaning of your communication is the response you get.**

The meta model

Today the meta model is generally thought of as 12 language patterns and any associated questions that seek to restore unhelpful distortions, generalisations and deletions. Therapists such as Virginia Satir and Fritz Perls were very effective at spotting and restoring distortions, generalisations and deletions to support powerful and effective change with their clients. As with many NLP tools and techniques modelled from therapy, meta model language is just as useful in everyday life. Distorting, deleting or generalising away important details can result in us giving ourselves, or reinforcing, all sorts of negative beliefs and ideas.

For example:

I can never get anything right (Generalisation)—to which the response might be, 'What never? Can you think of something that you have got right once?'

He didn't look at me today. This means he is angry (Distortion)—to which a response might be, 'Can you think of something else that him not looking at you could mean?'

Things are really bad (Deletion)—to which a response might be, 'Specifically what things are really bad?'

When first learning to use the meta model it is not important to learn all the names of the different patterns. Just allow yourself to begin by noticing the patterns that people use and you will easily begin to pick up greater understanding as you start to explore the ideas in the model. Being aware of how this happens with language can give you some powerful ways of interacting with and understanding other people.

Noticing the existence of the meta model in the speech of others, and asking questions that help people to restore the details of experience that have been missed, can help people to make significant changes or see the world in a different way.

On the following page (in Toolbox 26) you can find a table of all of the meta model language patterns. This is a very detailed language model and you don't need to take it in all at once. Start by just paying attention to the details that people miss out when they make statements or say things, and revisit the patterns a few at a time. One good way to do this is have your radar up for generalisations and then when you hear one look it up on the table. Do the same thing for distortions and deletions. NLP Toolbox 25 gives you a Quick Start to get you going.

NLP Toolbox No. 25

Quick Start—basic questions for meta modelling

You do not need to be too clever or complicated when first using the **meta model**. Keeping it simple can be just as effective. The simple questions below can be just as effective as using more complex ones. Have a go at using the questions with yourself first. This will give you a really good understanding of the potential impact of these approaches.

When you notice a deletion ask: *Tell me some more about that …*

When you notice a generalisation say: *Is this always the case …?*

When you notice a distortion ask: *How do you know that …?*

NLP Toolbox No. 26

Meta model language patterns

Although on the surface this set of language patterns looks very similar to the table for Milton model patterns in Chapter 5, on closer inspection you will see that where the Milton model gives you ways to deliberately create distortions, deletions and generalisations in order to influence others, the meta model gives you questions to restore and influence the distortions, deletions and generalisations in the language of others.

Name of meta model pattern	Example	Example questions that can be used to get more details or to open up the other person's thinking
Deletions Finding out what is behind the words someone has used		
Simple deletion	When something has been left out *I can't do it* *This is impossible*	Seek more detail *What can't you do?* *What specifically is impossible?*

NLP Toolbox No. 26 continued ...

Name of meta model pattern	Example	Example questions that can be used to get more details or to open up the other person's thinking
Comparative deletions	People will often talk themselves out of things by making comparisons using *good, better, less,* etc. *She is better than me*	*What is she better than you at?*
Unspecified verb	When an action has been omitted *She stopped me working*	Bring into the discussion the action that has been deleted or misapplied *Specifically how did she stop you working?*
Lack of a referential index	When the person(s) or object to which the statement refers has not been specified or is unclear *We must implement the curriculum this way* *They don't care*	Clarify who is being talked about *Who says that?* *Who doesn't care?*
Distortions Unpicking semantic errors		
Nominalisations	Nominalisations turn verbs into nouns *We have a bad relationship*	Respond by turning the noun back into a verb *How would you like us to relate to each other?*
Presuppositions	Where there is an inbuilt idea or assumption that is not stated *If you understood what is involved in this then you would not question what I say*	Identify what lies underneath *What makes you think that I don't understand what is involved?*

Name of meta model pattern	Example	Example questions that can be used to get more details or to open up the other person's thinking
Cause–effect	Where the speaker establishes a causal link without all of the details *You make me so cross*	Ask about how this process happens *How specifically does what I do cause you to be angry?*
Complex equivalence	When two experiences are seen as one *Because she didn't speak to me she hates me*	Challenge the link between externally observed behaviour and internal state *Has anyone not spoken to you before?*
Mind reading	Where someone claims to know what someone else is thinking or their internal state *Her problem is that she thinks that ...*	Challenge the source of the information *How do you know that ...?*
Generalisations Changing someone's map of the world		
Modal operators of necessity	Words like *must, should* and *ought* are often used to delete large amounts of information to justify an argument. They work by referring to past positions *We must do it like this* *We really shouldn't ...*	Reframe to the future *What would happen if we didn't?* *What would happen if we didn't?*
Modal operators of possibility	Words like *can/can't* and *will/won't* work in similar ways to modal operators of necessity by benchmarking to past experience *I can't ...*	Reframe to the present or the future *So what stops you?* *What would you get if you did?*

NLP Toolbox No. 26 continued ...

Name of meta model pattern	Example	Example questions that can be used to get more details or to open up the other person's thinking
Modal operators of possibility	Words like *can/can't* and *will/won't* work in similar ways to modal operators of necessity by benchmarking to past experience *I can't ...*	Reframe to the present or the future *So what stops you?* *What would you get if you did?*
Universal quantifiers	Universal quantifiers are typically words such as: *all, every, never, always, only, everyone, everything.* *Nobody listens* *Mrs Smith never gives me any help*	Look for a counter example *What nobody at all?* *Has there ever been a time when Mrs Smith has helped you?*
Lost performative	A value judgement that is stated without reference to who actually said it *Boys just can't listen* *It's wrong to ...*	Seek the source of the judgement *Who says that boys can't listen?* *Who says?*

The meta model takes practice to master. Begin by using the tools in the meta model toolbox above and then when you feel more confident expand your repertoire of questions and techniques.

The art of questioning

The subtitle of this chapter is How to be elegant with questions. Remember that there is nothing elegant in giving someone a hard time—all you will get is resistance. Learning to ask good questions means more than just noticing the patterns in the sentences that people use and having a set of possible questions with which to respond. You should always have a clear idea of what it is that you are seeking to achieve from the question and, if you are dealing with a difficult problem, be sensitive to the fact that people may need to feel that they can trust you before you get specific in your questioning. Avoid giving a third degree interrogation. When people first began to explore the **meta model** they found that they were able to literally challenge just about anything that anyone said. This is often referred to as **meta murder**. Remember to be in rapport with the other person. A lack of communication always indicates a lack of rapport. Be aware of your voice tone—make it more gentle as you ask your question.

Why?

One particular question to apply with great caution is **why?** There is something about the word in the English language that requires us to look back to the past. This level of meaning simply isn't there in many other languages. In English, however, it can have the impact of demanding a justification from the person who is being questioned. For this reason, why? is best used only carefully and should definitely be avoided when using the meta model. For example, if you were to notice a generalisation and then ask 'Why do you think that?', rather than seek more detail, you are likely to get a justification as a response rather than restoring the lost information. Of course, we are not suggesting that you also lose the very appropriate use of the word to stimulate critical enquiry. Most subjects would be pretty hard to teach effectively without it. Rather avoid the word when questioning about behaviour or competence.

Research Zone

How and when to ask questions for maximum impact

Much is known about how effective questioning should be done in the classroom and what its importance is. Specifically (Muijis and Reynolds, 2005):

- Questioning should take up a significant part of the lesson.

- Interaction through questioning is particularly important at the start of the lesson and much research suggests that there should be a review of learning at the beginning.

- Non-evaluative questioning is important to ensure participation and motivation.

- Effective teachers tend to use open questions (questions with many possible answers) rather than closed questions (questions with only a single possible answer).

- Effective teachers ask process and product questions with a high proportion of process questions. Product questions focus on a particular problem whereas process questions draw out the processes or procedures that need to be understood to solve a problem.

- Teachers need to be aware that the waiting time for a response to a higher order question will be longer than for a lower order question. Amongst new teachers leaving insufficient time is a more frequent fault than giving too much time (Rowe, 1986).

Muijis, D. and Reynolds, D. (2005) (2nd edn) *Effective Teaching: Evidence and Practice*, London: Sage
Rowe, M. B. (1986) Wait time: Slowing down may be a way of speeding up, *Journal of Teacher Education*, 80: 4: 206–211

Conversational belief change

Have you ever had someone say something to you and it completely changed your experience and later led you to choose different ways of acting? Robert Dilts, one of the early developers of NLP, became fascinated by this process and modelled the thinking processes of a number of famous historical figures to identify the sort of language patterns that they were using. At the heart of the notion of reframing is the idea that **the map is not the territory**. In other words people frame their experience and therefore their behaviour as a result of their language. For this reason this sort of NLP is sometimes referred to as conversational belief change. It works like this. Because our internal map of the world is the result of filtering out and generalisation, distortion and deletion, our ideas, beliefs and self-talk will in some way limit what we think of as possible because key information or perspectives are missing. There is always another way of seeing things. Reframing offers the ability to make a linguistic distinction between the intention of the person and their behaviour. Doing this allows you to find newer more appropriate behaviour and suggest these. Often people have not changed simply because they haven't thought of another possibility.

> At the heart of the process of reframing is the ability to make a linguistic distinction between the intention of the person and their behaviour. Doing this allows you to find newer, more appropriate behaviour and suggest these. Often people have not changed simply because they haven't thought of another possibility.

Dilts identified 14 key patterns that he called **sleight of mouth** patterns. These patterns make use of a range of processes that restore details, give a bigger picture or help people to adopt a different perspective. Below we have used an example of a limiting belief that you might hear a colleague say—however, the techniques are of course just as applicable for limiting beliefs of children and learners in general. The four patterns below are based on some of Dilts' work.

In the following examples the limiting belief *I have found this sort of thing so hard to do for such a long time that I really can't change* has been responded to with a range of different reframes.

1. Intention reframe: Redirecting people's thinking by identifying the purpose or intention behind a belief

Limiting belief:

I have found this sort of thing so hard to do for such a long time that I really can't change.

Example response:

Being honest with yourself is a really positive strength to have.

Positive intention: honesty

or

I really admire your ability to recognise what needs to change.

Positive intention: recognising what needs to change

In this example the listener has fed back two possible positive intentions behind the belief in order to place the belief in a positive rather than a negative frame. Often simply reframing something in a positive light can give children, parents and other teachers all kinds of opportunities in their own minds that can allow them to move forward more positively. This approach can be particularly effective with difficult students and in challenging situations.

2. Chunk down reframe: breaking elements of the belief down into smaller chunks

Limiting belief:

I have found this sort of thing so hard to do for such a long time that I really can't change.

Example response:

Instead of trying to change everything at the same time, if you were to tackle one small step at a time perhaps you could find it much easier and even begin to enjoy the changes.

Focuses on the reducing the scale of the problem: whole belief → small steps

Example response:

If you'd had the belief for only a short time this would make it less of a problem, so maybe you can recall what it was like when you had just got this belief.

This example focuses on reframing the time-related aspect of the limiting belief: long time → short time

3. Change the frame size: encouraging the re-evaluation of the belief from a bigger or smaller perspective

Limiting belief:

I have found this sort of thing so hard to do for such a long time that I really can't change

Example response:

Many people before you have had the same thoughts. In fact the more people who make changes the easier change will appear to be.

or

When you look back in the future you will have trouble remembering that you ever thought this.

Helping people to have a wider perspective or focusing on one aspect of the belief can change the way people see the problem really easily; a bit like one of those puzzles where you can only see part of the picture and have to guess what the object is.

4. Consequence reframe: Directing the speaker's attention to the effect of the belief

Limiting belief:

I have found this sort of thing so hard to do for such a long time that I really can't change.

Example response:

Being aware that something is going to be challenging can allow you to anticipate problems and make it much easier to do in the end.

This type of reframe focuses in on our tendency to connect things as being part of a cause-and-effect relationship that are in fact unconnected. In the example above this has been done by offering an alternative positive cause-and-effect relationship.

When we have a limiting belief we will often think that this way of thinking is the only one, and will close down our peripheral vision so that we ignore other possibilities. Suggesting counter examples creates a wider viewpoint. Even if the particular example is not agreed with, the fact that there are clearly other ways of seeing the problem opens the frame and creates the presupposition that change is possible.

Top tips

Have your reframing and meta model radar fully engaged in the following situations and be ready to ask a killer question, or just reframe, with more possibilities:

■ During parents' evenings

■ When being asked to do something that really won't work by a senior manager

■ When dealing with those smarty pants kids in years 10 and 11 who say awkward stuff that they can't really be told off for

■ When a child is upset to help them think outside of the problem and be more positive

■ Just because you can

NLP Toolbox No. 27

Reframing an inner critical voice

You know when you have that little inner voice that just won't let you do something, is critical or leads you to think that something is beyond you? Funny isn't it how one part of you can be so out of line with what you really would like to do. The technique below is a really great way to deal with those inner voices. As with any of the self-development techniques, find somewhere where you know you will feel comfortable and relaxed and can take the time to explore your inner world.

1. Think about the inner voice that has or is being critical or negative. Imagine yourself back listening to this voice. Notice all the details of the voice tone, the rhythm of the word and the speed and pitch of the voice.

2. Ask your inner voice to describe its positive intention and what it hopes to achieve for you in being difficult or critical. Listen carefully to the answers you get. Continue to ask your inner voice these questions until you are able to agree with the positive intention.

3. Thank the part of you that this voice comes from for having the positive intention.

4. Ask this part of you to come with you on a search for other possibilities. You could ask: 'If there were a number of different possible ways to achieve these intentions that were just as effective or even better than what you are doing right now, would you give them a go?' Wait for a yes answer that you are happy with.

5. Look elsewhere inside you to find that part of you that is creative or the part of you that is happy to find different ways of doing things. Think of a time when you used this part really effectively. Ask this creative part to help you to think of many possible behaviours

you could choose from. Allow the voice to choose the three best ones that it likes and is convinced will work.

6. Imagine yourself in the future doing each of these three things one a time in a suitable place. Take time to see, hear and feel exactly what you experience in the future. When you have explored all of the possibilities ask your inner voice to choose one or more of the options.

More ways to start improving your classroom practice with NLP

- Choose a day on which to notice generalisations, deletions and distortions in what the children say to you and respond by asking a detail restoring question

- When dealing with a challenging or difficult comment from a student instead of responding directly, ask a question or 'reframe' what they have said in another way. For example, 'I don't want to do this …' *Specifically what is it that you do want to do?*

- Learn to have some 'rescue' questions that you can always use to respond to a situation when you might otherwise be lost for words (e.g. *Tell me more about that? What else? So what's important to you? What stops you?*)

- Get children to list or talk about their beliefs about learning and use some reframing to help them to think differently

Chapter 11
The teacher within

How who you are affects what you do

Who are you? What's important to you? Do you know and do others know? What is it that leads you to act on a particular behaviour in the classroom or to make that assertion in the staff room? Why do you teach like that?

At first glance these sorts of questions can seem merely philosophical or at best a diversion. The reality is that our **values**, sense of purpose and **beliefs** drive our behaviours, particularly when we are in conflict or in times of stress or challenge. Although we like to see ourselves as rational beings it is our personal values that are at the heart of why we do what we do. For this reason values are often referred to as 'hot buttons' because whatever you do is almost always done because of a drive to fulfil a value. For example, you may like to go swimming because looking after your health is important to you, or you might specifically choose swimming over other team sports because for you 'independence' is more important. In the classroom values are underpin our actions and behaviours, and affect the way we plan our lessons, the choice of topics, the spoken and unspoken rules that we have, how we deal with different children and the judgments that we make on progress and attainment.

Understanding your values and making those values explicit to others can transform the way in which you live your life and the way in which others respond to you. Knowing what your values are, being able to define them and reflect on their relative importance can be the key to a happier and more successful life and career. Over the years, working with hundreds of teachers, we have found this to be one of the most critical and, at the same time, most neglected areas of development, and yet it is one which many have found central to moving their practice forward and their lives on.

Working with values

Although our values are very important and underpin so much of what we do, and how we go about what we do, very few people are fully aware of their values and what is important to them. In fact most people tend to be on a sort of autopilot most of the time. We usually have a clue as to what we want but very often fail to understand why it is that we want what we want. Knowing your values will enable you to:

- Be aware of what it is that you need to do to ensure that you feel good
- Gain the awareness to make better decisions and to make those decisions based on what is really important to you
- Become more in control of your emotions, feelings and actions

Research Zone

Moral purpose, values and spirituality

The central importance of values and moral purpose for effective school improvement have been demonstrated time and time again, and there is now a substantial body of work to support this (e.g. Fullan, 2003; 2005; Leithwood et al., 2006). There is also strong support for the importance of the moral and spiritual dimensions for school leadership and in teaching (West-Burnham 2002; 2004; West-Burnham and Huws Jones, 2007). Critically it has been suggested that it is important for leaders in schools to practise and develop the behaviours that go with the values associated with moral purpose (Fullan, 2001) and that significant breakthroughs in development come not just from doing but also from 'thinking about the doing' (Fullan, 2007).

Fullan, M. (2001) *Leading in a Culture of Change*, San Francisco: Jossey-Bass

Fullan, M. (2003) *The Moral Imperative of School Leadership*, Thousand Oaks, CA: Corwin Press

Fullan, M. (2005) *Leadership and Sustainability: System Thinkers in Action*, Thousand Oaks, CA: Corwin Press

Fullan, M. (2007) Leading in a system of change, Paper prepared for Conference on Systems Thinking and Sustainable School Development, Utrecht, February, OISE/University of Toronto

Leithwood, K., Day, C., Sammons, P., Harris, A. and Hopkins, D. (2006) *Seven Strong Claims About Successful School Leadership*, Nottingham: National College for School Leadership

West-Burnham, J. (2002) *Leadership and Spirituality*, NCSL Leading Edge Seminar Thinkpiece

West-Burnham, J. (2004) Leadership and personal effectiveness, Paper written for a seminar at the Royal Garden Hotel, London, November, Nottingham: National College for School Leadership

West-Burnham, J. and Huws Jones, V. (2007) *Educating for Understanding: Spiritual and Moral Development in Schools*, London: Network Continuum Press

What sort of thing are we talking about?

Usually when teachers begin to explore their practice and skills the emphasis is on what is visible: their behaviours, their ways of working and the way in which they structure their environment. All of these are extremely important and there is much in NLP that can support teachers, particularly in terms of presentation skills and influencing skills. In this chapter, however, we aim to help you to go deeper; deeper into your experience of life and your inner world.

Robert Dilts, one of the early developers of NLP, did a lot of work on people's experience of life and noted that there are levels of personal experience. On one level we experience the world in terms of the actual physical environment around us. In the classroom this level of experience consists of the room we teach in, the resources we have in that environment and the

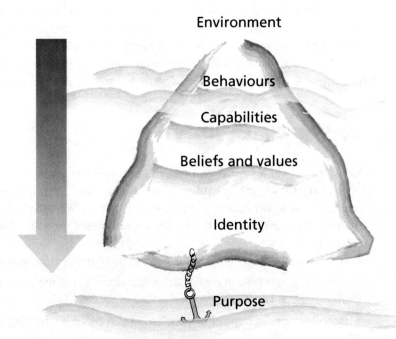

Environment

Behaviours

Capabilities

Beliefs and values

Identity

Purpose

way in which we organise that environment, including the planning of lessons. This first level of perceptual experience is an important one and has drawn the attention of many researchers in the world of education. Indeed, much time is spent in teacher training to support the development of an understanding of this aspect of highly effective teaching. On another level are the observable behaviours that we use: the way in which we carry out our lesson plans, the way in which we deal with students and the approaches and language that we use. Sometimes people use the metaphor of an iceberg, where the visible aspects that are easily perceived are those above the waterline.

If we think about those things that lie deeper under the surface we arrive at our beliefs, values, identity and purpose. The exercise (Toolbox 18 *Working the iceberg* in Chapter 7) may help you to gain a greater understanding of this concept if you need to do this in a practical way before moving on.

Beliefs are held in place linguistically and are the result of many generalisations, distortions and deletions of life experiences.

Of all the levels of experience, values play a pivotal role in shaping both the quality of our personal experience and our behaviours. In fact, whatever you do in the classroom is usually done to fulfil a value although you may not be consciously aware of it. Take a moment to think about the last lesson that you taught. What was significant about the way you went about that lesson? Now ask yourself, 'What's important to me about that?'

NLP Toolbox No. 28

Uncovering your values

The purpose of this exercise is to uncover and discover your values in relation to a specific area of your life. In the exercise below we have chosen education, but you could do this in relation to any area of your work or life. You may want to ask a colleague to help you do this or you could simply explore it on your own.

Ask your colleague to ask you: *What's important to you about 'education'?*

Get them to note down word-by-word **exactly** what the answer is in your own words (this is very important). If they don't quite catch what you said, or are unsure of the exact phrasing, tell them that they can ask you to repeat what you said. The answers should be written down as they are expressed without changing the wording.

They should then ask: *What else is important to you about* 'education'?

The questions should be repeated until **at least 10 values** are listed.

_____'s Values in Relation to Teaching are:
(enter your name)

1. ....

2. ....

3. ....

NLP Toolbox No. 28 continued ...

4. ....

5. ....

6. ....

7. ....

8. ....

9. ....

10. ....

Away from and towards values

All the things that we do are a means to achieving an end. The end is invariably driven by the desire to fulfil a value. However, values come in two general sorts: **towards** and **away from**. Towards values are those that drive us to move towards feelings of pleasure, comfort, etc.; away from values drive us to move away from feelings of discomfort or pain. In the classroom it might look like this:

Towards value	Away from value
It is important to me that all children are included	*It is important that things are never disorganised*

The distinction between towards and away from values is never a simple one and there is often a little of both in all of our values. In the examples above the value of 'including' has, for example, the need to avoid not-including as part of it. Likewise being driven to 'never be disorganised' includes the desire for organisation. Whether we express our values as being towards or away from is a matter of preference and can often be the result of early life experiences. In this context happiness can be seen as a state in which we are both achieving our towards values and avoiding our away from values. When we get the opposite in life we tend to feel unhappy and discontented.

Although our values are driving our everyday behaviours in the present, most of them were acquired years ago. Many will have been established in early childhood. Values that drive you towards pleasure may have been acquired as a result of a reward or positive emotional experience. Values which create an away from tendency are likely to be the result of negative experiences, emotional traumas or of past decisions that resulted in negative consequences. Sometimes away from values are helpful or are still appropriate; other times they may no longer be working for us and may need to be re-evaluated in the light of more recent experiences.

For example, you may want to ask yourself:

In the light of my adult life experience, do I really want to be driven by a fear of not getting something or would it be more beneficial to focus on the towards aspect of this value and orientate myself towards getting something positive?

Working with teachers we have often found this to be an area of development for those who have been in teaching awhile and who still have difficulty with behaviour management. It works something like this:

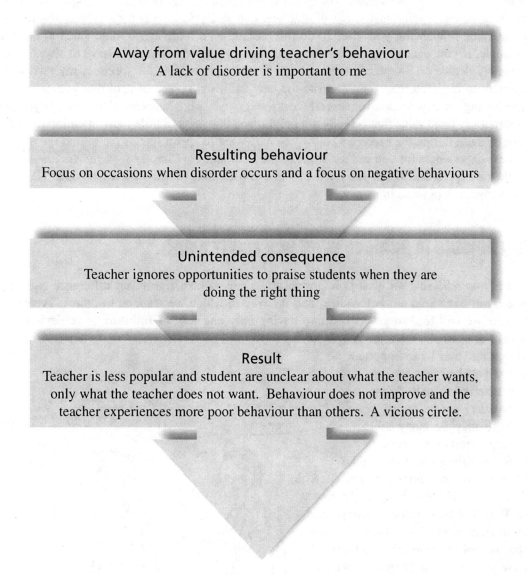

Away from value driving teacher's behaviour
A lack of disorder is important to me

Resulting behaviour
Focus on occasions when disorder occurs and a focus on negative behaviours

Unintended consequence
Teacher ignores opportunities to praise students when they are doing the right thing

Result
Teacher is less popular and student are unclear about what the teacher wants, only what the teacher does not want. Behaviour does not improve and the teacher experiences more poor behaviour than others. A vicious circle.

In this case we have, with much success, encouraged teachers with similar values to refocus not only on the towards aspect of the value:

Order is important to me

But also to think about what is important about the towards value, for example:

Everyone learning is important to me

By doing this many find it much easier to refocus on positive and consistent reward-based behaviour management processes. By placing the attention on the positive towards value, teachers will often start to notice students doing what they have asked and rewarding them rather than constantly returning to negatives. Doing this not only reinforces what is actually wanted—it will also influence all students to seek reward. For more on positive reward see Chapter 4, *Dolphin aquarium*.

Dealing with out of date values

Our values, beliefs and core identity (or purpose in life) can easily become misaligned or out of date. If you come across a value that is out of date you can easily make a conscious decision to no longer have that value influencing your life. To do this, decide on a more appropriate value to have instead. For example, if you want to replace an early childhood value which says, 'I have to always put others first', simply decide on a replacement, such as, 'I look after myself first because my own well-being is important to me.' You may want to write the new value on a piece of card that you carry with you. Practise having the new value over several weeks and notice what happens. Occasionally you may find a stubborn away from value that is really not helpful and that needs a little more attention to shift. If you find one of these during the exercises below you may want to spend some time to find the memory that holds these experiences for you and use some of the techniques in Chapter 8, *Memories are made of this*, to recode the experience. When you are happy that you are able to establish a new value make sure that you put something positive in its place.

Being flexible to achieve what you really want

Spending time reflecting on what is important to us can make a significant difference and help us to become more flexible in our behaviours, and the way in which we respond to others. Typically as we grow older we will tend to get locked into having only one way of fulfilling or achieving a particular value. For example, for some people 'trying new things out' may be an important value and yet they may be limiting themselves to only doing this when they are on holiday, when there may be many different opportunities at work or home for fulfilling this value. Take a look at the list of values that you came up with when you did the thought experience above. Which of those values are important to you in all aspects of your life and which are specific only to your job as a teacher? Now ask yourself, how often do I take the opportunity to fulfil these values when you are working as a teacher, or you are limiting yourself to a few tried and tested ways of implementing your values?

Ask yourself
Are your values orientated towards teaching or learning?

Sometimes a value may still be relevant—however, how we go about fulfilling that value may need to be brought up to date. Look at your list of values and decide which of them are most important to you. Circle the ones that are most significant and which you would describe as your **core values**. Because you will be seeking to update and realign your values as you go about your daily work and life it is a good idea to work on only one or two at a time. Allow a few days to focus on which value you want to work on and give yourself time to explore what this means for you. Thinking about your top values you could ask yourself:

What are the behaviours that I use to fulfil these values?

To what extent is the environment I create in the classroom a reflection of what is important to me?

What do I want to change?

If there were more appropriate behaviours what would they be?

Once you have decided on the area that you want to realign, or update, list all the behaviours that you can think of that will help you to fulfil your value-for-the-day. When you have done that, be objective and ask yourself which behaviours really support this value and its meaning for you today. Underline any behaviours that might be inappropriate or out of date and note those which are really perfect but which you have not yet started to do. Make this an ongoing process that you integrate into your day by giving yourself reminders. You could even write the perfect behaviours down on a small piece of card and carry it with you. Remind yourself to keep on track.

Your hierarchy of values

As you begin to work with your values you will start to notice how some values are more important to you than others. Being aware of this hierarchy and being able to rank your values in order of importance is something which can help you to understand where you are going in your life and help you to prioritise when faced with difficult decisions or challenges. Sometimes we may even get the ranking in the wrong order. For example, for some people how they appear is ranked lower than getting pleasure and satisfaction. They may at the end of the day sit in front of the television and simply slob the night away with food and drink. Although this may at first seem relaxing, when the summer approaches they may feel bad about their appearance and get into a manic attempt to lose weight and engage in a panicky regime of exercise and dieting. The end result may be disillusion followed by a return to old habits. In contrast, others might remain aware of their values and what is important to them throughout the year and ensure a more balanced and happy life. Working out your own hierarchy of values is easy.

Working out your values hierarchy

- First, take your list of values that you worked on earlier. Imagine if you could be absolutely certain that from now on one of those values from your list would always be fulfilled. Which value would it be? Whichever one you choose becomes your number 1 value. Write it down.
- Now continue. Imagine that you can choose another value from the same list and be sure that it would also be always fulfilled from now on. What value would it be? Write it down—this is your number 2 value.
- Continue in the same way until you have ranked all of your values in order of importance to you.
- Re-write your values in order of importance.

1. ....

2. ....

3. ....

4. ....

5. ....

6. ....

7. ....

8. ....

9. ....

10. ....

Now think about an aspect of your life or work that you are currently unhappy about. To what extent does this area of your life or work reflect your hierarchy of values? What is missing? Are you focusing on your most important values enough? Think about the behaviours that you currently use in this part of your life. To what extent do they reflect your values? What do you need to do instead? The tools described above are given in Toolkit 29 below in a more detailed form that can be used for yourself or to support colleagues. The values elicitation and hierarchy tool is an extremely useful one to explore as part of a whole staff or department training day and can add real depth to school improvement planning and teacher development.

Research Zone

Teacher identity and values

Two central questions constantly emerge as being at the heart of teacher education and professional development. First, what are the essential qualities of an effective teacher and, secondly, how can we help people to become, more effective teachers? In recent years a growing body of research has supported the idea that teacher education needs to go beyond skills and pedagogy (although these are of course important) and work on areas of professional identity and mission (e.g. Korthagen, 2004). Several studies suggest that teacher education needs to support trainee teachers to understand how their values and sense of identity impact on both their teaching practice and on the development of pedagogic knowledge and understanding (see e.g. Gudmundsdottir, 1990; Atkinson, 2004). The importance of values and ethics is also noted by Pachler et al. (2003) who suggest that as well as becoming immersed in the 'science of teaching' new teachers should also pursue the examination of values, ethics and wider educational goals. Significant research into how NLP can support teacher development in relation to professional identity is currently underway (see Dragovic, 2007).

Atkinson, D. (2004) Theorising how student teachers form their identities in initial teacher education, *British Education Research Journal*, 30: 3: 379–394

Dragovic, T. (2007) Teachers' professional identity and the role of CPD in its creation—a report on a study into how NLP and non-NLP trained teachers in Slovenia talk about their professional identity and their work, International Society for Teacher Education, 27th Annual International Seminar at University of Stirling, Scotland, 24–30 June

Gudmundsdottir, S. (1990) Values in pedagogical content knowledge, *Journal of Teacher Education*, 41: 3: 44–52

Korthagen, F. A. J. (2004) In search of the essence of a good teacher, *Teaching and Teacher Education*, 20: 1: 77–97

Pachler, N., Daly, C. and Lambert, D. (2003) Teacher learning: reconceptualising the relationship between theory and practical teaching in master's level course development, Proceedings: Forum for *Quality Assurance in Distance-Learning*, University of London: Institute of Education

Being a leader in the classroom

Numerous popular texts on leadership and management have been written in recent years. In most of these a common theme emerges: the importance of values in leadership and the importance of making your values explicit not just in the behaviours you choose but also in the way you talk about what is important to you. Making your core values explicit to your 'followers' seems to almost magically help them to align their behaviours and actions with what you want from them, whether you have been explicit about those behaviours and actions or not. The same applies in the classroom. Working with many teachers we have often found that there is a mismatch between what they externalise as being important to them and what is perceived by the children they teach as being important. This mismatch exists at quite a deep level and is often related to the identity of the teacher and the student and the basic needs and expectation of the students. For children the need to feel safe and nurtured comes above all others but although most teachers would also approach their careers from this perspective, they rarely communicate the values that relate to this very deep level of identity to their students.

Top tip

Work out what your core values are in the classroom and what is really important to you. When you have done this share these values with the children that you teach. You might even want to put them on the wall so that they become public. You could even get the children in your classes to do the same thing and explore where there are misalignments and common goals.

NLP Toolbox No. 29

Taking stock of where you are now

This exercise will help you to explore whether your current values and beliefs are in line with the rest of your experience. You can do it in relation to a specific area of your work or life or in relation to the whole of your experience at the moment. The tool can be used with someone else supporting you as a coach or you can 'coach' yourself through the process.

Purpose (Spirituality)

Identity

Belief and Values

Capabilities

Behaviour

Environment

Instructions

Write the name of each of the six different levels on the left on six different sheets of paper. Lay out the six sheets of paper on the floor in front of you going from Environment through to Purpose. Put the sheets in order. Starting with Environment stand on each level and think/feel only in that level. If you have someone helping you to do this then this person acts as coach to help you explore each level in relation to where you are now. Make brief notes to capture this information.

NLP Toolbox No. 29 continued ...

Purpose: *What am I here for?* What is my purpose?	
Identity: *Who am I?* What is my mission?	
Beliefs and values: *Why?* What motivates me? What do I believe about myself/others? (values and meanings)	
Capabilities: *How?* What strategies and states do I currently have available? (maps and plans)	
Behaviour: *What?* Which specific behaviours do I have that support me and which behaviours do not support me? (actions and reactions)	
Environment: *Where? When?* Where are my external constraints and opportunities? What are they?	

When you have worked through all of the levels, step back from the whole picture and notice which of the areas is not currently working for you. Step back into that area and think about what you now need to do to change this. Continue with this process until you feel more balanced and have a plan of action. Finally return to the values level and consider whether your values are up-to-date enough to achieve what you want to achieve.

This is a really powerful technique for working with a whole team on school improvement planning, or even a whole school staff. Instead of standing on spaces, get groups to consider the areas through discussion and record their thoughts on flip charts before sharing with everyone. If you are using it in this context you may like to start with purpose. Again return to values at the end.

Some forward-thinking schools we have worked with have adapted this approach to support the implementation of pupil voice programmes. Using a tool like this in this context can help to ensure that teacher and student perceptions are more aligned, particularly at the identity and behavioural levels.

NLP Toolbox No. 30

Who are you? Exploring your core identity

Above our values and beliefs about the world sits our core identity: that essence of who we are that never changes whatever we do and whatever life throws at us. Getting in touch with this part of ourselves can help us to align what it is that is really important to us and how we go about getting this right.

1. Make a list of those aspects of your personality that remain constant whatever you are doing, in every situation.

2. Ask yourself:

   What sort of person am I?

   What parts of me have been true for as long as I can remember, even when I was young?

3. Explore within your mind what it means to be this.

4. To be sure that these characteristics of you always remain constant see if you can identify a counter example

   Can you boil this all down to a single word, or phrase?

   X (your name) is someone who always …

5. Think of a time when you were not able to express this aspect of yourself? How did it feel?

6. Where are you now? Are you able to express this core you? What could you do about it?

7. Thinking about your classroom at this identity level, how can you align your core identity with the identity of the students that you teach?

Research Zone

How our brain 'decides' how we are going to behave

There is much neuroscience to support the idea that consciousness happens too late in the cognitive process to have a direct influence on how we behave (see e.g. Halligan and Oakley, 2000). In other words, by the time we have experienced the cinematic projection in front of our eyes we have already carried out the action (see Chapter 14, The magic number 7 for more detail on this). A number of writers believe that this automatic response to stimuli prior to conscious awareness is affected by what are known as **schemata**. Schemata are hierarchical and interrelated representations of the sequences of processing operations that are involved in well-learned behaviour. Within cognitive psychology (Norman and Shallice, 1984) these are seen as being triggered 'automatically' by environmental inputs. Some writers (Brown and Oakley, 2004) argue that it is the previous encoding of sensory representation in associative memory which provides a basis for recognition (Kosslyn, 1996).

Research Zone continued ...

Creating new representations ahead of encountering situations may therefore modify our behaviour when we actually come to the new situation. We believe that **values** are a phenomenological manifestation of this process. In other words, when we speak of values as triggers for behaviours and become aware of this process we may be becoming aware of some of our many schemata. By ensuring that the schemata we wish our 'automatic' mind to use are in our recent associated memory we may be helping to ensure their selection when we encounter something in the environment around us that triggers a response.

Brown, R. J. and Oakley, D. A. (2004) An integrated cognitive theory of hypnosis and high hypnotisability, in M. Heap, R. J. Brown and D. A. Oakley (eds), *The Highly Hypnotizable Person: Theoretical, Experimental and Clinical Issues*. New York: Brunner-Routledge

Halligan, P. W. and Oakley, D. A. (2000) Greatest myth of all, *New Scientist*, 168: 35–49

Kosslyn, S. M. (1996) *Image and Brain*, Cambridge, MA: MIT Press

Norman, D. A. and Shallice, T. (1986) Attention to action: willed and automatic control of behaviour, in R. J. Davidson, G. E. Schwartz and D. Shapiro (eds),*Consciousness and Self-regulation: Advances in Research and Theory*, 4: 1–18, New York: Plenium

Ways to start improving your classroom practice with NLP

- Ask yourself 'What is important to me?' more often when planning lesson content and topics. Combine this with some second position thinking (see Chapter 7, Knowing me, knowing you) and ask these questions from the student's perspective

- After doing a values audit, design a professional development plan that helps you to fill the gaps between what you aspire to and your skills. Get some feedback

- Write your values on a display in the classroom and share them with the students

- Find out what is important to your students and get classes and groups of students to write out their values in relation to the subject, their lessons and learning

- Compare values with the children you teach to help everyone understand what the underlying motivations are. This builds strong and effective relationships and can save a lot of behaviour management time

- Help children to develop themselves by using Dilts' logical levels Schema to help them to uncover their own values and motivations. Get them to write about themselves in relation to each of the levels

Chapter 12
You can do it ... and it's about time

How to keep motivation on target

Can't find time?

If you could literally find time, where would it be?

Excuse me, have you got time to ...? How many times have you heard this and not had the time? Interesting, isn't it? We talk about time as if it were a commodity that you can dish out at will.

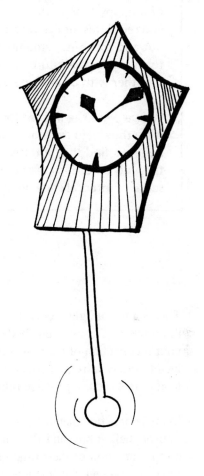

There is no doubt that we are sophisticated creatures when it comes to handling time. For other animals, time just passes with the sunrise or sunset. Other animals live in the moment, with no conscious plan for the future. In contrast, we have evolved a unique mechanism that allows us to travel back and forth in time in our minds. Pause for a moment and think about the last really important thing that happened to you ... amazing how easy it is for you to find yourself 'back in the moment' or imagining an event that hasn't even happened yet, isn't it?

At the heart of NLP is the idea of **modelling** excellence that other people demonstrate and applying it to ourselves. From this perspective, we can come to understand how time operates, then improve our ability to use our amazing 'time talents'. All of us who teach create schemes of work or other time-related plans. Those of you who teach any historical concepts will be familiar with the notion of time lines—where events, past or future, are placed on a line in order to make them comprehensible. An interesting question is where does this idea of a line of time come from, and why does it feel so natural? NLP modelling has identified two ways in which people process time. Understanding these methods provides a unique and powerful tool for self-development, goal achievement and much, much more.

Find your natural time processing pattern

As you begin to use the techniques outlined below, you can begin to become aware of how your mind creates a virtual space around you, where your 'time thoughts', past and present, are stored. People tend to have one of two distinct types of time processing as their natural preference. Amazingly, you have the power to choose between these and can even change your perception of time events within them. Have you ever asked a pupil a question and seen them stare off into space before they come back to you with the answer? This is no coincidence—they are accessing their storage of that memory (a picture, a sound or a feeling).

Just do it

Find a comfortable, quiet place and imagine, create or feel the space around you. Next think of a happy time in the past: teenage years are good, a birthday or special event perhaps. As you recall this, notice where in the space around you that memory would be if you could reach out and touch it. Remember this location. Now follow the same process for an event one or two years in the future: next Christmas or your birthday. You now have two points. Join them together with an imaginary line and you will have discovered your preferred time processing.

Where were the images for the past, present and future? Were some of them behind you or were they all in front of you? As you spend more time exploring this part of your mind you will begin to find that you have identified one of two patterns. In NLP we call these **in time** and **through time**. Each of these patterns has different behavioural characteristics and a different sense of internal state associated with it.

In time

This is any configuration whereby the line of time in your mind passes through your body. Usually with this pattern your recollection of the past is behind you and your imagined future is in front of you. A person with this pattern will tend to feel their experience fully in the present.

Many people find that just being asked to point in the direction of their future and their past is enough to draw out a representation of their time line. If this works less well for you, you can just imagine your line anyway. Just pretend and imagine where the line would be if you did know. Allow your unconscious mind to find the locations for the past, present and the future.

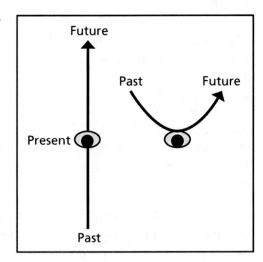

Through time

Through time is any configuration where the time line is not through the body—usually with the past on one side and the future on the other. From this perspective, all of your life appears laid out in front of you.

One way to double-check someone's preferred time line is to ask the person to think of a single happy memory. This can be quite difficult for someone with a through time preference, as they may tend to group or cluster their memories by type when accessing them. For an in time preference person, it is much easier to access single memories by type, as the nature of their preferred time processing pattern leads them to experience time in single episodes, a bit like rolling a videotape backwards and forwards but only hearing one moment at a time.

Characteristics of people with each type of time processing pattern

In time

- can get caught up in 'the here and now'
- may have part of their history unavailable to them unless they imagine turning their heads to look behind them
- sees memories through their own eyes (rather than as a photograph)
- likes to have options 'in the moment'
- may need to be kept on track or set themselves artificially early deadlines to ensure completion
- work and play are synonymous

Through time

- time is perceived as continuous and uninterrupted
- memories often are dissociated (as if looking at a photograph)
- are on time and feel they 'know time' well
- often cluster single memories and associate them with an internal state (e.g. may find it hard to think of a single happy memory at first, because all the happy memories are grouped together)
- good at staying on track
- less ability to focus in the present and be 'here, now'
- have a need for closure and to 'get the show on the road'—work and play are separate areas

Is it possible to use both time lines? Absolutely. Many people find that they will operate from one time line for certain tasks or activities and yet are using a different time line on other occasions. The time line tools below give you some ways to think about using and gaining flexibility over your time line.

Fun with your time line

Awareness of your preference is a powerful tool to have. You can choose to change your time line and adopt an alternative pattern for a particular moment or period of time. In doing so, you can take on the characteristics of your non-preferred mode. This is easy—just imagine your preferred time line and watch it move. You may find it helpful to visualise your time line on the floor and watch it turn in a new direction. If you have an in time preference remember to step back off your time line; if you have a through time preference, remember to literally 'step into' the present and see the future directly ahead.

Re-orientating your time line can particularly benefit through time people who may need to develop better listening skills. In timers are great listeners, as they find it easy to be in the here and now. Conversely, in time people may benefit from the long-term planning perspective that they can achieve by adopting a through time perspective. Time line tools and techniques can be done in the physical space around you or just in your own mind. If you, or the person you are working with, are confident in creating internal imageries they can be done with your eyes closed. Alternatively, they are just as powerful and effective when done in the physical space around you.

Noticing whether memories are clustered or separate

Have you ever had someone mention something to you and then find yourself, without thinking, adopting an internal state that was unconnected with what was just said? As you explore your time line you will begin to notice that some of your memories are clustered, or **gestalt**-ed. Being aware of this is particularly helpful for through time people. Because people with a through time preference have their memories arranged in front of them, they are more likely to have stronger experiences of negative or painful memories than people with an in time preference. Simply being aware of this process gives you the flexibility to adopt a different perspective where you need to. People with an in time preference will also gestalt their memories, but will experience negativity within memories as a result of more frequently associating (seeing it again through their own eyes) into the past experience. In contrast, through time people will often experience their memories as dissociated (seeing the experience as if an observer). In general, through time preference people more frequently gestalt their memories. In the Chapter 8, Memories are made of this, we experienced the subtle distinctions that encode our memories with emotions and feeling in more detail, and you will learn how to manage and work with these.

Just do it

Relax and think of happiness. Once you have accessed this internal state, take a moment to see if you can access a happy memory on your time line. Did you find a single memory? Or was the experience more one of noticing a cluster of memories? In your mind switch time lines—if you are in time imagine all of your memories in front of you. If you are through time place them all on a line behind you. Now repeat the experience of thinking about happiness and look for the happy memories. What's different?

Spend your time noticing the feelings that you now have and how they are different. If you are unused to noticing your internal state you may need to do this several times to notice the subtle distinctions and changes.

How could this be useful?

The language of time

Have you ever had the experience of feeling fine about doing something until someone came along and said something like, 'You must be a bit concerned about this, aren't you?' A core concept in NLP is the idea that the language we use strongly affects our brain and therefore our internal states and behaviours. In Chapter 5, *Don't think about chocolate cake*, we explored how the unconscious mind is affected by language. Time related language has a powerful effect particularly on our beliefs about what we are capable of and, therefore, has an effect on our potential to achieve. When we think of events we have a natural tendency to order them into a time sequence. These are mainly expressed in a verb form:

I talked to her

I talk to her

I will talk to her

These temporal language shifts can have an immediate impact on the listener by shifting them forwards or backward on their time line. This has a particularly strong effect in conversation because the person speaking is always in the present. Notice the differences between the following sentences and reflect for a moment on the potential internal state that they generate:

You are going to be anxious

You are anxious

You used to be anxious

It is well worth thinking carefully about the time related language that we use, particularly in the classroom, as it is easy to give someone a limiting belief about a future action when our actual intention was merely to express empathy or understand.

I'm sure that many of you are beginning to feel worried about the exams that are coming up but let me assure you that your worries are unfounded!

Overcoming these linguistic traps is easy and just requires a little thought at the moment of offering support. Stop and think of the best state that a person could have when doing the task that you are offering support on. Then ensure that you phrase your support accordingly.

Now that we have covered all of these topics in detail you can look forward to feeling confident on this topic as you move into the examination period.

If you find yourself having to refer to the anxiety that was experienced, do just that and place the feelings in the past.

So how much more confident are you, now that we have talked it through, that those old feelings of anxiety can be easily replaced by confidence?

Note the **double bind** at the start of the sentence that presupposes a change and increase in confidence (see Chapters 5 and 10 for more about presuppositions).

Research Zone

The grid in your head

For a number of years research has indicated that the hippocampus does far more than simply place memories in time (O'Keefe and Nadel, 1978). Alongside newly discovered 'grid cells', which are located in the cortex, the hippocampus also traces our movements through space. Therefore, whenever you remember an event you are also remembering the spatiotemporal context in which that event took place (Knierim, 2007). In rats it has been shown that each grid cell projects a visual lattice of triangles and fires when the animal is on any triangle's corner. Researchers suggest that grid cells provide spatial data that enables the hippocampus to construct the context necessary for the forming and storing of autobiographical memories. The regular geometric (almost crystalline) structure of the reported neutral response property is one of the most remarkable pieces of research in recent years. So far nothing else like it has been found in the brain (see Hafting et al., 2005; Sargolini et al., 2006).

Research Zone continued ...

Hafting, T., Fyhn, M., Molden, S., Moser, M.-B. and Moser, E. I. (2005) Microstructure of a spatial map in the Entorhinal Cortex, *Nature*, 436: 801–806

Knierim, J. J. (2007) The matrix in your head, *Scientific American Mind*, 18: 3: 42

O'Keefe, J. and Nadel, L. (1978) The hippocampus as a cognitive map <www.cognitivemap.net> accessed 7 July 2007

Sargolini, F., Fyhn, M., Hafting, T., McNaughton, L., Witter, M. P., Moser, M.-B. and Moser, E. . (2006) Conjunctive representation of position, direction and velocity in entorhinal cortex, Science, 312: 758–762

NLP Toolbox No. 31

Walking around anxiety

Do you have something coming up in the future that you are anxious about? For example, qualifications, a parent–teacher conference, interviews, etc. If so, then this is a really useful tool to begin to use.

1. First, imagine that your time line is laid out on the ground. Position the past behind you and the future in front of you. Make sure that you are standing on your time line at the point that represents 'now' for you. Decide where, on the future part of your time line, the event that you are anxious about lies and notice how you feel about it. What are you saying to yourself? What emotional feelings and physical sensations do you have? Where in your body are any physical feelings and sensations located?

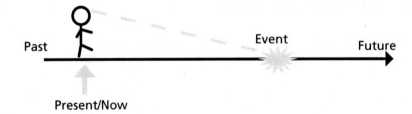

2. Next, take a step to one side of your time line and walk towards the future until you are past the event in question. Step back onto your time line (at a point in the future), looking back towards the event, as if it is something that you have already achieved. Notice how your feelings change when you reconsider the event from the point of view of already having achieved it.

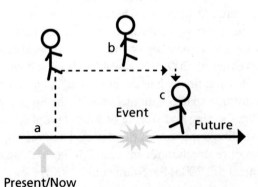

3. Finally, walk back along your time line to 'now' and look at your chosen event again. Notice how your anxiety has decreased. You might want to score this on a scale of 1 to 10 and become aware of how much it has reduced. You can repeat this process until you are completely comfortable with the level of your anxiety, or until you find that you are now looking forward to the event with more positive feelings or simply in a matter-of-fact way.

More ways to start improving your classroom practice with NLP

■ Teach some of the time line walking exercises to students who need to plan revision or plan a whole project or activity. This is fun for primary and secondary students

■ Use the walking a time line exercise in Toolbox 31 to walk through a lesson that you are to deliver but which you feel a bit unsure about the structure

■ Use the time line for working up schemes of work and walking through the learning

■ Get children to create a revision of the year's work time line, with content labelled on spaces on the floor, and get them to walk the learning from the year through in pairs reviewing the topics

NLP Toolbox No. 32

Walking your time line and adding resources

You can also use your time line to help you to set and achieve goals and to overcome barriers and challenges. Two really powerful tools that you can explore are given below. These tools can also be used when supporting children with revision, goal setting and coping with examination worries.

1. Imagine what you want to happen. Do this in detail, in full sensorama. Create a picture in your mind. See everything as if you were really there. Make the colours bright, clear, in focus and all around you. Next, be aware of the feelings and sensations in your body. Begin to create good feelings about the event and allow them to fill your body. Make sure you have fun doing this. As you generate these feelings, notice what sounds are also there. Adjust the volume and decide on the location of the sounds. Hear the event in full stereo (or even surround-sound) rich and full. What smells and tastes can you sense?

2. Imagine where in the room your goal can be found. Walk to that point and look back at where you started from, noticing what it feels like to have achieved your goal.

NLP Toolbox No. 32 continued ...

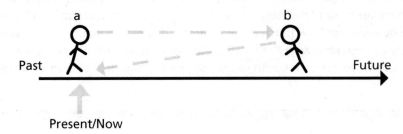

3. Return to 'now' on your time line and begin walking forwards (you can do this physically or just in your own mind). Imagine all the things that you will do and overcome. At some point you will feel the need to pause, as you begin to experience a barrier or potential challenge. At this point, step off your time line and look at yourself in the situation, as if you were an observer.

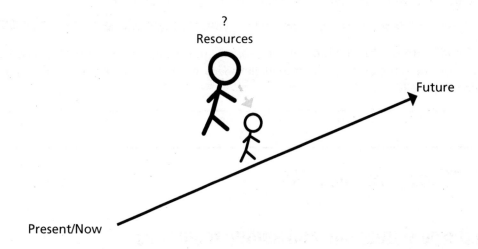

Think of all the internal or external resources (including people) that you need to use as you overcome the challenge. Once you have completed this, imagine taking these resources back onto the time line with you. Notice how different your challenge now appears. Continue walking on your time line towards your goal and repeat Step 2 as often as you need to, in order to reach your goal resourcefully.

4. Once you are standing on your goal again, imagine it as a beautiful picture and hold it in front of you. Imagine all the details (what you will see, hear and feel) as you achieve your goal. Finally, pull a golden thread from the picture and connect it to your heart. Take four deep breaths and breathe life into your goal.

5. Drop the picture onto your time line, leaving the thread connected and walk backwards seeing the thread extend as you go. Continue walking backwards, only as fast as you need to collect all your internal resources. Do this until you find yourself back at your 'now' point. Notice how motivated and connected you now are to your goal and how positive you feel.

Past

Present/Now

It can be good to have someone facilitate this with you. This can be done at a purely process level (with you keeping the details to yourself) so that your facilitator remains unaware of exactly what you are working on.

Research Zone

Neuron migration–the birth and journey of neurons

We grow new neurons when we need them and they travel for three to four weeks to arrive where they are needed, providing that there is effective communication between the neuron and its destination. Up until recently neuroscientists believed that the neurons we are born with are the only ones that we ever have. In 1962, Joseph Altman identified neurogenesis (the birth of new neurons) in the hippocampus of adult rats. In later experiments he showed that neurons migrate from the hippocampus to other regions of the brain. Fernando Nottebohm (Nottebohm et al.,1994) later demonstrated that male canaries show an increase in neurons in their forebrains during mating seasons, when they are required to learn new songs to attract females. Neurogenesis and migration have been shown to take place in monkeys and in the adult human brain (Eriksson et al., 1998).

After birth a neuron migrates to where it is needed. They travel along long fibres called radial glia, which link the inner structures of the brain to the outer layers. This migration takes between two and three weeks. New neurons travel using chemical signals that help them to navigate to their intended location (see e.g. Gilmore et al., 2002). However, not all neurons are successful and it is estimated that only 30% or so end up where they are needed. Although there is currently no evidence that mapping the complete journey to be travelled to a future goal stimulates and helps to facilitate effective neuron migration, most researchers agree that mental rehearsal is a potentially valuable technique for enhancing performance (see Druckman and Swets, 1988).

Druckman, D. and Swets, J. (1988) *Enhancing Human Performance*, Washington, DC: National Academy Press

Eriksson, P. S., Perfilieva, E., Björk-Eriksson, T., Alborn, A.-M., Nordborg, C., Peterson, D. and Gage, F. (1998) Neurogenesis in the adult human hippocampus, *Nature Medicine*, 4: 1313–1317

Gilmore, D. T., Maischein, H.-M., Nusslein-Volhard, C. (2002) Migration and function of a glial bubtype in the vertebrate peripheral nervous system, *Neuron*, 43: 577–588

Nottebohm, F., O'Loughlin, B., Gould, K., Yohay, K., and Alvarez-Buylla, A. (1994) The life span of new neurons in a song control nucleus of the adult canary brain depends on time of year when these cells are born, *Proceedings of the National Academy of Sciences*, 91: 7849–7853

Chapter 13
It's in your eyes ... among other things

How paying attention to small pieces of body language and eye movements can help you to build rapport, influence and communicate more effectively

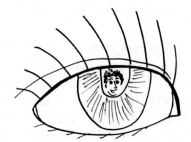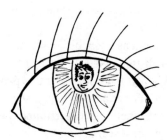

Isn't it amazing just how many pop songs there are about 'eyes' or which talk about what can be understood from eyes or the meaning of communication with our eyes? Eye movements are fascinating once you begin to pay attention to them, as is pupil dilation and the liquidity of the surface of the eye, which is constantly varying to create a more or less shiny surface.

In schools we rarely have long meetings and if we want to get our way with other staff and influence them—particularly when it comes to senior staff who often have control over budgets, timetables and the like—we need to be really efficient when it comes to reading the signs in relation to how our suggestions are being received. The skills below were one of the first things that Richard learnt about NLP and were his stock in trade at the final school where he worked in inner London. [Apologies Byron (headteacher)—this is going to cost me a free inset day I can tell!]

Sensory acuity

One of the key NLP skills is the ability to pay attention to small changes in people's facial expressions and body language. This is referred to as **sensory acuity**. It is important to remember, however, that there are no absolutes where this is concerned. Where the slight tightening of a muscle around the eye may indicate one internal emotion for one person it may indicate something quite different for another. What is fascinating to notice is that people tend to be consistent as individuals when it come to these 'display' signals, and indeed (as has been shown by Paul Ekman) there are many universal indicators of emotion. The first person to notice and begin to scientifically analyse this phenomenon was Charles Darwin in his book *The Expression of Emotion in Man and Animals* (1872). NLP practitioners have spent much time exploring this area to develop the rapport-building technique of **matching**. In doing so the importance of the individual expression of micro-signals became clearly apparent. As mentioned above, it is important not to jump to conclusions about a piece of body language, micro-facial expressions or an eye movement. You need to begin by hypothesising and then testing your hypothesis to see if repetition of what has been done consistently correlates with this emotion in someone. Once you have made a connection, you will be able to use this information to improve your communication with the other person. In NLP the process of noticing, checking and cataloguing an individual's micro-expressions and body language is known as **calibration**.

> In NLP the process of noticing, checking and cataloguing an individual's micro-expressions and body language is known as calibration.

One day I (Roger) noticed that one of my employees in the training centre office had developed a very subtle but distinguishable red patch on her neck, which suddenly appeared just before she asked for a day off. A few weeks later the same thing happened. Having calibrated this very individual display signal for embarrassment in a particular context, the next time this happened I amazed her by offering her a day off before she had asked. In our sales training we get salespeople to calibrate the strength, emotional warmth, movement and temperature of their customer's handshake. If you know someone well this can allow you to gauge how well a meeting went or how well it might go before you start. Again, remember that calibration is important—everyone is different (see Chapter 3, *We like like*).

You can develop your sensory acuity and calibration using some of the exercises in Chapter 15, *Instant training day*. As with most NLP you need to experience it to learn and to develop the skills. Most of your calibration, when you are learning this process, will relate to what people are saying and the subtle changes that you see. For example, if you see a very small muscle change or facial colour change when someone talks about something that irritated them, and this is often the same, you can log this for a time when you need to suggest something to this person. If you are then in conversation and make a suggestion which results in this signal, you then have the information to adapt and respond by modifying your suggestion before the person has responded.

Examples of things to take notice of and calibrate to

- Muscle movement around the eyes
- The muscles at the corner of the mouth
- How open and closed the eyes are
- Pupil dilation
- Changes in the liquidity of the surface of the eyes
- Changes in facial colour
- Eye movements
- Head tilt
- Breaths
- Combinations of all of the above

Research Zone

Micro-facial expressions

Research into facial expressions and communication suggests that very small changes in facial expression can communicate internal emotion. Furthermore, it is suggested that such facial expressions are not culturally determined, but rather are universal and thus have a biological origin, as suggested by Darwin. Ekman has reported micro-facial expressions that could be used to reliably detect lying. He has also developed the facial action coding system (FACS) to taxonomise all conceivable human facial expression (Ekman, 1985; 2003).

Ekman, P. (1985) *Telling Lies: Clues to Deceit in the Martketplace, Politics and Marriage*, New York: Morton
Ekman, P. (2003) *Emotions Revealed*, London: Phoenix

Eye movements

There is no doubt that one of the most fascinating and, at the same time, controversial aspects of what Bandler and Grinder modelled in the 1970s was **eye accessing cues**. In their work they began to notice that there appeared to be a correlation between where people's eyes look and the kind of sensory language they are using. More particularly, they suggested that people's eyes move around when they are thinking and internally processing (prior to speaking), and that you can often see a correlation between what they then say and where their eyes went before they spoke. The next time you are having a conversation with someone, pay particular attention to what happens to their eyes when they are thinking, particularly after you have asked them a question. Do you see any patterns or themes?

Early NLP writers suggested that when people move their eyes (for example, after they have been asked a question) you can with some certainty predict what sort of internal processing is most dominant (either visual, auditory or kinaesthetic) and that this is then often reflected in the language that people use when they are then speaking. In terms of the neuroscience, and what we know goes on inside the brain, this is an unproven and highly suspect concept. Some suggest that it is more likely that eye accessing cues are the external representation of individual phenomenological experience and therefore are an external manifestation of mind rather than brain function. However, even using eye accessing cues for a short time you will begin to experience the effects on rapport and your ability to influence others. Although you will come across much literature on the web about this subject, the truth is there have not been any robust studies that explore this phenomenon and there is a really good PhD waiting to be done in the area. Those studies that have taken place have not fully taken into account the importance of calibration in the process and therefore have sought to look for universals. Working with eye accessing cues it is clear that there is often as much variation from the general pattern as there is a demonstration of it. However, skilled calibration and observation of the micro-movements of eyes may give you useful information and definitely seems to increase rapport.

NLP Toolbox No. 33

Taking a snapshot

When you are working with others or listening to someone talk, take a moment to be a camera and take a snapshot of their whole body. It's easy to do—just imagine the shutter click and get your mind to visualise in that instant the frozen frame that you just saw. Take snapshots regularly, particularly when people are talking about the things that they like or dislike. As you become more skilled at this you will begin to notice more micro details, expressions and changes that are regularly associated with certain feelings and types of thinking for particular people.

This tool is explored in more detail in Chapter 15, *Instant training day*, where you can find a training exercise to develop your sensory acuity further.

What does this have to do with rapport and influencing others? Well, it all comes back to sensory acuity. If you notice a pattern or micro-signal that is consistently followed by a repeat behaviour or language pattern, that gives you more information to work with in terms of the flexibility of your own behaviour and things to match. Bandler and Grinder suggested that when the eye looks up this implies some involvement of visual internal representation and accessing of what they called the visual representation system. When the eyes look to the side, auditory processing is dominant. When they look down, feelings, sensations or emotions are being accessed. A defocused straight-ahead gaze has been suggested to sometimes indicate recently remembered visual information.

Just do it

Exploring the feel of different eye positions

Keep your head still and straight. Move your eyes to each of the eye positions indicated on the chart below. Hold each position for about 30 seconds. You may want to get someone to time this for you so that you don't get distracted.

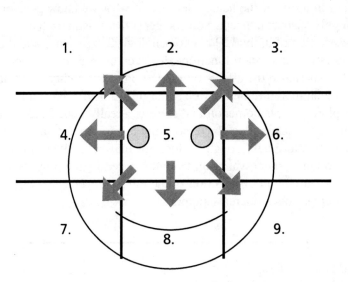

Notice the different experience that you personally have in each of the positions. Which positions are more comfortable or more natural? Did you get any associations in the different positions? What changes in feeling or internal state did you notice? What else happened?

Develop this experience further by thinking about a problem that you currently have or something that you are working on. Hold the eye positions as before while you think about this problem or situation. Notice what effect these different eye positions have on your thinking and feeling. Pay particular attention to how an unfamiliar eye position affects what happens to you inside. Are any feelings, sounds or internal images invoked by certain eye positions? What happens when you move eye position? Which changes in position have an effect and which do not?

The NLP eye accessing cues model

NLP writers suggest that eye movements and positions do not create internal representations and experiences but rather reflect, and are therefore an indication of, aspects of neurological information processing. Many suggest the following pattern structure as a starting point for learning to recognise and make use of this phenomenon. The basic notion is that when people's eyes move upward this indicates some sort of visual information processes. When a person's eyes move to the side this is suggestive of auditory processing. A downward eye movement is associated with either kinaesthetic or bodily information accessing or some form of internal self-talk or 'discussion/questioning'. It is also proposed that there may be an association between left or right eye movement and the processes of constructing or remembering information. Again, the caveat is that calibration to an individual's patterns is a key part of the process.

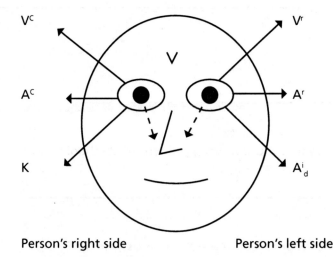

V	Visual
A	Auditory
K	Kinaesthetic
c	Constructed information
r	Remembered information
i	Internal source of information
d	Digital (self-talk, words)

Person's right side   Person's left side

It is not suggested that eye movements always follow this pattern or that they are consistent for everyone. Rather it is necessary to check the reliability of correlations that appear to exist for each individual person.

> NLP does not suggest that these eye movements always follow this pattern or are consistent for everyone. Rather it is necessary to check the reliability of correlations that appear to exist for each individual person.

Developing your sensory awareness of the small display signals that people exhibit when they are thinking, listening or communicating can help you to become in tune with others, communicate more effectively and know when you are on the way to achieving your outcomes. As we have said before the best way to learn NLP is to experience it. Essentially mind knows how to do this stuff—most of the time these kinds of processes have happened at an unconscious level. Bringing them into the 'conscious' part of your experience will give you more flexibility and confidence when working with others. The exercise below is as much an opportunity to test the NLP model for yourself as it is to begin to deepen your listening and communication skills. Ask one of the questions at a time and put your attention completely on your partner's eyes. You can photocopy this page if you like and record the eye movements that you see.

Test the NLP accessing cues model for yourself

Find someone to work with on this. First get the person to sit comfortably and then look straight ahead. Next ask each of the questions in turn, giving them plenty of time to answer. Draw a line to show the movement of their eyes as they think and process your question before and during their answer. Your lines should move in the direction of the positions in the eye accessing cues model (left or right horizontal, left and right diagonals both up and down).

☺	1. What does the prime minister look like?
☺	2. Picture a giraffe
☺	3. What was the first thing that you saw when you arrived at school today?
☺	4. What does the sound of your favourite piece of music sound like?
☺	5. What noise does a cow make?
☺	6. Think of someone you know saying your name?
☺	7. How do you feel?
☺	8. If you have got something wrong what do you say to yourself?
☺	9. How hot do you like your bath?
☺	10. What does your favourite food taste like?

Strategies

Observing eye movements and making use of this information to improve communication is just the beginning of NLP theory and **modelling** in relation to eye accessing cues. The interconnection of eye movements represents a whole field of study known as **strategies**. In NLP these are believed to relate to the pattern of subjective internal processing between stimulus and response and are often modelled and mapped using the letters indicated above. Strategies are claimed to form the formulae of effectiveness or ineffectiveness in relation to behaviour, communication and cognitive processing (Bandler and Grinder, 1979). NLP details techniques for identifying **strategies** and for installing more resourceful strategies. One strategy that is commonly referred to in the literature is **NLP spelling strategy**.

Test	Operate	Test	Exit
$A^e \rightarrow$	$V^c \rightarrow /V^r \rightarrow$	$K^{i+} \rightarrow$ or $\rightarrow$	K^e/A^c
		or $K^i \downarrow$	

Here it is suggested that excellent spellers will on hearing a word A^e (auditory external stimulus) first construct a visual representation of that word V^c, compare it to a recalled visual image V^r and then test this by accessing feelings processed internally K^{i+} (good feeling) K^{i-} (bad feeling). This continues in a loop until there is an external exit point (K^e/A^c writing of the word and simultaneous construction of the sound of the word) to complete the sequence. This strategy was modelled by observing the eye movements of excellent spellers (within the context of individual calibration). Today it is quite widely accepted that good spellers use internal word pictures as part of their spelling strategy; however, the origin of this idea is less well known.

The idea of stimulus and response has been the basis of behavioural psychology since Pavlov did his experiments in the 1920s.

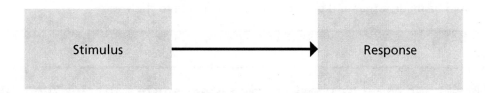

In their definition of the NLP model, Bandler and Grinder drew on the work of Miller, Galanter and Pribram (1960) who proposed the TOTE model. This is an elaboration on the original stimulus–response concept adopted by behaviourist psychology. TOTE (literally: test, operate, test, exit) presents the idea of the existence of a test–operate loop that takes place between external stimulus and behavioural response. In NLP, Bandler and Grinder suggested that we all have the capacity to modify steps in the chain of events between stimulus and response and thereby adapt/change/choose new behaviours in relation to any given stimulus. Through their work on eye accessing cues and other studies of language and representational systems (VAKOG), Bandler and Grinder suggested that these steps were related to sensory processes. As yet this hypothesis remains unproven. However, cognitive neuroscience supports the importance of associated memory in information processing and in the automatic selection of schemata (see Research Zone on page 141).

NLP Toolbox No. 34

Using the NLP spelling strategy

1. Write the word that you want the child to learn on a piece of card (laminated A4 sheets of paper used with dry wipe marker pens are a really good resource for this).

2. Have them experience a pleasant feeling. Something that makes them feel safe, successful, warm, something that makes them feel like saying YES. This is easy to do. Simply say: *image a time when you felt … [add in whatever works (e.g. successful etc.)]*

3. While they maintain this feeling, hold the card high up to your right so that it is in the top left corner of their field of vision, so that their eyes follow the card up into this position (some teachers have even begun to put spellings up in the top left corner of their whiteboard because they have found this strategy to be effective).

4. Tell them to take a snapshot of the word in their mind, just as if they were a camera ('click'). Ask them to create a mental image of the word on the card in their mind. Get them to add some distinguishing features (for example, add colour, change the background, choose a font or style, etc.) and to keep seeing the word in their mind's eye until the image is really clear.

5. Turn the card round to the blank side. With their eyes in the same position ask them to spell the word imagining that the word is still there.

6. Take the snapshot as many times as necessary.

7. Look up again at where the image is stored and write down what you see. Look up again and check that it is correct.

Students can be encouraged to make their mental images clearer by changing the submodalities (see Chapter 2, *Blockbuster movies* and Chapter 8, *Memories are made of this*). For example, it could be made larger and brighter or even be made to flash.

More ways to start improving your classroom practice with NLP

■ Run the NLP spelling strategy for yourself when you come across new words and phrases in your subject area that you need to learn yourself

■ Encourage a visual approach to learning spellings with the children that you teach

■ Run the spelling strategy with those children who are stuck in a 'spell as you speak mode' and reinforce this when teaching new words to them

Research Zone

Eye movements and cognition

Before we get a whole postbag of letters we should state quite clearly that this is the area of NLP for which there is the least parallel evidence from neuroscience and psychology! However, a toe-dip into the literature on saccadic and other eye movements shows conclusively that there is a clear connection between eye movements and cognition and internal processing. Specifically, eye movements studies have provided insights into how the brain integrates perception and action planning (Goldberg et al., 1990), have proved useful in the investigation of the interaction between cognitive and sensorimotor brain systems (Sweeney et al., 2007) and have demonstrated that eye position signal modulates brain function during memory guided movements (De Souza et al., 2000). Surprisingly studies involving primates have demonstrated that one step in the process of turning a target location, as seen by the eye, into a motor action involves the modulation of neural activity by changing eye position signals (Andersen et al., 1985; Zipser and Andersen, 1988; Boussaoud and Bremmer, 1999). It appears that eye movements may not only reflect neural activity but may also be integral to it. Recent evidence from neuropsychology demonstrates that when you remember a past event, you also remember the spatiotemporal context in which that experience occurred. This process is a function of place-tracking neurons called 'grid cells' (Hafting et al., 2005).

Andersen, R. A., Essick, G. K., Seigal and R. M. (1985) Encoding of spatial location by posterior parietal neurons, *Science*, 230:456–458

Boussaoud, D. and Bremmer, F. (1999) Gaze effects in the cerebral cortex: reference frames for space coding and action, *Experimental Brain Research*, 128: 170–180

De Souza, J. F. X., Dukelow, S. P., Gati, J. S., Menon, R. S., Andersen, R. A. and Vilis, T. (2000) Eye position signal modulates a human parietal pointing region during memory-guided movements, *Journal of Neuroscience*, 20: 15: 5835–5840

Goldberg, M. E., Colby, C. L., Duhamel, J. R. (1990) Representation of visuomotor space in the parietal lobe of the monkey, *Cold Spring Harbor Symposia on Quantitative Biology*, 55: 729–739

Hafting, T., Fyhn, M., Molden, S., Moser, M.-B. and Moser, E. I (2005) Microstructure of a spatial map in the entorhinal cortex, *Nature*, 436: 801–806

Knierim, J. (2007) The matrix in your head, *Scientific American Mind*, 18: 3: 42–49

Sweeney, J. A., Luna, B., Keedy, S. K., McDowell, J. E. and Clementz, B. A. (2007) fMRI studies of eye movement control: investigating the interaction of cognitive and senorimotor brain systems, *Neuroimage*, 36: 54–60

Zipser, D. and Andersen, R. A. (1988) A back-propagation programmed network that simulates response properties of a subset of posterior parietal neurons, *Nature*, 331: 679–684

Evidence that eye movements are related to internal processing and language

It has been shown that eye movements are, in some circumstances, an external manifestation of internal processing (Brandt and Stark, 1997; Hebb, 1968; Laeng and Teodorescu, 2002); specifically that eyes tend to return to the spatial source of recently presented information. This is the case even when that spatial information is irrelevant for performing the task (Richardson and Spivey, 2000). Furthermore, visual images and spoken descriptions elicit similar eye movements during mental imagery in both the light and in complete darkness (Johansson et al., 2006). Laeng and Teodorescu (2002) have demonstrated that eye scanpaths during visual imagery re-enact those of perception of the same visual scene. Therefore, eye movements that occur during mental imagery are not 'epiphenomenal' (a secondary phenomenon) but actually

Research Zone continued ...

assist the process of image generation. Of particular relevance to NLP is evidence which suggests that linguistic expressions drive eye movements (Altmann, 2004). Altmann demonstrated that those eye movements which are triggered while linguistic expression is taking place are based in the location of the internal representation of the scene being described, not on the actual location of the item in the scene (Altmann, 2004; Altmann and Kamide, 2004). Altmann and others (e.g. Richardson and Spivey, 2000) suggest that traces of spatial association are part of the encoding of the representation and that this drives the eyes towards a location.

Altmann, G. T. M. (2004) Language-mediated eye movements in the absence of a visual world: the 'blank screen paradigm', *Cognition*, 93: B79–B87

Altmann, G. T. M. and Kamide, Y. (2004) Now you see it, now you don't: mediating the mapping between language and the visual world, in J. M. Henderson and F. Ferreira (eds), *The Interface of Language, Vision, and Action: Eye Movements and the Visual World*, New York: Psychology Press

Brandt, S. A. and Stark, L. W., (1997) Spontaneous eye movements during visual imagery reflect the content of the visual scene, *Journal of Cognitive Neuroscience*, 9: 27–38

Hebb, D. O. (1968) Concerning imagery, *Psychological Review*, 75: 466– 477

Johansson, R., Holsanova, J. and Homqvist, K. (2006) Pictures and spoken descriptions elicit similar eye movements during mental imagery, both in light and in complete darkness, *Cognitive Science*, 30: 6: 1053–1079

Laeng, B. and Teodorescu, D. S. (2002) Eye scanpaths during visual imagery reenact those of perception of the same visual scene, *Cognitive Science*, 26: 207–231

Richardson, D. C. and Spivey, M. J. (2000) Representation, space and Hollywood squares: looking at things that aren't there anymore, *Cognition*, 76: 269–295

Eye movements, communication and rapport

In relation to communication and rapport it has been demonstrated that the coupling of eye movements takes place between a speaker and a listener. In a recent experiment (Richardson and Dale, 2005) participants talked, without previous preparation, about a television programme whose cast members they viewed on a screen. Later, other participants listened to the monologues of these people while they viewed the same screen. The eye movements of both the speakers and listeners were recorded. It was found that listeners' eye movements matched the speakers' eye movements at a delay of two seconds. Furthermore, the 'more closely a listener's eye movements were coupled with a speaker's, the better the listener did on a comprehension test'. In a further experiment low-level visual cues were used to manipulate the listeners' eye movements. These 'influenced their latencies to comprehension questions'. The conclusion reached by the researcher was that 'just as eye movements reflect the mental state of an individual, the coupling between a speaker's and a listener's eye movements reflects the success of their communication'.

Richardson, D. C. and Dale R. (2005) Looking to understand: the coupling between speakers' and listeners' eye movements and its relationship to discourse comprehension, *Cognitive Science*, 29: 6: 1045–1060

The NLP spelling strategy

Dilts (1995) reports studies that support the efficacy of the spelling strategy. Thomas Malloy at the University of Utah Department of Psychology carried out studies with groups of 'average' spellers. The first group was taught the NLP spelling strategy (looking up and to the left), the second a sounding out using phonetics and auditory rules, and the third group were used as a control and no new strategies were given. The visual recall of the spellers is reported as having improved by 25% with 100% retention one week later. The second group, who had been taught the auditory strategy, improved 15%, (however, this score dropped by 5% in the following week). The control group showed no improvement. In another study in 1985 at the University of Moncton in New Brunswick, in Canada, similar results were found and results suggested that looking up to the left enhances spelling and is twice as effective as simply asking students to visualise words. Furthermore, looking down to the right appeared to inhibit success.

Dilts, R. and Epstein, T. (1995) *Dynamic Learning*, California: Meta, Capitola

Eye movement desensitisation and reprocessing (EMDR)

EMDR is a psychotherapeutic approach developed by Francine Shapiro (Shapiro, 1995). Although some use EMDR for various problems, its research support is primarily in relation to disorders that stem from distressing life experiences (Briere and Scott, 2006). As with NLP, EMDR's most controversial component is the use of approaches such as eye movements. In EMDR these are combined with bilateral sound or bilateral tactile stimulation. Recent reviews have highlighted evidence that eye movement in EMDR does produce a differential effect (Servan-Schreiber, 2002). When compared to no eye movement, eye movements produce changes in physiological measures including reductions in blood pressure, galvanic skin response and heart rate (Wilson et al., 1996). On the other hand, a meta-analysis which looked at the contribution of eye movements to treatment effectiveness concluded that they made very little difference with the exception of those individuals who had a formal diagnosis of post-traumatic stress disorder (Davidson and Parker, 2001). Some NLP tools such as 'unwiring a synaesthesia' also make use of eye movements to change responses to memories.

Briere, J. and Scott, C. (2006) *Principles of Trauma Therapy: A Guide to Symptoms, Evaluation, and Treatment*, Thousand Oaks, CA: Sage

Davidson, P. R. and K. C. H. Parker (2001) Eye movement desensitization and reprocessing (EMDR): a meta-analysis, *Journal of Consulting and Clinical Psychology*, 69: 2: 305–316

Servan-Schreiber, D. (2002) Eye movement desensitization and reprocessing: is psychiatry missing the point?, *Psychiatric Times*, 14: 7: 36–40

Shapiro, F. (1995) *Eye Movement Desensitization and Reprocessing: Basic Principles, Protocols and Procedures*, New York: The Guilford Press

Wilson, D., Silver, S. M., Covi, W. G., Foster, S (1996) Eye movement desensitization and reprocessing: effectiveness and autonomic correlates, *Journal of Behavior Therapy and Experimental Psychiatry*, 27: 3: 219–229

Commentary

No neuroscience research currently directly supports the NLP eye movement model. However, specific NLP related neurological studies have yet to take place. Experimental psychology research in the late 1980s and early 1990s that examined NLP eye movement concepts did not find a basis for acceptance of the model (Buckner et al. (1987); Baddeley and Predecon, 1991). However, it can be argued that these studies did not take full account of calibration and subjective individual variation within the model, nor could they take into account more recent fMRI evidence of the relationship between eye movement and brain function. Where, from a practical perspective, eye accessing cues appear to work and individual consistencies can be observed, it would seem most likely that these represent a display of individual subjective experience and therefore are a largely phenomenological rather than a neurological phenomenon.

Research Zone continued ...

Baddeley, M. and Predebon, J. (1991) Do the eyes have it?: a test of neurolinguistic programming's eye-movement hypothesis, *Australian Journal of Clinical Hypnotherapy and Hypnosis*, 12: 1: 1–23

Buckner, M., Meara, N. M., Reese, E. J. and Reese, M. (1987) Eye movement as an indicator of sensory components in thought, *Journal of Counseling Psychology*, 34: 3: 283–287

Chapter 14
The magic number 7

Understanding the limits of consciousness and the contemporary research context around NLP

The use of fMRI scans and other technology for neuroscience research has greatly enhanced our understanding of how the brain works, and has provided us with the opportunity to place the research done by Bandler and Grinder into some sort of contemporary research context. This chapter aims to put NLP into the context of latest research into consciousness and cognition and explain more clearly what sort of knowledge NLP is.

How did you do that?

Do you remember turning the last page of this book? When did you decide to turn the page or did it just seem to happen? Were you conscious at the time? Prepare yourself for a bit of a shock! The truth is that our experience of consciousness is almost certainly a complex and elaborate self-deception. Recent neuroscience research demonstrates that although we like to think that we are in charge of our actions and our thoughts, the reality is that a large amount of our actual behaviours, actions and perceptions of the world around us are carried out automatically by the unconscious brain. In neuroscience this process is known as **automaticity** and many people in the field of neuroscience and psychology point to evidence that shows that consciousness happens too late in the cognitive process to have an effect on the mental processes that it appears to be associated with.

> Our experience of consciousness is almost certainly a complex and elaborate self-deception. Recent neuroscience research demonstrates that although we like to think that we are in charge of our actions and our thoughts, the reality is that a large amount of our actual behaviours, actions and perceptions of the world around us are carried out automatically by the unconscious brain.

Our thoughts, feelings, beliefs and attitudes, which have usually been considered to come from our conscious mind, are actually the product of unconscious processes. Consequently, consciousness is merely the projection of very recent past events, thoughts and actions, like being in big multiplex cinema complete with smell-o-vision and touch-o-vision.

Just as when you are in the cinema, a great deal went on behind the scenes to script, write and perform the movie before you ever saw the film. The only difference is that with your conscious mind it all happened very fast and in a single storm of activity. Obviously, this

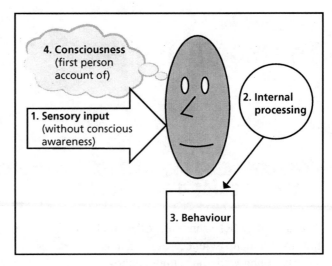

process is a lot more complex than the diagram above, but you get the picture. If you want a more detailed scientific explanation you can read the Research Zone below (which contains a detailed account of thinking in relation to the internal processing that is thought to take place). In this context it is clear that what NLP describes is the nature of our first person account of consciousness and how it feels to experience those internal processes that we have some awareness of, rather than a model of 'how' the brain works. Unfortunately, this 'how the brain works' view of the world (which is erroneous and misleading) has, all too often, been the way in which NLP has been presented by some trainers and writers. We hope that this chapter will put things in a more accurate and scientifically reasonable context. Why? Because NLP definitely works! Even if some previous explanations of why have been, to put it bluntly, somewhat wacky!

Just do it

The next time that you are talking to someone try to predict what your next word will be. If thoughts and decisions are the products of consciousness then this should be fairly easy to do.

The truth is you don't know what you are going to say next until after you have actually said it.

How did you decide to read the last few words? If you think about it, it just happened. How, though, did you make the decision and what part of you did that? The reality is that present thoughts, actions and feelings are slave to what was already present in your mind before you had an awareness of what was decided 'back there' in your unconscious mind!

Your actions and behaviours are the result of ideas and experiences that you or others put into your unconscious mind earlier.

Furthermore, the more you have repeated or embedded an idea, belief, set of routines or routine behaviours, the more likely it is that that particular program or **schema** will be the one which is fired up and create a behaviour or a thought pattern.

What fMRI scans and research demonstrate is that information comes into your brain at an unconscious level, and is then sorted though a whole set of functions and processes which include your associated memories and experiences of having done something or experienced something similar in the past. If there is something unusual that requires some higher level processing then we begin to get consciousness about the experience, during which we are able to feed back into the process modifications and thoughts. In fact, many argue that all of our brain information processing activities occur at an unconscious level. It is only later that these give rise to a continuous conscious experience. You've probably had that feeling of driving a car and are lost in your thoughts and then suddenly some brake lights come on ahead of you. Suddenly you are back in that moment, fully aware of where you are. If nothing novel or unusual happens you can just carry on automatically without any conscious awareness.

BLUE ELEPHANT

You were probably unaware of the process of reading and making sense of words until the words 'blue elephant' appeared and higher reasoning functions were required. When we have the opportunity to consciously create representations of what we will do in the future, or of actions that we about to do, it is clearly very important to make this work to our benefit as any representations that we create have almost certainly been fed back into the system as information for use in processing before we are even aware of them!

Have you ever noticed how if you dwell on a negative outcome you just seem to end up getting it, as if you were on a torpedo trajectory towards that outcome with no way of affecting the guidance system? In one of our training sessions we were asked by a participant, 'So is there no place in NLP for negative thoughts?' Well, what do you think? The truth is that the same processes apply to positive thinking as they do to negative thoughts. As you will have discovered from previous chapters, effective strategies for positive mental imagery and internal language are the bedrocks of NLP tools and techniques.

Note: For an up-to-date and detailed cognitive theory of information processing and consciousness see Brown and Oakley (2004).

NLP Toolbox No. 35

Present state to desired state

In the moments when we appear to have free will, what we pay attention to really matters. The present state to desired state tool is really effective, both when working through issues or problems with yourself or when coaching or supporting others.

1. Identify the problem or the issue

2. Spend one minute discussing or going through the problem and talking about all the difficulties that you or the person that you are working with face

3. Take a quick break

4. Spend at least four minutes talking through or thinking about what you would like instead. Imagine that outcome has already been achieved and outline in detail what it is like—what you see, hear and feel

What happens?

NLP techniques imply and promote the idea that there is a direct relationship between language and internal processing/neurological functioning—a notion that has been controversial and often criticised. However, the idea that there is a link between consciousness, cognitive processing and language is becoming clearer and more widely accepted as research develops. In particular, for many years the debate about the origin of speech has been an equally controversial one. Champions of the role of evolutionary inheritance over cultural influence (such as Noam Chomsky) were only able to point to languages themselves for evidence. However, in the 1990s a speech gene *FOXP2* was discovered and, more recently, it has been demonstrated that some songbirds learn songs in a similar way to the way in which children learn to speak. These similarities between birdsong and human language appear to extend all the way to a molecular level (Marcus and Fisher, 2003; Haesler et al., 2004). Alongside this, within the emerging field of cognitive linguistics, it is suggested that there is a direct relationship between cognitive processes and the use and development of language and language structures (see e.g. Croft, 1998; Fauconnier, 1994; 1997). Recent research into mirror neurons and language suggests that action verbs may have a distinct role in causing relevant mirror neurons to resonate (Tettamanti et al., 2005).

Research Zone

Automaticity and cognitive theories of information processing

The concept of automaticity is central to recent theories of cognition and information processing in the brain. Where we used to see consciousness as the key controlling element in behaviour we now understand that routine behaviours are controlled by the activation of low-level 'control structures' known as schemata. These interact competitively until one schema 'wins' and a resulting behaviour occurs. Schemata are hierarchically organised and nested internal representations that describe the sequence of processing which is involved in well-learned behaviours (Norman and Shallice, 1986). Schemata are triggered automatically by inputs from the external environment and therefore do not require our attention to be activated and for behaviour to occur. Therefore, much of what we do happens automatically, with our conscious awareness triggered only when something novel or unusual occurs. This results in our phenomenological sense of 'will' or consciousness (Norman and Shallice, 1986). However, this experience of consciousness happens too late in the cognitive process to effect the processing itself and is therefore happening after the fact (see Halligan and Oakley, 2000). Consequently, all experience can be said to be the result of automaticity at one level or another.

Neuroscientific research suggests that incoming information from our senses is extensively analysed before the activation of any attentional mechanisms. These systems then determine which information will provide the basis for further processes or the activation of behaviour (see e.g. Velmans, 2000). Following a pre-attentive process, what is described by some (Brown and Oakley, 2004) as the primary attention system (PAS) establishes the most meaningful interpretation of the environment and uses this interpretation to produce representations that allow for behaviour control. Primary representations serve as triggering inputs for cognitive networks and action schemata resulting in external behaviour and the subsequent experience of consciousness. Where existing knowledge is insufficient to fire schemata immediately, such as novel situations, it is thought that a high-level secondary attention system (SAS) takes control. This system manages planning, goal-setting, decision-making and problem solving (Brown and Oakley, 2004). Halligan, Brown and Oakley suggest that it is secondary attention system processing that is the source of the 'first person' account of consciousness and our sense of self (Halligan and Oakley, 2000; Brown and Oakley, 2004).

In relation to hypnosis in general, and suggestion specifically, Brown and Oakley propose that there are two routes to suggestion: the automatic activation of low-level schemata by an external input and the indirect activation of low-level schemata by the secondary attention system. In the case of the second of these two routes, this is said to encompass deliberate use of SAS strategies (e.g. 'thinking with' suggestions or goal-directed imaging)—what in NLP we would term the deliberate overloading of the conscious mind through the use of hypnotic language and hypnotic techniques. In relation to the NLP concept of the deliberate matching of metaprograms to influence others, etc. it is possible that metaprograms and other observable preferences are the linguistic and phenomenological manifestation of triggers for some schemata and that therefore by deliberately making use of the preferred metaprograms (etc.) of others we may be providing an external stimulus that results in the automatic activation of low-level schemata resulting in the acceptance of suggestions and resulting compliant behaviour.

Brown, R. J. and Oakley, D. A. (2004) An integrated cognitive theory of hypnosis and high hypnotizability, in M. Heap, R. J. Brown and D. A. Oakley (eds), *The Highly Hypnotisable Person: Theoretical, Experimental and Clinical Issues*, London: Routledge

Halligan, P. W. and Oakley. D. A. (2000) Greatest myth of all, *New Scientist*, 168: 35–49

Norman, D. A. and Shallice, T. (1986) Attention to action: willed and automatic control of behaviour, in R. J. Davidson, G. E. Swartz and D. Shapiro (eds), Consciousness and Self-regulation: *Advances in Research and Theory*, 4: 1–18, New York: Plenum

Velmans, M. (2000) *Understanding Consciousness*, London: Routledge

The magic number 7—the limits of consciousness

Richard Bandler and John Grinder did not have the benefit of fMRI scans nor the latest neuroscience when they developed their model. However, they did base their research on what was, at the time, cutting edge thinking in psychology and linguistics. One of these areas of thinking (as discussed earlier in the book) was Noam Chomsky's transformational grammar, which was an attempt to gain an understanding of the relationship between language and psychological processing. The other work that strongly influenced their thinking was the work of George Miller. At this time George Miller was the Co-Director of the Centre for Cognitive Studies at Harvard University and Professor of Psychology at Rockefeller University. John Grinder was a research assistant in George Miller's laboratory before taking up a professorship in linguistics at the University of Santa Cruz in California. Even 50 years on, Miller's research is still recognised as having validity and importance—quite an achievement in the world of psychology.

In a series of groundbreaking experiments in the 1950s, Miller demonstrated conclusively that there was a limit on our capacity for processing information. Specifically he showed that this limit was seven plus or minus two pieces of information. In other words, once we go beyond the of range five to nine pieces of information our conscious mind is taken beyond our ability to process and we begin to filter information out (Miller, 1956). This results in a loss of information and a focus on a more limited range or band of detail. In terms of our perception of consciousness and our first person account of being here and now, this results in us appearing, in our mind's eye, to drop out of consciousness and go inside to the world of internal imagery and representations. It is this phenomenon that is built upon in the process of hypnosis. Language that requires us to go inside because it has 'overloaded' our consciousness takes our reasoning functions off line and leaves us open to suggestion and influence (or at least this is how it appears from the point of view of our perception of consciousness).

Just do it

Think of a colour. Close your eyes and really focus on the colour so that it becomes vivid in your mind. Now get up have a walk round and notice what you notice. Do this for at least two minutes.

What happens?

While you were doing this where were all the other possible colours of the rainbow? Most people find that when they do the 'Just do it' above they find the colour they were thinking of jumps out all around them. Come to think of it, where was your left little toe when you were doing the colour experiment?

The truth is that it would be impossible for us to pay attention to everything that is going on around us—we would be overloaded. Consequently, this natural filtering process takes place all the time. Bandler and Grinder undertook a number of years of research in this area. Specifically they focused on excellent communicators. As a result of this research they noticed two key processes. Firstly, that the basic filtering processes which could be observed in the language of the people they studied followed Chomsky's broad concepts of distortion, generalisation and deletion. In other words the seven plus or minus two filtering process resulted in either the distortion of the meaning of events, the generalisation of what had happened or the deletion of information. Secondly, they noticed that this process effectively filtered out whole chunks of key information from our conscious awareness, and that effective communicators made use of this phenomenon to influence others. As a result of this they defined a key presupposition of NLP, namely that: **the person who sets the frame controls the communication**. That is to say, whoever establishes what is to be noticed or discussed sets the attentional filters for the people being spoken to, and therefore the communication that follows is a result of that filter being established. This is true for everyone: children, parents, other teachers.

> The person who sets the frame controls the communication. That is to say, whoever established what is to be noticed or discussed sets the attentional filters for the people being spoken to.

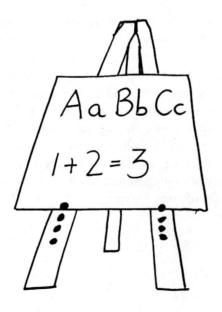

The NLP communication model

All of the elements of NLP are sometimes drawn together into what is known as the **NLP communication model**. This model is based on the idea that our senses—seeing, hearing, touch, taste and smell—take in vast amounts of information, far more than we can pay attention to. Some people have suggested that this may be as much as two million pieces of information at any one time. As Miller demonstrated, however, our 'conscious mind' is only able to make use of approximately seven pieces of information (plus or minus two) at any one moment in time.

The NLP communication model

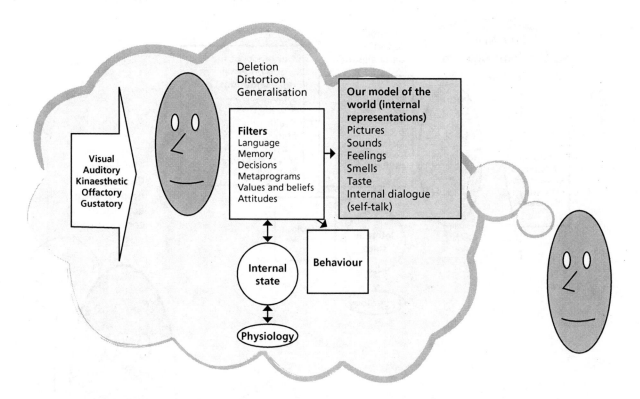

Bandler and Grinder's research focused on language patterns, people's experience of internal representations and what happens when you work with language and internal representations. The language patterns of the people that Bandler and Grinder studied seemed to demonstrate that filtering of experience, at a conscious level, took place in a number of ways. They categorised these using the headings **values and beliefs, metaprograms, decisions, language, memories** and **attitudes**. When viewed from this linguistic perspective, the experience of consciousness appears to be one in which our 'conscious mind' filters the information from events creating maps by distorting, deleting and generalising according to the language we use about our attitudes, values, beliefs, decisions, past experiences, etc.

As discussed above, these models have often been erroneously associated with the working of the brain; and it is the presentation of these ideas as a concept of brain function that has often got NLP into hot water with psychology and neuroscience. With the benefit of recent advances in neuroscience (particularly theories of automaticity, cognitive information processing and consciousness) we are now able to see more clearly where much of Bandler and Grinder's work fits in relation to what we know about the brain and information processing. In this context the NLP communication model can be seen as a map of the final stage of the cognitive process (our subjective first person experience of consciousness and specifically a map of our experience of the engagement of our sense of being).

The NLP communication model can be seen as a map of the final stage of the cognitive process (our subjective first person experience of consciousness and specifically a map of our experience of the engagement of our sense of being).

Where the NLP Communication Model fits in relation to the process of consciousness

4. 'Consciousness' - First person account of

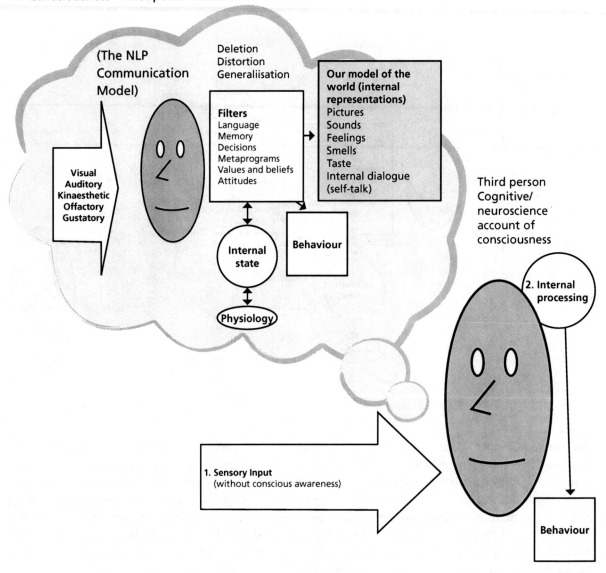

What is becoming clearer now, as a result of recent neuroscience and cognitive research, is that what Bandler and Grinder were in fact mapping was the subjective experience of consciousness and how it appears (from a first person perspective) to feed back into automatic processes (i.e. what happens in most people's experience, most of the time—in Step 4 in the diagram above (the thought bubble). In a sense, although this 'map' reflects many underlying processes, it can never represent the 'technically' accurate description that can be provided through a cognitive, neurological, 'third person' account. Seen in this context the NLP communication model is not a neurological model, but rather a practical model that helps us to understand how we can communicate more effectively with other people, and a map of the subjective experience of consciousness when communicating. At the end of the day, NLP is still evolving and being researched and the advent of NLP university-based research programmes is continually helping to refine and add rigor and depth to what is without doubt one of the most interesting and potentially useful fields in personal and human resource development.

Research Zone

Key influences on NLP

We know that many of you are engaged in academic study as trainee teachers or as part of master's degrees and research qualifications. Therefore, for those of you who may be interested in writing about NLP, we have included the following section.

Academic definitions of NLP

Defining Neuro-linguistic Programming in academic terms is not simple. NLP is a constantly evolving collection of personal development tools that can be applied to self or to others. However, NLP also seeks to model human functional processes, therapeutic techniques and excellence in general. Researchers point to the way in which NLP has drawn equally on ideas and concepts from outside of academia, as well as from within it (see e.g. Tosey and Mathison, 2003a; 2003b). Recent evidence from neuroscience suggests areas of overlap and support for a number of elements in the NLP model (Mathison, 2007). Generally, however, researchers in the field tend to support the study of NLP from a phenomenological perspective (Mathison, 2006), one which emphasises conscious experience and exploration of people's inner worlds over psychological or neuroscientific evidence. Some point to the potential of NLP modelling as a research methodology in itself and to the potential application of NLP to education (Tosey and Mathison, 2003; Tosey et al., 2005). Significant research projects are underway in both the Open University (see Dragovic, 2007) and the University of Surrey (see Tosey and Mathison, 2007).

Although NLP has been criticised for being a collection of tools and approaches with no real theoretical coherence (Craft, 2001), as Tosey and Matheson (2007) point out, originally 'NLP was described as a methodology [Bandler and Grinder 1975a], the purpose of which was to investigate exemplary communication, not to create a body of practice' nor did it set out to inform learning theory per se. Furthermore, despite any apparent lack of coherence, recent neuroscience research into hypnosis and suggestion (see Brown and Oakley, 2004) can be said to help place NLP models of communication firmly in the context of phenomenological studies of first person accounts of consciousness. Alongside this, the establishment of a cognitive theoretical understanding of hypnosis and hypnotic phenomena (e.g. Brown and Oakley, 2004) supports many NLP tools and techniques [e.g. Milton model language patterns] as does evidence in relation to positive mental imagery and performance (Neck and Manz,1992) [NLP well-formed outcomes], micro facial expressions (Ekman, 2003) [NLP sensory acuity techniques], memory reconsolidation (Miller and Matzel, 2000) [recoding of memories] and mirror neuron networks (Rizzolatti et al., 1996) [rapport and matching].

Research Zone continued ...

Influences on Bandler and Grinder

Both in its literature and in its practical application, NLP draws on a wide and eclectic mixture of references, theories and models. Most influential of all of these are the cybernetic concepts of Gregory Bateson (1972), the hypnotherapeutic approaches of Milton Erickson (Bandler and Grinder 1975b; 1975c), Gestalt therapy (Perls et al., 1951) and Virginia Satir's approaches to family therapy (Bandler and Grinder, 1975a). The hypnotherapeutic influences on NLP are particularly strong and are often linked in NLP literature to Korzybski's writings (1933) and seminal papers on primary and secondary awareness (Miller, 1956), and the TOTE model elaboration on the original stimulus–response concept adopted by behaviourist psychology (Miller, Galanter and Pribram, 1960). NLP has also embraced the TOTE model. Central to this is the proposition that we all have the capacity to modify steps in the chain of events between stimulus and response and thereby change/choose new behaviours in relation to any given stimulus. In NLP this concept is applied to the notions of **strategies** and modelling. The classic stimulus–response process described in Pavlovian classical conditioning (Pavlov, 1927) by which any stimulus or representation (either internal or external) may become connected to a response also appears within the NLP model in the technique of **anchoring**. Bateson also applied classical conditioning in the notion of the **context marker** and its role in the creation of restrictions within cybernetic explanation and in the concepts of learning I, II and III (1972).

According to the 'neo-dissociation' theory of hypnosis (Hilgard, 1974) the consciousness that solves a problem may well be different from the consciousness that reports the solution. It is this split in consciousness that NLP tools and techniques target and make use of. Evidence suggests that the prefrontal cortex has a key role in this split between awareness and automatic information processing and in this sense NLP tools are sometimes described as tools for your prefrontal cortex. It seems that those techniques that affect the emotional state, and a person's feeling, may well be triggering prefrontal cortex functioning that in some way is affecting the raw emotional activity of the amygdala. The use of internal imagery and visualisation are to be found in a number of related personal development fields, most notably in sports psychology. NLP employs a much more detailed concept called **submodalities** (Bandler and MacDonald, 1988). These are employed primarily in techniques that seek to change **beliefs** and **re-code** memories and past experiences. Submodalities are the numerous qualitative distinctions (such as bright or dim) that occur within visual, auditory, kinaesthetic, olfactory and gustatory internal perception. Within the NLP model these are seen as having a direction relationship to physiological response. Representation systems are believed by practitioners to be connected in series known as **strategies**. These strategies are claimed to form the formulae of effectiveness or ineffectiveness in relation to behaviour, communication and cognitive processing (Bandler and Grinder, 1979). The elicitation of strategies is in part achieved through the interpretation of **eye accessing cues**, a process which (although theoretically controversial) remains widely used and accepted as useful by practitioners (see Hall and Boddenhamer, 2003a). For a critical history of the development of NLP in relation to its application to human resource development, see Tosey and Mathison (2007).

Bandler, R. and Grinder, J. (1975a) *The Structure of Magic I: A book About Language and Therapy*, Palo Alto, CA: Science and Behaviour Books

Bandler, R. and Grinder, J. (1975b) *Patterns of the Hypnotic Techniques of Milton H. Erickson, M.D.* vol i, Cupertino, CA: Meta Publications

Bandler, R. and Grinder, J. (1975c) *Patterns of the Hypnotic Techniques of Milton H. Erickson, M.D.* vol ii, Cupertino, CA: Meta Publications

Bandler, R. and Grinder, J. (1979) *Frogs into Princes*, Moab, UT: Real People Press

Bandler, R. and MacDonald, W. (1988) *An Insider's Guide to Sub-modalities*, Cupertino, CA: Meta Publications

Bateson, G. (1972) *Steps to an Ecology of Mind*, London: Paladin, Granada

Brown, R. J. and Oakley, D. A. (2004) An integrated cognitive theory of hypnosis and high hypnotizability, in M. Heap, R. J. Brown and D. A. Oakley (eds), *The Highly Hypnotisable Person: Theoretical, Experimental and Clinical issues*, London: Routledge

Craft, A. (2001) Neuro-linguistic programming and learning theory, *The Curriculum Journal*, 12: 1: 125–136

Dragovic, T. (2007) *Teachers' Professional Identity and the Role of CPD in its Creation—A Report on a Study into How NLP and Non-NLP Trained Teachers in Slovenia Talk About Their Professional Identity and Their Work*, International Society for Teacher Education, 27th Annual International Seminar at University of Stirling, Scotland, 24–30 June

Ekman, P. (2003) *Emotions Revealed*, London: Phoenix

Hall, L. and Boddenhamer, B.G. (2003) *The User's Manual for the Brain, Volume I: The Complete Manual for Neuro-linguistic Programming Practitioner Certification*, Carmarthen: Crown House

Hilgard, E. R. (1974) Towards a neo-dissociationist theory: multiple cognitive controls in human functioning, *Perspectives in Biology and Medicine*, 17: 301–316

Korzybski, A. (1933, 1994) *Science and Sanity: An Introduction to Non-Aristotelian Systems and General Semantics*, Lakeville, CT: The International Non-Aristotelian Library Publishing Company

Mathison, J. (2006) *Phenomenology*, Surrey University <http://www.nlpresearch.org> Centre for Management Learning and Development

Mathison, J. (2007) *Mirror neurons: a neurological basis for making sense of the words, feelings and actions of others*, Surrey University: nlpresearch.org, Centre for Management Learning and Development

Miller, G. (1956) The magical number seven plus or minus two: some limits on our capacity to process information, *Psychological Review*: 63: 81–97

Miller, G. A., Galanter, E. and Pribram, K. (1960) *Plans and the Structure of Behaviour*, New York: Holt Rhinehart and Winston

Miller, R. R. and Matzel, L. D. (2000) Memory involves far more than 'consolidation', *Nature Reviews Neuroscience*: 1: 214–216

Neck, C.P. and Manz. C.C. (1992) Thought self-leadership: the Influence of self-talk and mental imagery on performance, *Journal of Organizational Behavior*, 13: 7: 681–699

Pavlov, I. (1927) *Conditioned Reflexes*, London: Oxford University Press

Perls, F., Hefferline, R.F. and Goodman, P. (1951) *Gestalt Therapy: Excitement and Growth in the Human Personality*, London: Souvenir Press

Rizzolatti, G., Fadiga, L., Gallese, L. and Fogassi, L. (1996) Premotor cortex and the recognition of motor actions, *Cognitive Brain Research*, 3: 131–141

Tosey, P. and Mathison, J. (2003a) Neuro-linguistic programming and learning theory: a response, *Curriculum Journal*, 14: 3: 371–388

Tosey, P. and Mathison, J. (2003b) Neuro-linguistic programming: its potential for learning and teaching in formal education, Paper presented at the European Conference on Educational Research, University of Hamburg, 17–20 September 2003

Tosey, P. and Mathison, J. (2007) Fabulous creatures of HRD: a critical natural history of Neuro-linguistic Programming, Paper for the Eighth International Conference on HRD Research and Practice Across Europe, 27–29 June, Oxford Brookes Business School

Tosey, P., Mathison, J. and Michelli, D. (2005) The potential of neuro-linguistic programming, *Journal of Transformative Education*, 3: 2: 140–167v

NLP Toolbox No. 36

Generate some new behaviours

This visualisation technique is a great way to advance your experience of NLP. You can use this whenever you want to add more choices or new behaviours. This technique is extensively used in professional sports coaching throughout the world to improve performance. First, find a quiet and relaxing place where you know that you will be able to work in your own mind without being disturbed.

NLP Toolbox No. 36 *continued* ...

1. Take a moment to look up to your right and in your 'mind's eye' notice someone who looks exactly like you. It is this other you that will be engaged in all of the learning and changes that take place in this activity. To get the best out of this technique check at the end to make sure that you have put into place all the changes, new behaviours and thoughts necessary for you to feel happy that you have done a complete job.

2. To ensure that you are able to maintain a separation between you and the 'other you' while you create the new behaviours, you can imagine that you are standing behind a sheet of plexiglass. This will allow you to feel detached from the activities that the other you is experiencing.

3. Think of something that you really want to be able to feel motivated to do in the classroom or in your wider work in school—something simple for this exercise. As you begin to develop your skills you will be able to apply the technique to many aspects of your life.

4. Pay attention to the other you. Take a moment to notice what the other you sees and what it will look like when the task is finished.

5. Now see your other self doing the task easily and effortlessly with all the new behaviours and thoughts included. Notice what the other you sees, hears and feels. The other you can keep looking at the image of the completed task. Notice how that other you feels more comfortable and positive the closer it gets to completing the activity. The other you can now see the benefits of having done the task. Hear the encouraging words that the other you's internal voice says, right now.

6. If what you see isn't totally complete just allow a light mist to descend over your inner vision and allow your unconscious mind to make any adjustments that may be necessary.

7. When you are ready the mist can disappear allowing you to see all of the changes that have been made. Allow yourself to be sure that you want to be the person that is your other self and that that person has completely internalised all the skills and changes that need to take place.

8. Now allow the plexiglass screen to fall away and let the other you float into you—some people find it helpful to reach out to embrace the other you—you may feel an internal change in energy.

9. Now imagine yourself faced with that task sometime in the future. Notice how you are feeling and thinking now. What are the differences? If you need to you can revisit the process and add anything extra whenever you want to.

Chapter 15
Instant training day

How to plan and deliver your own NLP training

As we were finishing the book, one of Roger's NLP practice group sessions in Chichester was given the chance to go gliding by an NLP master practitioner that Roger had trained. At this event was a a teacher we had trained earlier who was very keen to talk about the book. 'You know what it needs,' she said, 'some advice on doing the training yourself back in your own school.'

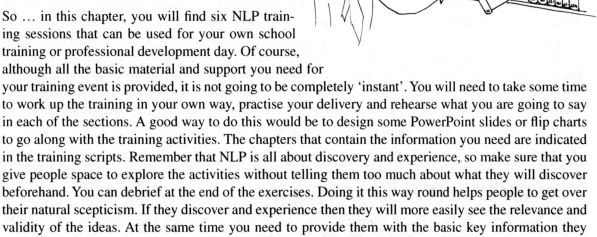

So ... in this chapter, you will find six NLP training sessions that can be used for your own school training or professional development day. Of course, although all the basic material and support you need for your training event is provided, it is not going to be completely 'instant'. You will need to take some time to work up the training in your own way, practise your delivery and rehearse what you are going to say in each of the sections. A good way to do this would be to design some PowerPoint slides or flip charts to go along with the training activities. The chapters that contain the information you need are indicated in the training scripts. Remember that NLP is all about discovery and experience, so make sure that you give people space to explore the activities without telling them too much about what they will discover beforehand. You can debrief at the end of the exercises. Doing it this way round helps people to get over their natural scepticism. If they discover and experience then they will more easily see the relevance and validity of the ideas. At the same time you need to provide them with the basic key information they need up front. We advise that you read the book carefully before embarking on leading any training and make sure that you have particularly studied the chapters that relate to the exercises that you are leading. If you are fairly new to NLP it is a good idea to re-read the relevant chapters again before you begin any training event—or even better, experience some NLP training yourself first. This will help you develop your own vocabulary and script.

> We advise that you read the book carefully before embarking on leading any training and make sure that you have particularly studied the chapters that relate to the exercises that you are leading.

The six activities covered in this chapter are:

- Present state, desired state
- Calibration
- Rapport
- Spatial anchoring
- Putting goals into your future using your time line—or 'making it happen'
- The Walt Disney creativity strategy

Getting started

For each technique, we have given you a structure that many NLP trainers use, called the 4MAT model (McCarthy, 1981). In its simplest form, you structure your training for each of the activities around the following four questions:

1. WHY would you want to know this?
2. WHAT is it about?
3. HOW do you do it?
4. WHAT does it get you?

Using this structure helps to ensure a logical progression and that the material is covered from all possible angles. We have already done this for you, so all you need to do is to follow the training script through each of the stages. In designing your training day, it may be useful to focus on the WHY—thinking about what in particular your staff need help with, situations that are challenging, or other priorities linked to the school development plan or other strategic plans. If your workshop is to be about dealing with conflict (for example) simply debrief the exercises accordingly by asking participants (at the end) to think of ways that the tools could be useful or how they plan to use them. Debriefing to flipcharts in groups or from the front is a good way to approach this. The same could be done if the focus of your session is about communication, or managing parents, etc. The six units below are designed to be totally flexible, so that you can run them as a whole day together, or you could pick and mix any of the aspects that are particularly relevant to your staff group. However, once you understand the key principles you will be able to apply the same techniques to many of the Toolboxes and Just do its throughout the book. Toolbox No. 15, *Puppet master's parents' evening* works well as an additional session. Indeed, many of the Toolboxes can easily be adapted for a training session.

Top tips for training NLP techniques

- Remind the group of the importance of rapport (once you have taught them about it, of course). Remember body position, breathing, language and voice tone are a few easy ones to match and mirror.

- It is useful to have the instructions written up in advance, either on handouts or an overhead projector, so that the participants can refer to them when practising an exercise.

- Ensure that facilitators stand alongside their partners. This creates better rapport as the facilitator takes the journey with their partner.

- Practise the technique yourself several times and read the relevant chapters before you lead the session. Ensure that you are in a resourceful state yourself; use a spotlight to sort yourself out first!

- Music can be really useful to manage transitions and pull the group back together. You can even anchor the group to a specific piece of music that will always mean it is time to come back from an exercise. Choose something that has a strong beat and a happy and light mood. This works great in the classroom too.

- Think about the language you use to make sure that you are always presupposing success in the words you use to set up the exercises. There are some good tips and examples to help you do this in Chapter 5, *Don't think about chocolate cake.*

The exercises below are laid out in the four sections described above. Specific things that you **might** say as a trainer are indicated in italics. Diagrams show how the activities should be set up.

Training exercise 1

Present state, desired state—becoming outcome focused

(Estimated time needed: 30 minutes)

Part 1 (Why): Introduction—some possible questions to ask at the start

You could introduce this exercise by including some of the information about consciousness from Chapter 14, *The magic number 7*. The idea that 'what we pay attention to' is important is key to this exercise. Questions that you might ask to help people see the relevance of this exercise could include:

- Would it be useful to have a new way to approach problems?
- How many times have you spent hours in a meeting going round and round a problem without a solution?
- How many times have you thought and thought about a problem and not seemed to have got anywhere?
- How many times has a solution appeared when you have not been focused on the problem?
- Would you like a simple way of changing the way you approach problems?

Part 2 (What): Explanation: information we need to explain the NLP technique

When we focus on our problems we tend to think in particular ways both independently and when we work in groups. This often becomes a habitual way of thinking. This is a useful approach to shift from problem thinking to outcome thinking. When issues are approached in this way creative solutions appear. We use a different way of thinking when we focus on what we want as the end result, rather than the problem or even the how of getting there. Taking ourselves in our imagination to the outcome and thinking about what it would be like—what we would hear, see and feel when we have the outcome— helps us find new ways of getting there.

Part 3 (How): Activity—set up the exercise

1. Ask the participants to pick an issue/problem that is current for them. In NLP we often use a scale of 1 to 10 to grade problems we are going to deal with, where 1 represents a small problem and 10 represents a massive issue. For teaching purposes and to facilitate a positive experience it is best to use problems up to 3 or 4 on the scale. These are the best size problems for running an exercise and will enable participants to understand the benefits of this change in approach without getting stuck in larger issues before they have had some practice. Tell the participants to select such a problem.

2. Put participants into pairs, A and B, and ask them to take turns so they each experience the whole process.

3. Person A briefly outlines the issue (allow only one minute for this so that they don't get caught up in the problem). Person B listens and notices how A reacts (body language, voice tone, animation, mood, etc.) as A describes the issue (B is not to offer solution or opinions, just listen attentively).

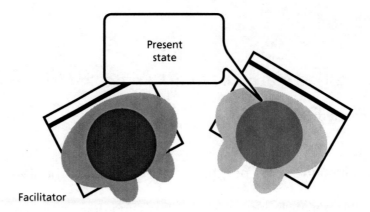

Facilitator

Present state

4. B asks A what is sometimes called the 'miracle question':

   IF YOU WOKE UP TOMMORROW AND THE ISSUE WAS SOLVED WHAT WOULD IT BE LIKE?

   WHAT WOULD YOU HEAR, SEE AND FEEL?

   WHAT WOULD YOU BE SAYING TO YOURSELF?

You could write these on a flip chart or have them ready on your PowerPoint.

5. Person A answers the question, B listens, and notices how A reacts (body language, voice tone, animation, mood, etc.) as A describes the outcome (B is not to offer solutions or opinions, just listen attentively). The facilitator should allow the person to talk for about four minutes about the 'desired state'.

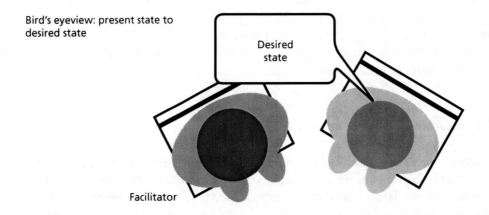

Bird's eyeview: present state to desired state

Desired state

Facilitator

6. Person A and B then swap over.

Part 4 (What if): Debrief—what do we get from this learning?

1. Collect reactions and feedback from the exercise. Go beyond like or dislike for the activity to what is learned about how we tackle issues from this exercise. Make sure you ask open questions. A good way to start is to simply ask, 'What happened?'

2. Explore things further: What are the differences? How does the issue seem now? Have solutions appeared? On the 1–10 scale is there a difference in the way you now approach the issue?

3. Facilitate a discussion on how when we focus on the outcome we begin to perceive the issue in a different way. Solutions may even appear or our perception of the problem changes.

4. How could this be applied in class, meetings or other areas of life?

Training exercise 2

Calibration

(Estimated time needed: 40 minutes)

Part 1 (Why): Introduction—some possible questions to ask and ideas to introduce at the start

Re-read Chapter 13, *It's in your eyes* and Chapter 3, *We like like*, so that you understand the principles.

Bandler and Grinder discovered that people make minute changes in their body language from moment to moment, and that those changes have meaning IF you have enough sensory acuity to notice them. In any one-to-one situation, there is information available providing you have tuned your senses to notice. Sensory acuity and calibration (taking mental snapshots) are crucial skills in NLP, helping you to read accurately the non-verbal signals from another person and develop the flexibility to change your communication style to match the other person.

■ Would it be useful to be able to read those non-verbal signals, which indicate shifts in state?

■ How many times would it have been less stressful if you could have read non-verbal signs before something happened?

As teachers, you already do some of this unconsciously. Doing this exercise is about practising and increasing your skills.

Part 2 (What): Explanation—information we need to explain the NLP technique

This exercise has two parts. Firstly it aims to re-train the mind to take snapshots of a person during a communication. This is called calibration. Secondly, to notice the differences in the minimal cues which we give off (sometimes called non-verbal leakage).

There are many physical changes that happen as we communicate and as our thoughts and feelings change. We can learn to notice these differences and then we are able, with practice, to know how someone is reacting. The non-verbal clues come before words and so we have an opportunity to modify our approach and maintain positive communication. By training our mind to take snapshots we become more elegant at rapport (covered in the next exercise).

Part 3 (How): Activity—set up the exercise

The calibration exercise is much like the 'spot the difference' game we played as children. We are training our mind to take snapshots and compare one snapshot with the next. This begins a flow of information focused on communication.

1. Person A adopts a position either seated or standing. B takes a mental snapshot and then closes their eyes.

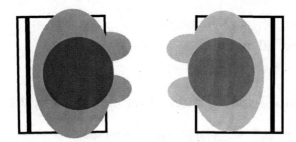

2. Person A then moves a part of their body, say an arm, says ok, and B opens their eyes and tells A what they have moved.

3. Repeat with smaller and smaller changes.

4. Continue repeating this until you can notice the movement of a finger by an inch or some other minimal move (you can go back and forth in turns).

Once you have mastered telling the differences have a go at calibrating a particular thought or mind state.

1. Pick two contrasting thoughts. Usually A thinks of someone they don't like and tells B. B takes a snapshot then A thinks of someone they like and tells B. B takes another snapshot.

2. Once B is confident they have the calibration, A chooses one of the people, thinks of them without telling B who it is and B tells A who they are thinking of. B must get this right three times in a row—then swap roles.

Once you have mastered this you can play with it, noticing more subtle changes.

Part 4 (What if): Debrief—what do we get from this learning?

1. Collect reactions and feedback from the exercise. Go beyond like or dislike for the activity, to what is learned about how much information there is coming from people when they communicate, as most of it goes unnoticed.

2. What are the differences? What changes did you notice in the second part of the exercise when paying attention following the changes? Have a PowerPoint slide or flip chart available with details of all the sorts of things that can be calibrated (skin tone, breathing, body language, facial expressions, voice tone, etc.).

3. Facilitate a discussion on how when we focus our attention on taking snapshots, much more information becomes available. How could this be applied in class, meetings or other areas of life?

Training exercise 3

Rapport

(Estimated time needed: 30 minutes)

Part 1 (Why): Introduction—some possible questions to ask at the start

- Would it be useful to be able to build relationships quickly?
- Would it be useful to be able to handle difficult people and get positive results from conflict situations?
- Would it be useful to know why it is that we get on well with some people and others we find more challenging?
- Would it be useful to quickly create a connection with an individual child so that you can help them learn or be in a more resourceful state?

Part 2 (What): Explanation—information we need to explain the NLP technique

The purpose of this exercise is to allow teachers to notice the differences between creating strong rapport and having little or no rapport.

As social creatures we seek relationships, and rapport skills give us the opportunity to hone that ability to create good relationships easily and effectively. In this exercise, we are concentrating on physiology and body posture. Later on, when you have mastered this, you will be able to create deep levels of rapport by matching words, voice tone and breathing.

Tell the teachers about the difference between matching and mirroring (you will find this information in Chapter 3, *We like like*). It is very useful for the facilitator to demonstrate the differences between matching and mirroring before the exercise begins. You may need a volunteer to help you with this.

Part 3 (How): Activity—set up the exercise

1. Ask the teachers to work in pairs.

2. Before they start the exercise, ask them to choose two topics to talk about, one which they agree upon and the other which they disagree about. It is important that they have decided on these topics before they begin the exercise.

3. They should begin with the topic they agree about. In this part, you will ask them to reduce the level of rapport—to sit in different body positions to each other, reducing the amount of eye-contact, and notice what occurs in this communication. It is important to allow this discussion to run for a minimum of five minutes.

4. In the second part, they should discuss the topic they disagree about. This time, ask them to maintain a high level of rapport—sit in the same body positions, increase the amount of eye-contact, match some of the breathing patterns (you can always tell when someone is breathing out because they are speaking!), and notice what occurs in this communication. It is important to allow this discussion to run for a minimum of five minutes.

Part 4 (What if): Debrief—what do we get from this learning?

1. Collect reactions and feedback from the exercise. As always, go beyond like or dislike for the activity to what is learned about how our body postures affect our communication.

2. Ask the teachers to describe how they felt when discussing the topic they agreed about with little or no rapport. Then ask them about discussing a topic they disagreed about with a high level of rapport.

3. How could this be applied in class, meetings or other areas of life?

Training exercise 4

Spotlighting (or spatial anchoring)

(Estimated time needed: 30 minutes)

Part 1 (Why): Introduction—some possible questions to ask at the start

■ Have you ever taught a class when you've not been at your best?

■ Have you ever wanted to have more energy or confidence in situations like meetings with colleagues or parents?

■ Would you like to know how to tap into your inner resources and be able to be in the right state at the right time, so that life and work and become less stressful?

■ Would it be useful to have a way to resource yourself during the day to stop yourself getting frazzled?

Part 2 (What): Explanation—information we need to explain the NLP technique

Re-read the chapter on anchoring (Chapter 9, *Anchors away!*) so that you understand the principles.

This type of anchor is particularly effective in the classroom. It allows you to be in a resourceful state and so be more effective in managing your classroom and students. You can access whatever states you need; enthusiastic, calm, confident, assertive or fun.

Creating spotlight areas for particular teaching activities also helps condition the expectations of your students. This is effective when a particular teaching activity is done from the same spot every time.

For instance, pick a spot in the classroom from where you would like to call order. Decide the states you would like to have for that activity, anchor them there with a spotlight, and always use that space. Over time, this will condition not only your state and response, but also the state and response from your students, on an unconscious level.

Part 3 (How): Activity—set up the exercise

To teach this, it is important that you are familiar with the basic anchoring process, the concept of association and dissociation and the use of submodalities to enhance a state or internal experience.

Successful anchoring is dependent on recalling strong, associated, positive memories and it is very important that you can model this to the group.

This will give them a strong reference for how the technique works. So, make sure that you have practised this technique yourself and that you are able to create spotlight states in yourself that are powerful. The best way to show teachers how this works is to demonstrate it in front of the group yourself and talk through what you are doing. If you feel confident enough and have practised this technique more extensively, you could use another person to demonstrate on.

The walk-through of this technique as you might model it:

1. Decide the states you are going to model for the group. Energised states are more visible as the non-verbal signals are stronger (e.g. colour change, breathing rate, etc.). Ensure that you can access these states and model them visibly for the group.

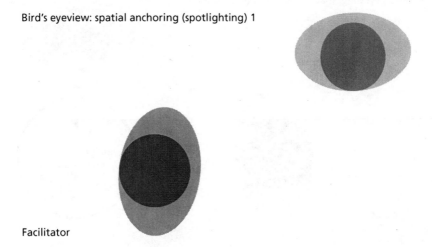

Bird's eyeview: spatial anchoring (spotlighting) 1

Facilitator

2. Imagine a circle on the floor. Choose the first state to go into the spotlight and tell the group what this is. Access the state, making the process visible for the group, describing a time when you felt that state strongly, using visual, auditory and kinaesthetic (VAK) descriptions, e.g. what you could *see*, *feel* (where in your body?), *hear*, etc. When the state is rising strongly, step into the circle for 10 seconds.

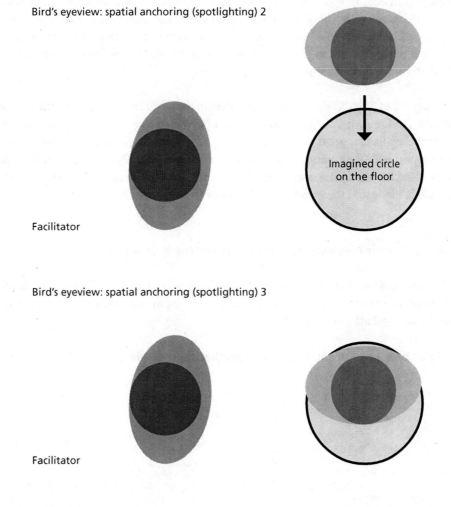

Bird's eyeview: spatial anchoring (spotlighting) 2

Facilitator

Imagined circle on the floor

Bird's eyeview: spatial anchoring (spotlighting) 3

Facilitator

3. Step out and imagine leaving that state in the circle. Break your state by thinking about something completely different, and now explain what you have done and the importance of this.

Bird's eyeview: spatial anchoring (spotlighting) 4

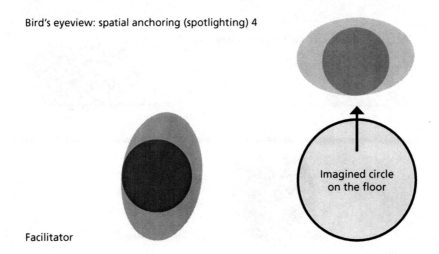

Facilitator

Imagined circle on the floor

4. Repeat this process for two other states, ensuring that you explicitly model how it is that you are re-creating the states strongly in yourself.

5. Break state to clear yourself completely. Now it is time to test the anchor!

6. Think of a situation when that resource would be useful (in the classroom, in meetings, etc.). Access this unresourceful time and state, step into the circle and then model the shifts that happen. Describe the differences that you are aware of. You may need to add stronger states if necessary. If you are confident about training this activity you could use someone from the audience. Make sure that you pick someone who is quite extravert and 'reactive' so that changes in their emotional state are visible to the rest of the group. This is easy to do—just look for someone who usually has noticeably different and contrasting facial expressions.

7. Send the group off in pairs to facilitate one another in this exercise. A very useful instruction here is that the facilitator may only allow the other person to step into the circle when they are convinced that they have a good, strong state. Another useful tip is for the facilitator to ensure that they are in rapport with their partner and access the desired state themselves, e.g. be enthusiastic if your partner is anchoring enthusiasm, confident if they are confident, etc. Finally, ensure that the facilitator stands alongside their partner, rather than facing them.

Part 4 (What if): Debrief—what do we get from this learning?

1. Collect reactions and feedback from the exercise. Go beyond like or dislike for the activity to what is learned about using their inner resources in different situations. What changes did they notice in themselves before and after this exercise?

2. How could this be applied in class, meetings or other areas of life?

Training exercise 5

Putting goals into your future using your time line—or 'making it happen'

(Estimated time needed: 30 minutes)

Part 1 (Why): Introduction—some possible questions to ask at the start

▨ Do you ever decide you want something and then find it doesn't happen, or make plans and targets that you don't follow through?

▨ If you have decided on your goals, would it be helpful for you to have a way of making them happen?

Part 2 (What): Explanation—information we need to explain the NLP technique

Re-read Chapter 12, *You can do it ... and it's about time.*

Just as we have memories of the past, we can also create 'future memories'. These are a full representation of what you want, already achieved, with pictures, sounds and feelings, and even smells and tastes. This technique is a way of making sure that your goals and outcomes become your reality. By using your time line, you can help your unconscious mind to have the right filters in place so that you are aware of all the things that will enable you to fulfil your goal. You may even find that after doing this exercise, your unconscious mind will generate ways of getting there that you hadn't even thought of.

Part 3 (How): Activity—set up the exercise

The best way to teach this technique is to demonstrate it yourself, with a commentary to make your processing explicit to the group. The group can then practise it in pairs. Remember to ensure that the facilitator stands alongside their partner and is in good rapport.

1. Decide on a goal that you want for yourself. In NLP we often use a scale of 1 to 10 to grade goals we are going to deal with, where 1 represents a small goal and 10 represents a huge life change. For teaching purposes and to facilitate a positive experience it is best to use goals up to 3 or 4. This is the best level to work at for running an exercise and will enable participants to understand the benefits of this technique.

2. Create an associated experience of having achieved that goal. What would you *see, hear, feel, taste* and *smell*? Be extravagant! Put everything that you can imagine into this representation. Feel it in your body—have big, bright, colourful pictures that are close to you. When you are satisfied that you have created a very desirable goal, move on.

3. Imagine you are holding your goal as you would a picture. Look at the picture. See yourself achieving that outcome. Make sure it is just as you would want it.

4 Imagine a line stretching in front of you out into your future. Notice how far along that line the goal belongs.

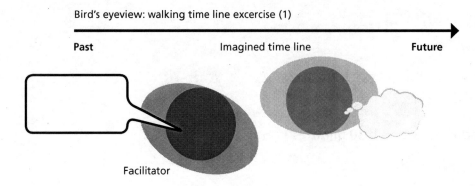

Bird's eyeview: walking time line excercise (1)

Past   Imagined time line   **Future**

Facilitator

5. Imagine attaching a golden thread from your goal to your navel that will draw you towards your goal and keep you on track, just like the thread that allowed Theseus to escape from the Minotaur's maze!

6. Walk forwards into your future along your time line, until you reach the place where the goal belongs. Allow the goal to gently slot into place. You may imagine hearing a click as it does so.

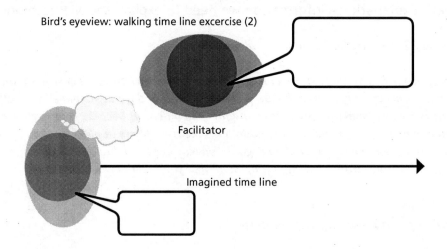

Bird's eyeview: walking time line excercise (2)

Facilitator

Imagined time line

7. Keeping your thread attached, say to the group: *I am walking back to now, only as fast as my unconscious mind can make all the adjustments needed to take me easily and effortlessly to my goal*. The facilitator will need to say these words correctly phrased for their partner when the group practise the technique, so have this on a flip chart.

i.e. Walk back to now, only as fast as your unconscious mind can make all the adjustments needed to take you easily and effortlessly to your goal.

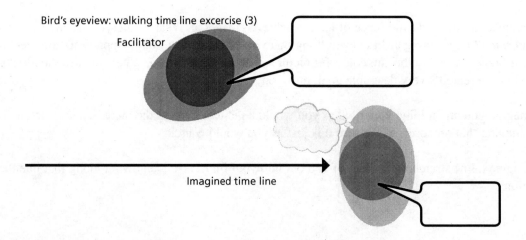

Bird's eyeview: walking time line excercise (3)

Facilitator

Imagined time line